MW00697926

TRILATERALS OVER WASHINGTON

VOLUMES I & II

by Patrick M. Wood and Antony C. Sutton

Printed in the United States of America

Republished 2017
Original Printing 1979

ISBN 978-0-9863739-2-3
Coherent Publishing, LLC
P.O. Box 52247
Mesa, AZ 85208

Additional Information & Updates
www.Technocracy.News

TABLE OF CONTENTS

Antony C. Sutton
(1925-2002)

Antony Sutton was a legendary scholar, researcher and author who studied at the universities of London, Göttingen, and California and received his D.Sc. from the University of Southampton. He was an economics professor at California State University, Los Angeles and a research fellow at Stanford University's Hoover Institution for War, Peace and Revolution from 1968 to 1973. During his time at the Hoover Institution, he wrote the massive 3-volume work, *Western Technology and Soviet Economic Development*. A prolific author, Sutton completed 25 books during his career.

Sutton's soft-spoken demeanor was not to be mistaken for his fierceness of spirit. He was so well-armed with the indisputable facts of historical study, that critics would seldom dare to engage him in debate, and if they did, they regretted it afterward.

No one understood the global elite, or resisted them more forcefuly, than Antony Sutton. His words still speak truth today:

> *"The power system continues only as long as individuals try to get something for nothing. The day when a majority of individuals declares or acts as if it wants nothing from the government, declares that it will look after its own welfare and interests, then on that day the power elites are doomed."*

FOREWORD

In what later appeared to be divine appointment, Antony Sutton and I bumped into each other in 1977 at a gold and investment conference in New Orleans. We both intended to eat a quiet breakfast but the coffee shop was jammed and the maître d' had declared European seating where you sit in whatever empty chair can be found. We were strangers, forced to meet over eggs and bacon. It took about fifteen minutes of casual conversation for us to realize that we were both investigating the Trilateral Commission and its seemingly undue influence over the **Carter** administration.

Trilaterals Over Washington, Volumes I & II was the fruit of our conjoined labors over the next several years and it literally changed the course of our lives. We were interviewed on hundreds of radio programs around the nation, spoke at conventions and large meetings, publically debated members of the Trilateral Commission on radio and in person, and methodically pushed forward with our research. In the end, we apparently hit one too many nerves as the largest national bookstore chain, B. Dalton Bookseller, permanently banned our books from their stores. Yes, banned in America. Dalton sent out a memo to all their stores and simply stated, "The book is out of print and the publisher is out of business."

Trilaterals Over Washington offers important historical understanding of what transpired in those early years. We were not only eye witnesses, but we were intensely focused on studying the writings, publications and activities of the Trilateral Commission and its members. Nevertheless, reading this book some 40 years later will reveal our limited vision in grasping the whole game plan. We knew for certain that the Commission was dedicated to creating a "New International Economic Order", but what did they really mean by the word "New"?

Neither Sutton nor myself fully grasped the enormity of "New". After Sutton passed in 2002, I was compelled to restart and continue my personal research into Trilateral Commission activities during the intervening years. I found that commission members had dominated all Presidential administrations since **Jimmy Carter**, including **George H. W. Bush, Bill Clinton** and **Al Gore** and George W. Bush where **Dick Cheney** was vice president. The Obama administration was saturated with Commission members in top positions.

This was the background against which I inadvertently stumbled upon a movement from the early 1930s called **Technocracy**. It immediately peaked my interest for several reasons, but most importantly because it was billed as a *new economic system* designed by prominent scientists and engineers of that era. They had taken it upon themselves to rescue the world from the Great Depression by replacing capitalism and free enterprise with a resource-based economic system that used energy as its accounting system instead of money. It also proposed the abandonment of private property, the dismissal of Congress and other legislative bodies, and the installation of non-elected scientists, engineers and technicians to run the entire continent. History had largely forgotten Technocracy, but after two years of intensive original research, I further discovered that it was the *only* replacement economic model that had ever been posited in history. In addition, its radical nature stood in distinct contrast to communism, socialism, fascism, progressivism and other "isms" of that day.

Could it be that Technocracy was the *"new"* in *New International Economic Order*? If so, could it be demonstrated that members of the Trilateral Commission were actually involved in implementing Technocracy? These questions are answered in great detail in my 2015 book, *Technocracy Rising: The Trojan Horse of Global Transformation*, which I have likened to the third installment of a trilogy that started with Volumes I & II of *Trilaterals Over Washington*. In short, *Technocracy Rising* closes the circle of nearly 40 years of research and perspective that started with a random meeting between two tired and hungry travelers who intersected in time and space, hundreds of miles from their respective homes.

THE INTERVENING YEARS OF TRILATERAL HEGEMONY

The Trilateral Commission dominated the Carter administration. Both **Jimmy Carter** and **Walter Mondale** were members. Carter's first appointment was his National Security Advisor **Zbigniew Brzezinski**. Subsequently, all but one of the top cabinet appointees would be Trilaterals. If you think this was a political coup, at least on the surface, it was, but not for the sake of politics. What the Commission wanted was to gain control over the most powerful trade machine in the world. In other words, political structure was only a means to an end and not the end in itself. This is easily demonstrated by subsequent actions: nine out of eleven U.S. Trade Representatives have been Trilaterals, six out of eight World Bank presidents were members, Federal Reserve chairmen included **Arthur Burns** (1970-1978), **Paul Volker** (1979-1987) and **Alan Greenspan** (1987-2006), and the list goes on.

Using this trade sledge-hammer, Commission members have orchestrated the creation of the World Trade Organization, the North American Free Trade Agreement (NAFTA), the wholesale conversion of the United Nations to Sustainable Development and global warming issues, and other similar, high-level and transformative strategies.

To demonstrate this process in finer detail, I am including below the full text of a paper that I wrote on China several years ago.

HOW THE TRILATERAL COMMISSION CONVERTED CHINA INTO A TECHNOCRACY

It was no mistake of history that China transformed from a Communist dictatorship into a neo-authoritarian Technocracy.

In this regard, the influence of the Trilateral Commission, its members and policies on the world stage can hardly be quantified. The Commission, founded by **David Rockefeller** and **Zbigniew Brzezinski** in 1973, drew membership from North America, Europe and Japan. Out of approximately 300 members, only 86 were originally from the United States, and yet they corporately devised and pushed policies that suited the entire membership, and did so under a virtual cloak of invisibility that lasts even into 2013.

Today, we reap the "benefits" of Trilateral manipulation. The European economy is trashed, Japan's economy is still smoldering from the mid-1990s and the U.S. is much worse off today than in the late 1960s. But, the political systems of these countries are not much better off than their economies. The fruit of decay in the United States is painfully evident with a fractured and contentious politic that defies reconciliation on even the most minor issues.

My friends at Coalition for a Prosperous America and Economy in Crisis, among others, are working hard to offset messed-up trade policies that put American industry in the toilet over the last 30 years. As long as we have some freedom of speech left, organizations like these are a welcome voice, even if they are shouted down by the global free-trade cartel.

However, people need to know where and how this all started, and who was responsible for it. Only by understanding the genesis of globalization can modern economics, politics and social trends be understood. Can anyone say, "Pin the tail on the donkey?"

Thirty-five years ago, in the November 1978 and April 1979 issues of *Trilateral Observer*, Antony C. Sutton and myself wrote the following analysis on China. We warned of the disastrous effects that would result if these policies moved forward, and we thoroughly exposed the members of the Trilateral Commission who were almost solely responsible for China's ascendant rise as a world power. That no one listened at the time is self-evident, because nothing changed and no one resisted.

CHINA IN THE TRILATERAL CROSSHAIRS

The policy of "normalization" of relations with Communist China — in effect a program to build China technologically into a super power — was implemented by **Zbigniew Brzezinski**. A high ranking Administration source is reported as saying: "This was Zbig's baby more than anyone else's."

From outside the White House (from a top policy maker who generally sides with **Cyrus Vance**):

"Zbig is really riding high now. He had the central role behind the scenes, and he was all alone in the press play. I'm told the President thinks Zbig did 99 percent of the work on China."

More likely, however, the China policy was formulated and implemented by a Trilateralist troika: **Jimmy Carter**, **Cyrus Vance** and **Brzezinski**. And this policy was only a continuation of a policy begun under a "Republican" Administration, that of Richard Nixon and **Henry Kissinger**, another Trilateralist.

The heady effect that these vast policy-making exercises have on these men, almost an infantile reaction, is well reported in the Washington Post on February 8, 1979 with the headline, *China Policy: A Born-Again Brzezinski*, describing how **Brzezinski** excitedly describes his meeting with Teng [aka Deng Xiaoping]:

> *FEBURARY 1979 — The eyes sparkle with excitement even days later. The arms erupt in sudden sweeping gestures when he talks about it. And that causes the photos — about a dozen of them — to fly out of Zbigniew Brzezinski's hands and scatter over the floor of his office as he is speaking.*
>
> *"Here's Cy... and here I am... and there is Teng right between us...."*
>
> *Brzezinski is talking in that quick. clipped, excited style that is his way, and he is pointing at one photo that remains in his hand while he bends to scoop up the rest, talking all the while.*
>
> *"It's amazing, when you think of it. The leader of a billion people — having dinner in my house just two hours after he arrived in this country!*
>
> *"I mean, it really is rather amazing!"*

TRILATERALISTS AND THE CHINA TRADE

An example of the influence of a mere handful of Trilateralists in creating self-serving policies many thousands of miles from the United States, can be illustrated by a recent conference in Japan. In early February 1979 a symposium on the China Trade was sponsored by the Japanese newspaper Nihon Keizai. The few speakers were mainly Trilateralists, and the Trilaterals agreed with one another's proposals thus creating a power bloc. Reporting in the U.S., the Washington Post (February 9, 1979) cited only Trilateralist speakers.

The key Japanese speaker was Trilateralist **Kiichiro Kitaura**, Chairman of Numuru Securities Company, Ltd.

What were **Kitaura's** proposals? They were:

- Internationalize the yen
- Consultations and cooperation between Japanese and American businessmen on ways to penetrate the Chinese market
- "Blending" Japanese and American technology

Of course, **Kitaura** thoroughly agreed with fellow Trilateralist **Philip Trezise** (from Brookings Institution) that Japan's large current account surplus should be invested abroad and not in Japan. **Trezise** was backed by another American Trilateralist, **Peter G. Peterson**, Chairman of Lehman Brothers, Kuhn Loeb, Inc., who, like **Kitaura**, urged more Japanese trade.

In brief, this important conference was dominated by Trilateralist thinking, and that was the only thinking reported, yet on the surface the Trilateral link is not apparent to the lay reader.

TRILATERAL BUILDUP OF COMMUNIST CHINA

Trilaterals proposed to build up Communist China. Trilateralist policy is clear cut. The West must aid the construction of Communist China: this is expressed in *An Overview of East-West Relations* (*Triangle Paper* No. 15, p. 57) as follows:

> *"To grant China favorable conditions in economic relations is definitely in the political interest of the West"* adding *"...*

there seems to exist sufficient ways for aiding China in acceptable forms with advanced civilian technology."

Triangle paper 15 also adds:

"The situation is different... where arms supplies or advanced military technologies are concerned, except for types of equipment that by their nature serve purely defensive purposes." (p. 58)

In fact, as we shall see later, Trilateral firms have exported even advanced military technology to Communist China.

Further, as part of one world, Trilateralists see an ultimate merging of free enterprise Taiwan with the Communist mainland. Even more remarkable, the paper envisages that Communist China will return to an expansionist aggressive policy under two conditions: as Communist China "gets stronger," if relations with the Soviets are "normalized."

The paper adds, "already now, the activity of Communist Guerrillas in Thailand and Malaysia, linked to each other and looking to China, persists and even seem to be on the increase." (page 59)

So far as Communist China is concerned, we may conclude that Trilaterals:

- Want to build Communist China into a military superpower,
- wish to do this with the full and clear understanding that China will likely resume its expansionist course in the Far East, and
- are willing to subsidize guerrilla activities in Thailand and Malaysia (much of the "civilian technology" currently being transferred has usefulness for guerrilla warfare.)

TECHNOCRACY RECOGNIZED

The transfer of technology was a key aspect of early Trilateral policy. Admittedly, their stated goal of "fostering a New International Economic Order" was not fully understood in 1978–79. However, by June 2001, at least one writer for Time

Magazine (Time was connected with the Trilateral Commission, by the way) got it perfectly in *Made in China: The Revenge of the Nerds* - China had been converted into a Technocracy! According to the author, Kaiser Kuo:

> *The nerds are running the show in today's China. In the twenty years since Deng Xiaoping's [Ed. Note: count backward to 1978–79] reforms kicked in, the composition of the Chinese leadership has shifted markedly in favor of technocrats. ...It's no exaggeration to describe the current regime as a technocracy.*
>
> *After the Maoist madness abated and Deng Xiaoping inaugurated the opening and reforms that began in late 1978, scientific and technical intellectuals were among the first to be rehabilitated. Realizing that they were the key to the Four Modernizations embraced by the reformers, concerted efforts were made to bring the "experts" back into the fold.*
>
> *During the 1980s, technocracy as a concept was much talked about, especially in the context of so-called "Neo-Authoritarianism" — the principle at the heart of the "Asian Developmental Model" that South Korea, Singapore, and Taiwan had pursued with apparent success. The basic beliefs and assumptions of the technocrats were laid out quite plainly: Social and economic problems were akin to engineering problems and could be understood, addressed, and eventually solved as such.*
>
> *The open hostility to religion that Beijing exhibits at times — most notably in its obsessive drive to stamp out the "evil cult" of Falun Gong — has pre-Marxist roots. **Scientism underlies the post-Mao technocracy, and it is the orthodoxy against which heresies are measured.** [Emphasis added]*

Thus, during the 1980s Technocracy (and scientism) took deep root not only in China, but also in South Korea, Singapore and Taiwan. Similar gains were seen in Europe during the 1990s and in the United States since 1973. The Trilateral Commission's utopian "New International Economic Order" is Technocracy, and China was the first modern experiment and transformation.

And, why not China? Dealing with a single Communist dictator was a lot easier than dealing with a parliament, congress or senate found in more democratic nations. The so-called "Neo-Authoritarianism" mentioned above is ample evidence that the champions of Technocracy knew full-well that it would be easier to transform an already authoritarian nation into Technocracy. In fact, as far back as 1932, original members of Technocracy, Inc. in the U.S. called for a dictatorship in the U.S. in order to implement Technocracy.

This is the rest of the story, of which I was a keen observer at the time. What I lacked in education and academic discipline was amply shored up by the consummate researcher and scholar, Antony C. Sutton, who was a professor of economics and a research fellow at Stanford's prestigious Hoover Institution for War Peace and Revolution in California. Sutton is widely recognized as the most detailed and prolific writer in the 20th century on the transfer of technology from the West to the East. [End of article.]

CONCLUSION

As you read through *Trilaterals Over Washington*, you will begin to understand the modern state of affairs in a new light. Dots will be connected. Patterns will be uncovered. Strategies will be revealed.

However, it is imperative that you read the conclusion to the saga of Trilateral hegemony, which is contained in *Technocracy Rising: The Trojan Horse of Global Transformation*. One reader wrote,

"For the first time, the core of the globalist agenda is clearly defined. A brilliantly researched piece of work by one of the most knowledgeable experts on the subject."

Another reader wrote,

I have been following the Trilateral Commission for some time. I first heard of it in 1977. This is the best, most comprehensive information I've read on the Trilateral Commission and all it touches: ever. Easy to read and easy to understand.

Thus, these three literary works are meant to, indeed must

be, read together to see the entire picture. (You are encouraged to follow up-to-the-minute analysis and developments on www.Technocracy.News.)

This is obviously not the end of the story, but at the very least it exposes the players, their strategies, achievements and aspirations. I will leave you with a poignant historical exhortation from the great American statesman, Daniel Webster (1782-1852):

> *"I apprehend no danger to our country from a foreign foe. Our destruction, should it come at all, will be from another quarter. From the inattention of the people to the concerns of their government, from their carelessness and negligence, I must confess that I do apprehend some danger. I fear that they may place too implicit a confidence in their public servants, and fail properly to scrutinize their conduct; that in this way they may be made the dupes of designing men, and become the instruments of their own undoing.* **Make them intelligent, and they will be vigilant; give them the means of detecting the wrong, and they will apply the remedy."**
> [emphasis added]

Indeed, dear friends, the rest is up to us.

Patrick Wood, 2017

TRILATERALS OVER WASHINGTON

VOLUME I

Chapter One

What Is The Trilateral Commission?

According to each issue of the official Trilateral Commission quarterly magazine *Trialogue*:

> *The Trilateral Commission was formed in 1973 by private citizens of Western Europe, Japan and North America to foster closer cooperation among these three regions on common problems. It seeks to improve public understanding of such problems, to support proposals for handling them jointly, and to nurture habits and practices of working together among these regions.*

This book attempts to tell the rest of the story, according to official and unofficial commission sources and other available documents.

The Trilateral Commission was founded by the persistent maneuvering of **David Rockefeller** and **Zbigniew Brzezinski. Rockefeller,** chairman of the ultra-powerful Chase Manhattan Bank, a director of many major multinational corporations and "endowment funds" and has long been a central figure in the mysterious Council on Foreign Relations (CFR). **Brzezinski,** a brilliant prognosticator of one- world idealism, has been a professor at Columbia University and the author of several books that have served as "policy guidelines" for the CFR. **Brzezinski** served as the commission's executive director from its inception in 1973 until late 1976 when he was appointed by President **Carter** as assistant to the president for national security affairs.

The word commission is puzzling since it is usually associated with instrumentalities set up by governments. It seems out of place with a so-called private group unless we can determine that it really is an arm of a government - an unseen government, different from the visible government in Washington. European and Japanese involvement indicates a world government rather than a national government. We would hope that the concept of a sub-rosa world government is just wishful thinking on the part of the Trilateral commissioners. The facts, however, line up pessimistically.

If the Council on Foreign Relations can be said to be a spawning ground for the concepts of one-world idealism, then the Trilateral Commission is the "task force" assembled to assault the beachheads. Already the commission has placed its members (some of whom have subsequently "resigned") in the top posts the U.S. has to offer.

President **Carter**, the country politician who promised, "I will never lie to you," was chosen to join the commission by **Brzezinski** in 1973. It was **Brzezinski**, in fact, who first identified **Carter** as presidential timber, and subsequently educated him in economics, foreign policy, and the ins-and-outs of world politics. Upon **Carter's** election, **Brzezinski** was appointed assistant to the president for national security matters. Commonly, he is called the head of the National Security Council because he answers only to the president - some say Brzezinski holds the second most powerful position in the U.S. **Carter's** running mate, **Walter Mondale**, was also a member of the commission. (If you are trying to calculate the odds of three virtually unknown men, out of over sixty commissioners from the U.S., capturing the three most powerful positions in the land, don't bother. Your calculations will be meaningless.)

On 7 January 1977 *Time Magazine*, whose editor-in-chief, **Hedley Donovan**, is a powerful Trilateral commissioner, named President **Carter** "Man of the Year." The sixteen-page article in that issue not only failed to mention **Carter's** connection with the commission but stated the following:

As he searched for Cabinet appointees, Carter seemed at times hesitant and frustrated disconcertingly out of character. His lack of ties to Washington and the Party Establishment - qualities that helped raise him to the White House - carrypotential dangers. He does not know the Federal Government or the pressures it creates. He does not really know the politicians whom he will need to help him run the country.

Is this portrait of **Carter** as a political innocent simply inaccurate or is it deliberately misleading? By 25 December 1976 - two weeks before the *Time* article appeared - **Carter** had already chosen his cabinet. Three of his cabinet members - **Vance**, **Blumenthal**, and **Brown** - were Trilateral commissioners; and the other non-commission members were not unsympathetic to commission objectives and operations. In addition, Carter had appointed another fourteen Trilateral commissioners to top government posts. As of 25 December 1976, therefore, there were nineteen commissioners, including **Carter** and **Mondale**, holding tremendous political power. These presidential appointees represented almost one-third of the Trilateral Commission members from the United States. Try to give odds to that!

Nevertheless, is there even the slightest evidence to indicate anything other than conspiracy? Hardly! **Zbigniew Brzezinski** spelled out the qualifications of a 1976 presidential winner in 1973:

The Democratic candidate in 1976 will have to emphasize work, the family, religion and, increasingly, patriotism...The new conservatism will clearly not go back to laissez faire. It will be a philosophical conservatism. It will be a kind of conservative statism or managerism. There will be conservative values but a reliance on a great deal of co- determination between state and the corporations.

*On 23 May 1976 journalist Leslie H. Gelb wrote in the not-so- conservative New York Times, "(**Brzezinski**) was the first guy in the Community to pay attention to **Carter**, to take him seriously. He spent time with **Carter**, talked to him, sent him books and articles, educated him." **Richard Gardner** (also of Columbia University) joined into the "educational" task, and as Gelb noted, between the two of them they had **Carter** virtually to themselves. Gelb continued: "While the Community* *as a whole was looking elsewhere, to Senators Kennedy and* **Mondale**...*it paid off.* **Brzezinski**, *with* **Gardner**, *is now the leading man on* **Carter's** *foreign policy task force."* Although **Richard Gardner** is of considerable academic influence, it should be clear that **Brzezinski** is the "guiding light" of foreign policy in the **Carter** administration. Along with Commissioner **Vance** and a host of other commissioners in the state department, **Brzezinski** has more than continued the policies of befriending our enemies and alienating our friends. Since early 1977 we have witnessed a massive push to attain "normalized" relations with Communist China, Cuba, the USSR, Eastern European nations, Angola, etc. Conversely, we have withdrawn at least some support from Nationalist China, South Africa, Rhodesia, etc. It is not just a trend -it is an epidemic. Thus, if it can be said that **Brzezinski** has, at least in part, contributed to current U.S. foreign and domestic policy, then we should briefly analyze exactly what he is espousing.

MORE JUST AND EQUITABLE

The Trilateral Commission met in Tokyo, Japan, in January 1977. **Carter** and **Brzezinski** obviously could not attend as they were still in the process of reorganizing the White House. They did, however, address personal letters to the meeting, which were reprinted in Trialogue:

> *It gives me special pleasure to send greetings to all of you gathering for the Trilateral Commission meeting in Tokyo. I have warm memories of our meeting in Tokyo some eighteen months ago, and am sorry I cannot be with you now.*

> *My active service on the Commission since its inception in 1973 has been a splendid experience for me, and it provided me with excellent opportunities to come to know leaders in our three regions.*

> *As I emphasized in my campaign, a strong partnership among us is of the greatest importance. We share economic, political and security concerns that make it logical we should seek ever-increasing cooperation and understanding. And this co-operation is essential not only for our three regions, but in*

the global search for a more Just and equitable world order (emphasis added). I hope to see you on the occasion of your next meeting in Washington, and I look forward to receiving reports on your work in Tokyo."

Jimmy Carter

Brzezinski's letter, in a similar vein, follows:

The Trilateral Commission has meant a great deal to me over the last few years. It has been the stimulus for intellectual creativity and a source of personal satisfaction. I have formed close ties with new friends and colleagues in all three regions, ties which I value highly and which I am sure will continue.

*I remain convinced that, on the larger architectural issues of today, collaboration among our regions is of the utmost necessity. This collaboration must be dedicated to the fashioning of a **more just and equitable world order** (emphasis added). This will require a prolonged process, but 1 think we can look forward with confidence and take some pride in the contribution which the Commission is making.*

Zbigniew Brzezinski

The key phrase in both letters is "more just and equitable world order." Does this emphasis indicate that something is wrong with our present world order, that is, with national structures? Yes, according to **Brzezinski**; and since the present "framework" is inadequate to handle world problems, it must be done away with and supplanted with a world government.

In September 1974 **Brzezinski** was asked in an interview by the Brazilian newspaper *Vega*. "How would you define this new world order?" **Brzezinski** answered:

When I speak of the present international system I am referring to relations in specific fields, most of all among the Atlantic countries; commercial, military, mutual security relations, involving the international monetary fund, NA TO etc. We need to change the international system for a global system in which new, active and creative forces recently developed - should be integrated. This system needs to include Japan. Brazil. the oil producing countries, and even the USSR,

to the extent which the Soviet Union is willing to participate
in a global system.

When asked if Congress would have an expanded or diminished role in the new system, **Brzezinski** declared "...the reality of
our times is that a modern society such as the U.S. needs a central
coordinating and renovating organ which cannot be made up of
six hundred people."

Brzezinski developed background for the need for a new
system in his book *Between Two Ages: America's Role in the
Technetronic Era* (1969). He wrote that mankind has moved
through three great stages of evolution, and is in the middle of the
fourth and final stage. The first stage he describes as "religious,"
combining a heavenly "universalism provided by the acceptance
of the idea that man's destiny is essentially in God's hands" with
an earthly "narrowness derived from massive ignorance, illitera-
cy, and a vision confined to the immediate environment."

The second stage is nationalism, stressing Christian equality
before the law, which "marked another giant step in the progres-
sive redefinition of man's nature and place in our world." The
third stage is Marxism, which, says **Brzezinski**, "represents a further vital and creative stage in the maturing of man's universal vision." The fourth and final stage is Brzezinski's *Technetronic Era*,
or the ideal of rational humanism on a global scale - the result of
American- Communist evolutionary transformations.

In considering our present structure **Brzezinski** states:

*Tension is unavoidable as man strives to assimilate the new
into the framework of the old. For a time the established
framework resiliently integrates the new by adapting it in a
more familiar shape. But at some point the old framework
becomes overloaded. The newer input can no longer be redefined into traditional forms, and eventually it asserts itself
with compelling force. Today, though, the old framework of
international politics - with their spheres of influence, military alliances between nation-states, the fiction of sovereignty, doctrinal conflicts arising from nineteenth century crises
- is clearly no longer compatible with reality.*

One of the most important "frameworks" in the world, and especially to Americans, is the United States Constitution. It is this document that outlined the most prosperous nation in the history of the world. Is our sovereignty really "fiction"? Is the U.S. vision no longer compatible with reality? **Brzezinski** further states:

> *The approaching two-hundredth anniversary of the Declaration of Independence could justify the call for a national constitutional convention to reexamine the nation's formal institutional framework. Either 1976 or 1989 - the two- hundredth an anniversary of the Constitution could serve as a suitable target date culminating a national dialogue on the relevance of existing arrangements...Realism, however, forces us to recognize that the necessary political innovation will not come from direct constitutional reform, desirable as that would be. The needed change is more likely to develop incrementally and less overtly...in keeping with the American tradition of blurring distinctions between public and private institution.*

In **Brzezinski**'s *Technetronic Era* then, the "nation state as a fundamental unit of man's organized life has ceased to be the principal creative force: International banks and multinational corporations are acting and planning in terms that are far in advance of the political concepts of the nation-state."

Understanding the philosophy of and monitoring the Trilateral commission is the only way we can reconcile the myriad of apparent contradictions in the information filtered through to us in the national press. For instance, how is it that the Marxist regime in Angola derives the great bulk of its foreign exchange from the offshore oil operations of Gulf Oil Corporation? Why does **Andrew Young** insist that "Communism has never been a threat to Blacks in Africa"? Why does the U.S. funnel billions in technological aid to the Soviet Union and Communist China? Why does the U.S. apparently help its enemies while chastising its friends?

These questions, and hundreds of others like them, cannot be explained in any other way: the U.S. Executive Branch (and related agencies) is not anti-Marxist or anti-Communist - it is, in fact, pro-Marxist. Those ideals which led to the heinous abuses of Hitler, Lenin, Stalin, and Mussolini are now being accepted as necessary inevitabilities by our elected and appointed leaders. This hardly suggests the Great American Dream. It is very doubtful that Americans would agree with Brzezinski or the Trilateral Commission. It is the American public who is paying the price, suffering the consequences, but not understanding the true nature of the situation.

ELEMENTS OF CONTROL

This book will carefully document the economic nature of the driving force within the Trilateral Commission. It is the giant multinational corporations - those with Trilateral representation - which consistently benefit from Trilateral policy and actions. Polished academics such as **Brzezinski, Gardner, Allison, McCracken, Henry Owen** etc., serve only to give "philosophical" justification to the exploitation of the world.

Don't underestimate their power or the distance they have already come. Their economic base is already established. Giants like Coca-Cola, IBM, CBS, Caterpillar Tractor, Bank of America, Chase Manhattan Bank, Deere & Company, Exxon, and others virtually dwarf whatever remains of American businesses. The market value of IBM's stock alone, for instance, is greater than the value of all the stocks on the American Stock Exchange. Chase Manhattan Bank has some fifty thousand branches or correspondent banks throughout the world. What reaches our eyes and ears is highly regulated by CBS, the *New York Times*, *Time* magazine, etc.

The most important thing of all is to remember that the political coup de grace is over - the virtual domination of the White House.

Fortunately, these commissioners are not infallible they make mistakes. They misjudge. They over- and under-estimate. They create crises to manage and then find menacing backlashes from those very crises.

"Management by crisis" has brought about the energy crisis, the International monetary crisis, and the banking crisis. All are clearly man-made, but all certainly threaten the creators. In the end, the biggest crisis of all is that of the American way of life. Americans never counted on such powerful and influential groups working against the Constitution and freedom, either inadvertently or purposefully, and even now, the principles that helped to build this great country are all but reduced to the sound of meaningless babblings.

CHAPTER TWO

THE POWER STRUCTURE OF THE TRILATERAL COMISSION PART I

A bare membership list of the Trilateral Commission does not suggest its massive political and economic power nor its outstanding scope and global ramifications. Understanding of the power base requires analysis of its membership.

The basic Trilateral structure is a power pyramid. At the tip of the pyramid we can identify a "financial brotherhood," comprising several old-line American families, the so-called American aristocracy, controlling major New York financial installations. Below this highest level is the executive committee for the United States, linked to executive committees in Europe and Japan. Then comes the Trilateral Commission itself: 109 members from North America, 106 from Europe, and 74 from Japan. Because these Trilaterals control the executive branch of the U.S. government, they also control U.S. policy. Furthermore, one of their ongoing projects is to dominate nine "core countries" in Europe and Japan, which, by virtue of their productive ability, account for 80 percent of world output. The "core" group will then dominate the remaining 20 percent of the world. The American multinational corporations (MNCs) provide country by country liaison, intelligence, and financial conduits, the sinews to bind a global New

World Order to the directions of the Commission.

As the *Washington Post* has phrased it:

Trilateralists are not three-sided people. They are members of a private, though not secret, international organization put together by the wealthy banker, David Rockefeller, to stimulate the establishment dialogue between Western Europe, Japan and the United States.

But here is the unsettling thing about the Trilateral Commission. The President-elect is a member. So is Vice-President-elect Walter F. Mondale. So are the new Secretaries of State, Defense and Treasury, Cyrus R. Vance, Harold Brown and W. Michael Blumenthal. So is Zbigniew Brzezinski, who is a former Trilateral director and, Carter's national security adviser, also a bunch of others who will make foreign policy for America in the next four years. [1]

COMPOSITION OF THE POWER PYRAMID

In outline form then, the Trilateral power pyramid has five levels and looks like this:

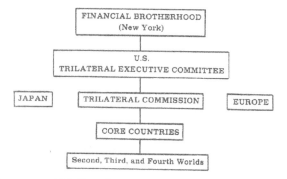

There are 109 North American commissioners (as of October 1977): of these 12 are Canadian and 97 are American citizens. American commissioners can be divided into three operational groups as follows: (1) operators, (2) propagandists and technicians, and (3) power holders. Let's take each group in turn.

Operators	Number of Commissioners	Percentage of Total U.S. Membership
Establishment lawyers	9	9
Politicians/bureaucrats	27	27
Trade unionists	6	6
Miscellaneous	5	5
Total	47	47

The common link among Trilateral operators is administration of power rather than power holding. Lawyers, politicians, bureaucrats, and trade unionists come and go in the halls of power. They retain administrative positions only as long as they are successful in using political power to gain political objectives. Operators do not, by and large, create objectives - this is an important point. One should label this group of operators "the hired hands." As Senator Mansfield once said of Congress, "To get along, you must go along." Trilateral operators are at the pinnacle of success in "going along."

Consequently, we find the following Establishment law firms well represented in Trilateralism:

CENTER FOR LAW AND SOCIAL POLICY

Paul C. Warnke

Philip H. Trezise

CLIFFORD, WARNKE, GLASS, McILWAIN & FINNEY

Paul C. Warnke

COUDERT BROTHERS

Sol M. Linowitz

Richard N. Gardner

O'MELVENY & MYERS

Warren Christopher

William T. Coleman, Jr.

SIMPSON, *THACHER* & *BARTLETT*

Cyrus R. Vance

WILMER, CUTLER & PICKERING

Gerard C. Smith

Lloyd N. Cutler

PROPAGANDISTS AND TECHNICIANS

Quite distinct from the operators, although their functions often overlap, are the propagandists (the media) and the technicians (academicians and research controllers). These groups provide the intellectual linkage between the power holders (we consider these next) and the power administrators (the operators).

Technicians design the plans needed to promote and implement objectives. They explain ideas to the public and even conceive ideas - within limits. Technicians and propagandists achieve personal success only insofar as they have ability to conceive and promote plans within the overall framework welcome to the power holders. A media source distributing unwelcome news or a researcher developing unwelcome conclusions is politely so informed - and usually takes the hint. Trilateralist technicians are experts at "getting the message."

We find the following "think tanks" linked to Trilateralism:

ASPEN *INSTITUTE FOR HUMANISTIC STUDIES*

Maurice F. Strong

Robert S. Ingersoll

BROOKINGS INSTITUTION

William T. Coleman, Jr.

Henry D. Owen

Gerard C. Smith

C. Fred Bergsten

Graham T. Allison, Jr.

Philip H. Trezise

Bruce K. MacLaury

CENTER FOR DEFENSE INFORMATION

Paul C. Warnke

COLUMBIA UNIVERSITY

Richard N. Gardner

GEORGETOWN UNIVERSITY, CENTER FOR STRATEGIC AND

INTERNATIONAL STUDIES
> **David M. Abshire**
> **William E. Brock**
> **William V. Roth, Jr.**
> **Gerard C. Smith**

HARVARD UNIVERSITY
> **Graham Allison**
> **Robert R. Bowie**

HOOVER INSTITUTION ON *WAR, REVOLUTION AND PEACE*
> **David Packard**

HUDSON INSTITUTE
> **J. Paul Austin**

MASSACHUSETTS INSTITUTE OF *TECHNOLOGY (MIT)*
> **Carroll L. Wilson**

MITRE CORPORATION
> **Lucy Wilson Benson**

RAND CORPORATION
> **J. Paul Austin**
> **Graham Allison**
> **William T. Coleman, Jr.**

WORLD WATCH INSTITUTE
> **C. Fred Bergsten**

These "think tanks" are financed by foundations which are also linked to Trilateralism:

ROCKEFELLER FOUNDATION
> **Cyrus R. Vance**
> **W. Michael Blumenthal**
> **Robert V. Roosa**
> **Lane Kirkland**
> **John D. Rockefeller IV**

TWENTIETH CENTURY FUND RUSSELL SAGE FOUNDATION
> **J. Paul Austin**

FORD FOUNDATION

Andrew Brimmer
John Loudon
CARNEGIE ENDOWMENT FOR INTERNATIONAL PEACE
William A. Hewitt
Hedley Donovan
Thomas L. Hughes
BORDEN FOUNDATION
Zbigniew Brzezinski
ROCKEFELLER BROTHERS FUND
David Rockefeller
ROCKEFELLER FAMILY FUND
David Rockefeller
John D. Rockefeller IV
WOODRUFF FOUNDATION
J. Paul Austin
WORLD PEACE FOUNDA TION
Robert B. Bowie
The following media outlets are also linked to Trilateralism:
NEW YORK TIMES
Cyrus B. Vance
CBS
Arthur B. Taylor
Henry B. Schacht
LOS ANGELES TIMES
Harold Brown
TIME. INC.
Hedley Donovan
FOREIGN POLICY MAGAZINE
Samuel P. Huntington
Thomas L. Hughes
Richard N. Cooper
Elliot L. Richardson
Marina von Neumann Whitman

Richard Holbrooke
Zbigniew Brzezinski
FOREIGN AFFAIRS
William M. Roth
C. Fred Bergsten
CHICAGO SUN-TIMES
Emmett Dedmon

POWER HOLDERS

So, by elimination, we are left with a third group:

	Number of Commissioners	Percentage of Total U.S. Membership
Multinational corporate directors	17	17
International bankers	11	11
Totals	28	28

However, even the power holders are not the ultimate power base - that is an even smaller group, the American aristocracy itself. Power holders lay down guidelines for the propagandists and the research directors, and pass through objectives to the operators for implementation. Remember, a Richard Nixon goes to see international banker **David Rockefeller**, not the other way around. **Henry Kissinger** accepted a gift of $50,000 from power holder Nelson Rockefeller, not the other way around. **Jimmy Carter** is invited to have lunch with **David Rockefeller**, not the other way around. A widespread myth in American society is that the president has completely independent power, that he is not beholden to some power base. Indeed, the president has power; but presidential power can in fact be applied only within carefully framed guidelines, and this has been the case at least since the days of President Grant.

So our Trilateral analysis looks like this:

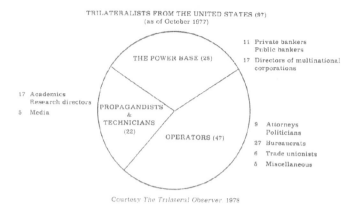

TRILATERALISTS FROM THE UNITED STATES (97)
(as of October 1977)

THE POWER BASE (28)

11 Private bankers
    Public bankers
17 Directors of multinational
    corporations

17 Academics
    Research directors
 5 Media

PROPAGANDISTS
&
TECHNICIANS
(22)

OPERATORS (47)

 9 Attorneys
    Politicians
27 Bureaucrats
 6 Trade unionists
 5 Miscellaneous

Courtesy *The Trilateral Observer* 1978

When we look at Trilateralists in the three Trilateral areas we can identify some differences, but these are not really of major distinction. Academics and industrialists are equally represented from all three areas. Media representatives and bureaucrats are more prominent from Europe. There are more American and European politicians than Japanese politicians. The diplomats are more likely to be European than American or Japanese.

So let's look more closely at these American commissioners, at names rather than numbers.

THE TRILATERAL LEGAL ESTABLISHMENT

Nine of the American Trilateral commissioners are Establishment lawyers, from highly influential major law firms. The "revolving door" area between so-called public service and private gain, where attorneys alternate between private practice and the federal payroll, clouds more precise identification. For some reason, probably accidental, two of the nine lawyers are partners in the major Los Angeles law firm O'Melveny & Myers: senior partner, **William T. Coleman Jr.** (also a director of **David Rockefeller's** Chase Manhattan Bank and a former secretary of transportation); and **Warren Christopher**, who was a partner from 1958 to 1967 and again from 1969 until joining the present **Carter** administration as deputy secretary of state. Other attorney Trilateralists are well known in and around the halls of power: **George S. Franklin, Jr.** started out in a Wall Street law firm, soon became associated with the **Rockefeller** family, and is today coordinator of the Trilateral Commission.

Primary Occupation of Trilateral Commission Members (Past & Present

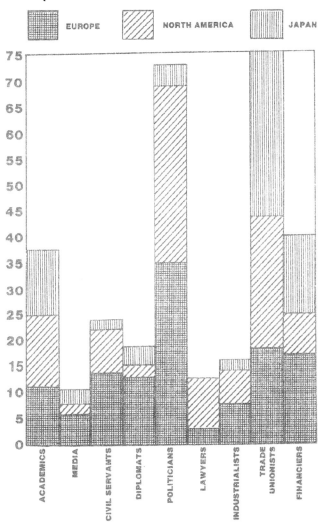

George W. Ball, member of the New York law firm of Cleary, Gottlieb, Steen & Ball, was recently chairman of the international banking firm Lehman Brothers International. **Gerard C. Smith**, formerly with the Washington firm of Wilmer, Cutler & Pickering is now ambassador-at-large for non-proliferation matters. **Lloyd N. Cutler** has also been a partner in Wilmer, Cutler & Pickering since 1962. **Cyrus R. Vance**, secretary of state, was formerly partner in the venerable firm of Simpson, Thacher & Bartlett of New York, whose then partners aided the 1917 Bolshevik Revolution 2 in the same way as **Cyrus Vance** is today pressing the African Marxist guerrilla cause upon Rhodesia and South Africa.

It is truly extraordinary how influential pro-Bolshevik actions in a mere handful of prestigious law firms can persist unpublicized and uninvestigated for over five or six decades. Commissioner **Paul C. Warnke**, presently director of the Arms Control and Disarmament Agency, was formerly a partner in the firm of Clifford, Warnke, Glass. McIlwain & Finney of Washington. In brief, Trilateral attorneys are from the major old-line Establishment law firms.

POLITICS AND GOVERNMENT

A sizeable group of twenty-seven Trilateral commissioners can be categorized as professional politicians and professional bureaucrats, thus reflecting the Trilateral need to control domestic government in order to fulfill Trilateral internationalist objectives. President of the United States **James Earl Carter, Jr.**, and Vice-President **Walter Frederick Mondale** are longstanding Trilateralists. **Carter** was brought in by **David Rockefeller** in 1973, as reported in *The Times* (London):

> *Governor Jimmy Carter, the 1976 Democratic Presidential candidate, has for reasons known only to himself professed to be an innocent abroad, but the record is somewhat different. As Governor of Georgia, a state aspiring to be the centre of the New South, he led the state trade missions abroad. While in London in the autumn of 1973 he dined with another American visitor, but by no means an innocent, Mr. David Rockefeller of Chas[J Manhattan Bank.*

> *Mr. Rockefeller was then establishing, with the help of Professor Zbigniew Brzezinski of Columbia University, an international study group now known as the Trilateral*

Commission. He was looking for American members outside the usual catchment area of universities, corporation law firms and government, was impressed by the Governor, if only because he had ventured abroad, and invited him to join. Governor Carter, perhaps because he was already eyeing the White House from afar, was only too happy to accept.

In any event. five senators also are Trilateral commissioners:

Senator Lawton Chiles. Democrat, Florida

Senator Alan Cranston. Democrat. California, Senate majority whip

Senator John C. Culver, Democrat. Iowa

Senator John C. Danforth, Republican, Missouri

Senator William V. Roth, Jr., Republican, Delaware

This neatly reflects the Democratic majority in the Senate. three Democrats and two Republicans; and it is notable that the Senate majority whip - a key Senate post - is a Trilateralist.

The following six Congressmen are Trilateralists:

John B. Anderson, Republican. Illinois.
Chairman House Republican Conference.

John Brademas. Democrat, Indiana; majority whip.

William S. Cohen. Republican. Maine,

Barber B. Conable, Jr. Republican. New York

Thomas S. Foley. Democrat. Washington;
chairman, House Democratic Caucus

Donald M. Fraser, Democrat, Minnesota; chairman, Democratic Conference and Americans for Democratic Action

Trilateralists also occupy key posts in the House, i.e., chairman of the House Republican Conference, majority whip, chairman of the Democratic Conference, and chairman of the House Democratic Caucus. In sum, Trilaterals have a lock on the legislative process.

The significance of this lock on the legislative process is brought into focus when we examine the political ideology of Trilateralism as expressed by **Crozier, Huntington,** and **Watanuki** in *The Crisis of Democracy.*

- The democratic political system no longer has any purpose.
- The concepts of equality and individualism give problems to authority.
- The media is not sufficiently subservient to the elite.
- Democracy has to be "balanced" (Le., restricted).
- The authority and power of the central government must be increased.

Weighing these totalitarian ideas which form the political philosophy of the commission against congressional membership in the Trilateral Commission, the reader will be tempted to ask, were these the political policies espoused by these politicians when elected to office?

Two present state governors are commissioners: **John D. Rockefeller IV** of West Virginia and **James R. Thompson** of Illinois. So are two former state governors, **William W. Scranton** of Pennsylvania, and **Daniel I. Evans** of Washington.

Finally, there are the permanent professional bureaucrats including **Elliot Lee Richardson,** now ambassador-at-large with responsibility for the UN Law of the Sea Conference (a major Trilateral objective); **Edwin O. Reischauer,** former ambassador to Japan and reportedly close to the **Rockefeller** family; **Russell E. Train,** former administrator of the Environmental Protection Agency; **Richard Charles Holbrooke,** now assistant secretary of state for Far Eastern affairs;

Gerald L. Parsky, former assistant secretary of the treasury for international affairs; **Richard N. Gardner,** now ambassador to Italy; **George Bush** former director of the Central Intelligence Agency; **Anthony Soloman,** now under-secretary of the Treasury for monetary affairs; **Philip H. Trezise,** former assistant secretary of state for economic affairs; and **Lucy Benson,** under-secretary of state for security assistance.

We can identify twenty-seven Trilateralists now or recently in the executive branch of the United States government and always in top policy making positions. Just how closely this elite monopolizes top administration jobs in Republican and Democratic administrations can be illustrated by looking back to President Ford's cabinet shuffle of November 1975. Under media headlines of "sweeping changes" in the cabinet, Ford "discarded" Secretary of Defense **Schlesinger**, who is now Secretary of Energy in the **Carter** administration. Ford also installed Trilateralist **Elliot Lee Richardson** as Secretary of Commerce, who is now Ambassador-at-Large in the **Carter** administration and previously had been undersecretary of state in the Nixon administration. Trilateralist **George Bush** was a Nixon appointee to CIA, and **David Packard**, a businessman Trilateralist, was an ardent Nixonite and formerly deputy secretary of defense.

In brief, top administration jobs - Republican and Democrat - are being filled from a talent pool dominated by the Trilateral Commission. This selective process of filling top Executive Department slots with Trilateralists has been deliberate and ruthless. Before President **Carter** formally took office, numerous Trilateralists were appointed as follows:

Zbigniew Brzezinski - assistant to the president for national security affairs

Cyrus Vance - secretary of state

Harold Brown - secretary of defense

W. Michael Blumenthal - secretary of the treasury

Andrew Young - ambassador to the United Nations

Warren Christopher - deputy secretary of state

Lucy Wilson Benson - under secretary of state for security affairs

Richard Cooper - under secretary of state for economic affairs

Richard Holbrooke - under secretary of state for East Asian and Pacific affairs

W. Anthony Lake - under secretary of state for policy planning

Sol Linowitz - co-negotiator on the Panama Canal Treaty

Gerald Smith - ambassador-at-large for nuclear power negotiations

Elliot Richardson - delegate to the Law of the Sea Conference

Richard Gardner - ambassador to Italy

Anthony Solomon - under secretary of the treasury for monetary affairs

C. Fred Bergsten - assistant secretary of the treasury for international affairs

Paul Warnke - director, Arms Control and Disarmament Agency

Robert R. Bowie - deputy director of intelligence for national estimates

If these appointments were from a single ethnic group, or graduates of a single university, or residents of a single state, or even members of a single club, the public outcry would have been immediate and deafening. In fact, their commonality is far more serious: Trilateralists represent a political philosophy alien to the American tradition. *The Crisis in Democracy* is devoted to the theme that the American system needs to be discarded and totalitarian central authority substituted. Why was there no public outcry? Simply because media reporting was superficial and stifled, people did and presently do not know.

TRADE UNIONS

Six prominent American trade unionists are Trilateralists (as of October 1977.)

Three early Commissioners were **I. W. Abel**, president United Steel Workers of America; **Lane Kirkland**, prominent in the AFL-CIO efforts to elect **Jimmy Carter** as president and **Leonard Woodcock**, formerly president of United Auto Workers Union and more recently chief U.S. envoy to China for the **Carter** administration. Three recent union Trilateralists are **Glenn E. Watts**, president of Communications Workers of America, **Martin J. Ward**, president of United Association of Journeymen and Apprentices of the Plumbing and Pipe Fitting Industry of the U.S. and Canada; and **Sol Chaikin**, president of the International Ladies Garment Workers Union. These prominent trade unionists need to read some modern history: a close association of unions and big business is the hallmark of a fascist economy. Notably, George Meany is not a Trilateralist and has retained an outspoken criticism of Wall Street globalists. Remember, too, that Meany has been a persistent critic of the Wall Street construction of a Marxist world. while all the businessmen Trilateralists, including such self- styled "conservatives" as **David Packard**, have been outspokenly pro- Soviet when it comes to subsidizing the Soviet military machine with American technology and aid.

THE MEDIA

Trilateralist media representation, although not large in numbers, is highly influential. Of five media commissioners, three are relatively insignificant: **Doris Anderson**, editor of Chatelaine Magazine; **Carl Rowan**, columnist and **Arthur R. Taylor**, formerly head of the CBS network, dismissed in October 1976.

Two media Trilaterals are highly influential: **Emmett Dedmon** is editorial director of the Chicago Sun-Times, published by Field Enterprises. The chairman of Field Enterprises, Inc. is **Marshall Field V**, who is also a director of First National Bank of Chicago. **Marshall Field V** operates Field Enterprises under an exhaustive agreement with his half brother "Ted." Frederick W. Field; and Field ownership is significant because of Trilateral connections with the First National Bank of Chicago. In any event Chicago Sun Times is the sixth largest newspaper in the U.S. (daily circulation 687.000.)

Another influential media Trilateralist is **Hedley Donovan**, editor-in- chief of *Time*. member of the Council on Foreign Relations and director of the Carnegie Endowment for International Peace. According to the U.S. Labor Party:

> *Donovan played a central role in the "faking of the President, 1976. Under his Trilateral direction, Time functioned as a black propaganda vehicle throughout the campaign and post-election period, painting* **Carter** *as an "outsider" with no connections with the corrupt politics of Washington, D.C.*

and Wall Street. This "image building" provided the crucial cover for the planned vote fraud, and Time played a crucial cover-up role as widespread evidence of the Nov. 2 fraud surfaced.

Trilateral disdain for the First Amendment is a factor working strongly against generally sympathetic media attention. On the other hand, Trilateralist intervention in day-to-day media operation, by use of the traditional telephone call, is probable, given the numerous Trilateral corporate directors in the media: **Henry B. Schacht** is a director of CBS; **Sol Linowitz** is a director of *Time*; **J. Paul Austin** is a director of Dow Jones; **Harold Brown** is a director of Times-Mirror Corporation; **Archibald K. Davis** is a director of Media General. Inc.; **Peter G. Peterson** is a director of Great Book Foundation and National Education TV; **William M. Roth** is a director of Athenum Publishers; and **Cyrus Vance** is a director of the New York Times. Their presence is ominous. However, any persistent intervention to kill or reorient stories will backfire. Most media people are professionals rather than propagandists.

Other Trilateral influence, albeit indirect, stems from appointments such as that of Sharon Percy Rockefeller to the Board of Directors of the Corporation for Public Broadcasting (CPB); Sharon is the wife of Commissioner **John D. Rockefeller IV**, governor of West Virginia. The CPB "closed shop" is already under fire in the media interesting as a minor example of the basic game plan to blur the distinction between "public" and "private" for Trilateralist profit.

ACADEMIC AND RESEARCH INSTITUTIONS

The media may be a Trilateral weak spot but its numerous links with the academic and research world are its strong points. The academic- research world is not only the "brains" of Trilateralism but the suppliers of many capable operators, that is, academics dissatisfied with the rewards of academe who search for the bright lights and the ego- satisfaction of power manipulation.

Among the more obvious of such academics are **Henry Kissinger** (Harvard); **Arjay Miller** (Stanford, formerly Ford Motor); **Paul McCracken** (University of Michigan); **John C. Sawhill** (president. New York University); **Harold Brown** (president, California Institute of Technology and director of Schroders, Ltd.); **Hendrik S. Houthakker** (Harvard); **Zbigniew Brzezinski** (Columbia); **Marina von Neumann Whitman** (Manufacturers Hanover Bank and University of Pittsburgh); **Gardner Ackley** (Michigan); **David M. Abshire** (Georgetown); **Graham T. Allison, Jr.** (Harvard); **Robert Bowie** (now deputy director of intelligence for National Estimates); **Gerald L. Curtis** (Columbia); and **Carroll L. Wilson** (MIT).

Finally, and by no means least, **Bruce King MacLaury**, head of Brookings Institution which provides the policy input for the **Carter** administration and **Thomas L. Hughes,** president of the ever-present Carnegie Endowment for International Peace.

CONTROL OF THE EXECUTIVE BRANCH BY TRILATERALISTS

This massive infiltration of government from the top down by an alien philosophy is typified by the National Security Council whose four members have a statutory function to advise the President with regard to "the integration of domestic foreign and military policies relating to the national security." Its four members are all Trilateralists:

JIMMY CARTER

WALTER F. MONDALE

CYRUS R. VANCE

HAROLD BROWN

Similarly the Council on International Economic Policy, has eleven members including three Trilateralists:

Cyrus R. Vance

W. Michael Blumenthal (Chairman)

Harold Brown

What does it all add up to? The Greek newspaper *Exormisis* summed it all up even before the 1976 election:

"A new kind of fascism emerges with Carter. The oppression will not have the form we used to know, but it will be the "de-politicization" of all citizens in the U.S., and the generating of all power in the executive branch, that is, the Presidency,

without the President giving any account to the Congress or anybody else except the multi-nationals, which have financed Carter's campaign...the accession to power of Carter, who tries to present himself as the protector of the poor and the weak, would mean a new era of dictatorial policies. "

CANADIAN TRILATERALISTS

North America" for Trilateralism includes only the United States and Canada, with a seeming distinct preference for Quebecois Canadians. A glaring omission from the commission is Mexico - there are no Mexican commissioners. Mexico, in spite of its enormous economic potential, is delegated to the "rest of the world" category. The twelve Canadian Trilateralists as of October 1977 are divided as follows:

Politics and Government	3
Corporations	3
Research Institutions	2
Banking	2
Trade Unions	1
Legal Establishment	1
Total	12

From the viewpoint of Canadian independence, Canadian Trilateral membership is disturbing because it includes two members of Parliament, **Gordon Fairweather** and **Mitchell Sharp** (former Canadian minister of foreign " affairs), along with the directors of three quasi-official research institutions, **Peter Dobell**, **Michael Kirby**, and **Louis A. Desrochers** (founding director of the Institute for Research on Public Policy). **Claude Masson**, head of the Division of Planning and Research at the Department of Trade and Commerce, Ottawa, is also a Trilateralist. In brief, there is a heavy Canadian representation from the equivalents of Brookings Institution. Canadian corporate representation includes **Robert W. Bonner** (British Columbia Hydro), **Maurice F. Strong** (Petro Canada), and **Jean-Luc Pepin** (director of

American multinationals in Canada, Le., Westinghouse Canada, Ltd.; Collins Radio Company of Canada, Ltd.; Celanese Canada, Ltd.; and others). Finally, Canadian banking Trilateralists are **Michel Belanger**, of the Montreal Stock Exchange, and **Alan Hockin**, formerly with Morgan Stanley and now executive vice president of Toronto Dominion Bank.

FORMATION OF A TRILATERAL ADMINISTRATION

The creation of a **Carter** administration image of anti-Establishment arianism while simultaneously creating a Trilateral administration is typically the deceptive operational approach taken by this self-appointed elite. Take the first half dozen appointments and look at their associations and allegiances. The administration was at some pains to show a competition for posts and promoted the idea that anti-Establishment and non-Establishment persons would be appointed. See, for example, the Wall Street Journal on 2 December 1976 concerning the meeting of sixteen candidates in Plains, Georgia. The initial sequence of appointments went like this:

APPOINTMENT NUMBER 1

Bertram Lance: president of National Bank of Georgia (Atlanta) to be director of Office of Management and Budget (OMB). This is a vital, central post for plans to centralize the U.S. economy. Lance is not a Trilateral and has since departed.

APPOINTMENT NUMBER 2

Cyrus Vance: Secretary of State, Trilateralist. At the time of taking office, **Vance** was a partner in Simpson, Thacher & Bartlett; a director of IBM, Pan American World Airways and Aetna Life Insurance; a member of the Democratic party, Foreign Policy Task Force, Council on Foreign Relations (vice-chairman of the board), and the Trilateral Commission; and also a former deputy director of defense.

APPOINTMENT NUMBER 3

Michael Blumenthal: secretary of treasury, also a Trilateralist. Who is **Blumenthal**? Like **Henry Kissinger**, he was born in Germany and came to the U.S. at the age of twenty-one. At the time of taking office, he was chairman of Bendix Corporation and formerly in the Kennedy administration as deputy for the secretary for economic affairs, member of the Trilateral Commission, and the Council on Foreign Affairs, and the Initiative Committee for National Economic Planning (with **Irwin Miller** and **Robert McNamara**.)

After this third appointment, there was definite feedback in newspapers and radio that the "liberals" felt they had been betrayed because appointments and rumors of appointments did not include them. The result? Jane Cahill Pfeiffer, vice president of IBM, strongly pushed for commerce secretary as Appointment Number 4 dropped out, and the next two appointments went to big government liberals:

APPOINTMENT NUMBER 4

Brock Adams: transportation secretary. Also a Trilateralist.

APPOINTMENT NUMBER 5

Congressman **Andrew Young** as ambassador to U.N. Trilateral.

APPOINTMENT NUMBER 6

Zbigniew Brzezinski: executive director of Trilateral Commission was appointed national security adviser. Who is **Brzezinski**? By explicit statement, Trilateralists reject the Constitution and the democratic political process; in *Between Two Ages*, **Brzezinski** (**Carter's** sixth appointment) wrote as follows:

> *The approaching two-hundredth anniversary of the Declaration of Independence could justify the call for a national constitutional convention to reexamine the nation's formal institutional framework. Either 1976 or 1989 - the two hundredth anniversary of the Constitution -could serve as a suitable target date culminating a national dialogue on the relevance of existing arrangements...Realism, however, forces us to recognize that the necessary political innovation will not come from direct constitutional reform, desirable as that would be. The needed change is more likely to develop incrementally and less overtly...in keeping with the American tradition of blurring distinctions between public and private institutions.*

According to **Huntington** of *Foreign Policy* magazine, an "election coalition" may be abandoned after political office has been achieved; a politician does not have to keep his word to the elec-torate. **Jimmy Carter** is a supreme example of Trilateralism in practice. When **Brzezinski** refers to "develop(ing) incremen-tally and less overtly" he is specifically recommending a decep-tive "salami-type" approach to abandonment of the Constitution. Perhaps some readers may consider this to be the essence of sub-version. If so, they had better do something about it, because no one in Congress has yet plucked up enough courage to even call for an investigation of Trilateralism.

As individuals, Trilateralists live in a make-believe world. They are part of the same crowd that squandered $300 billion and fifty thousand American lives over a decade in Vietnam, then scuttled out, tail between legs, while then Vice-President Nelson Rockefeller forbade public discussion and investigation of the Vietnam debacle. Have you seen a congressional investigation or public inquiry into this, the most scandalous waste of lives and materials in American history? Furthermore, Trilateral ambitions are greater than Trilateral intellects. While priding themselves on an international outlook, Trilaterals are, in fact, quite close-mind-ed and provincial in outlook. Their writing reflects this predict-able pattern:

a. It has limited, repetitive, and shallow themes and key words such as "interdependence, co-operation, global."

b. Opportunism is presented as altruism.

c. It espouses an amoral view of human motiva-tion.

(This author has personally heard a prominent Trilateralist call on a select audience to take pecuniary advantage of govern-ment handouts.)

Trilaterals represent an elite, kept afloat by sheer audacity and by the traditionally slow reaction of citizenry in a still reasonably free society. Unfortunately, reaction to elitism is usually stimu-lated only by overt oppression.

The basic game plan of the Trilaterals? To blur the separation between "private wealth" and "public service" for Trilateral advantage; public wealth is to be oriented to private Trilateral ends.

ENDNOTES

1. *Washington Post*, 16 January 1977.
2. See Antony C. Sutton, *Wall Street and the Bolshevik Revolution* (New York: Arlington House Publishers, 1974).
3. *Times* (London), 24 July 1976.
4. Michel J. Crozier, Samuel P. Huntington, Joji Watanuki *The Crisis of Democracy* (New York: University Press, 1975).
5. U.S. Labor Party, *The Trilateral Commission's Coup d'Etat* (New York: Campaign Publications, Inc., 1977), p. 13..
6. Exormisis, 23 July 1976.
7. Zbigniew Brzezinski, *Between Two Ages: America's Role in the Technetronic Era* (New York: Viking Press, 1973), p. 246.

CHAPTER THREE

THE POWER STRUCTURE OF THE TRILATERAL COMMISSION PART II

Moving up from the lower levels of the Trilateral Commission described in the last chapter, let us now focus on the higher echelons. Organizing and directing the overall activities of the commission itself is a North American executive committee, with yet another and virtually unseen power base behind it. The identity of this Trilateral power base varies according to the observer. Most American observers zero in on the international bank affiliation. While constitutional conservatives focus on the **Rockefeller** family and Chase Manhattan Bank as the culprits, liberal-leftists focus on bankers in general. A radically different interpretation is that of the U.S. Labor party. The latter considers the Rockefeller label to be a "cover," that Trilateralism is a "British conspiracy" operation to infiltrate the U. S., using **Henry Kissinger** as a conduit. Unfortunately, the United States Labor party seems intent on substituting Lyndon LaRouche, Jr., and a "dirigiste" economy for Trilateral authoritarianism and a Trilateral-directed economy, which will leave the average citizen no better off than he was before. Totalitarianism under any label spells loss of freedom.

THE NORTH AMERICAN EXECUTIVE COMMITTEE

Let's first look at the Trilateral North American Executive Committee and its members:

I.W. Abel: president, United Steel Workers of America; member, Executive Committee Trilateral Commission: member, War Production Board and War Manpower Commission, 1941-45. Election to the USW A presidency in 1965.

Robert W. Bonner (Canadian): chairman, British Columbia Hydro.

William T. Coleman Jr.: senior partner, O'Melveny & Myers; former secretary of transportation in the Ford administration; director of Chase Manhattan Bank.

Robert S. Ingersoll: director of First Chicago Corporation (and First National Bank of Chicago); Borg Warner, Kraft, Inc.; Weyerhaeuser Company; AtlanticRichfield; Caterpillar Tractor. Also deputy chairman of the University of Chicago Board of Trustees, trustee of Aspen Institute of Humanistic Studies and California Institute of Technology. Resigned from Borg Warner to become U.S. ambassador to Japan, then assistant secretary of state for Far Eastern affairs, then deputy secretary of state, Resigned March 1976. A typical example of "revolving door" elitism and the "closed-shop" nature of U.S. decision making.

Henry Kissinger: former secretary of state, now on the International Advisory Board of Chase Manhattan Bank.

Bruce K. MacLaury: president of Brookings Institution, formerly president of Federal Reserve Bank of Minneapolis and deputy under secretary of the treasury for monetary affairs.

Henry Owen: fellow, Brookings Institution, formerly State Department Intelligence Division.

Charles W. Robinson: senior managing director of Kuhn, Loeb & Company and former deputy secretary of state.

David Rockefeller: chairman, Chase Manhattan Bank and chairman, Council on Foreign Relations (CFR).

William M. Roth: Matson Navigation, Pacific National Life Assurance Company, Carnegie Institution, Committee for Economic Development.

William W. Scranton: former governor of Pennsylvania.

Mitchell Sharp (Canadian): former minister for external affairs.

The most startling observation is that three members of this twelve-man executive committee are Chase Manhattan people. (**Rockefeller** and **Coleman** are directors and **Kissinger** is on the International Advisory Committee.) Later we shall explore the Rockefeller-Chase Manhattan connection in more detail - it suffices at this point to note that

William Miller (chairman, Federal Reserve Board) was also on the Chase International Advisory Committee just before appointment to the Fed. Other Trilaterals on the Chase Manhattan Advisory Committee are the following:

> **Robert Marjolin**
>
> **Giovanni Agnelli** (Fiat)
>
> **Chujiro Fujino** (Mitsubishi)
>
> **Sir Reay Geddes**
>
> **William W. Hewitt** (Deere & Company)

In brief, no fewer than eight members of the governing boards of Chase Manhattan Bank are also Trilaterals. One can certainly question this unusual coincidence without being accused of either paranoia or oversimplification.

The twelve executive committee members can be further grouped as follows:

a. Two from Brookings Institution, the **Carter** "think tank" -

b. **MacLaury** and **Owen**.

c. Four former ministerial-level appointees - Commissioner **Kissinger, Scranton, Sharp** (Canada), and **Coleman**.

d. Two "revolving door" specialists - Commissioners **Ingersoll** and **Robinson**, both former deputy Secretaries of state.

e. Two ad *hoc* industrialists — Commissioners **Bonner** and **Roth**.

f.   One trade unionist - Commissioner **Abel**.

The founder of the Trilateral Commission, chairman of its executive committee, chairman of the Council on Foreign Relations, and chairman of the Chase Manhattan Bank - **David Rockefeller**. Comparing the October 1977 executive committee to that of March 1975 we find some significant differences: four members had quit to take highest level positions in the **Carter** administration: **Harold Brown** became secretary of defense; **Zbigniew Brzezinski** became national security advisor to President **Carter** (**Brzezinski** had been executive director of the Trilateral Commission from its inception); **Gerard C. Smith** became ambassador-at-large for non-proliferation matters; and **Paul C. Warnke** became director of the Arms Control and Disarmament Agency. As we have noted, many other commissioners moved into the **Carter** administration (including, of course, **James Earl Carter** and **Walter Mondale**); but it is significant that no fewer than one-third of the executive committee moved into the *top security slots in the new administration*.

In brief, we can note two outstanding characteristics:

g.   The Chase Manhattan Bank dominates the Trilateral Commission, and

h.   The Trilateral Commission dominates the U.S. executive branch.

In the words of the Washington Post (16 January 1977),

At last count, 13 Trilateralists had gone into top positions in the administration, not to mention six other Trilateralists who are established as policy advisers, some of whom may also get jobs. This is extraordinary when you consider that the Trilateral Commission only has about 65 American members.

THE TRILATERAL POWER BASE

Run your eye down the list of executive committee members. Who is the most powerful individual among them? There is no doubt that **David Rockefeller** dominates the executive committee, and thus the commission itself. Even if we are generous (or naive) and see the executive members as equals, then David

would surely be *primus inter pares*. It is, however, naive to see
David Rockefeller as an omnipotent dictator or the Rockefeller
family as an all-powerful monarchy. This is a trap for the unwary.
Our world is much more complex. We are looking at a family of
families, a collective of power holders with at least several hundred, perhaps several thousand, members, who collectively aim
to divert the world, not just the United States, to their own collective objectives.

Let's start at the beginning. The Trilateral Commission was
David Rockefeller's idea and promoted with David's funds.
(Leave aside for the time being the U.S. Labor party theory that
Trilateralism uses the Rockefellers as a "cover" for a "British con-
spiracy.")

An interview with **George S. Franklin**, commission coordinator, by Michael Lloyd Chadwick, editor of *The Freemen Digest*,
published in Provo, Utah, is the most authentic version of the
founding process which has yet surfaced. This portion of the interview follows:

*MR. CHADWICK: Mr. Franklin… you were a participant with
Mr. David Rockefeller, Robert Bowie, Zbigniew Brzezinski and
Henry Owen in forming the Trilateral Commission. Would you
provide us with a brief history of how it came into existence?*

*MR. FRANKLIN: David Rockefeller, in the winter and spring
of 1972, gave several speeches to the Chase Bank forums in
London, Brussels, Montreal and Paris. He recommended the
establishment of an international commission on peace and
prosperity which in fact is now the Trilateral Commission. He
didn't receive an enthusiastic response in these meetings and
he dropped the idea. He thought, If the Chase Bank Forums
don't respond favorably to my suggestion then it's probably
a lousy idea."*

*He then went to a Bilderberger meeting. Mike Blumenthal
was there (now Treasury Secretary), and he said, You know,*

*I'm very disturbed...Cooperation between these three areas -
Japan, the United States and Western Europe - is really falling
apart, and I foresee all sorts of disaster for the world if this*

continues. Isn't there anything to be done about it?" David then thought, I'll present the idea once more," which he did, and he aroused great enthusiasm. The next eight speakers said that this was a marvelous idea; by all means, somebody get it launched.

David wasn't quite sure whether these were all his friends. He wasn't quite sure if they were being polite or if they really thought it was a good idea. So he took Zbig Brzezinski back on the plane with him. Zbig thought it was a very good idea and had done some writing on it. Bob Bowie had done some writing on it too. When he got back, David asked me if I would go back to Europe and talk to some people more at leisure and see if they really thought this was a good idea. They truly did.

David and I went to Japan in June of 1972 and he talked to a lot of people there. They thought it was a good idea, so we had a meeting of 13-15 people at his place in Tarrytown (ed: New York).

It was decided to go ahead and try to organize and form it.

There is no reason to doubt that formation came about in any other way - at least we have no evidence that **Franklin** is hiding anything. But note that the way the Trilateral Commission was founded suggests a loose power coalition, sometimes in competition, sometimes in cooperation, rather than a small, tight, iron-fisted conspiracy run by the **Rockefellers**. [1]

SOURCE OF TRILATERAL FUNDS

Where did the funding come from? The source of funds is always a reliable clue to the source of power. Again to quote the Chadwick article:

In the meantime David Rockefeller and the Kettering Foundation had provided transitional funding.

In January of 1973 Gerald Smith, Max Kohnstamn, Zbigniew Brzezinski and George Franklin held consultations with Takeshi Watanabe and the Japanese planning group members in Tokyo. It was during this time period that approval of the highest political and financial circles was obtained.

In February of 1973 a formal proposal was submitted to the Ford Foundation to support the majority of the intellectual and research projects of the Commission. The funds were also to provide for administrative and promotional activities.

In February additional support was also obtained from several other foundations.

What is The Kettering Foundation? There are three "Kettering Foundations." This citation almost certainly refers to the Charles F. Kettering Foundation, Dayton, Ohio. **Charles F. Kettering**, the donor, was with General Motors for twenty-seven years and held among other positions, director-ships of Ethyl Corporation (important for transfer of petroleum technology to Hitler pre-World War II) and Sloan-Kettering Institute for Cancer Research (in mounting trouble over credibility of its cancer research programs). The assets on the early 1970s were about $93 million, with no grants to individuals, only to "high-risk programs" to "support the forces for world order and peace." [2]

Better known than the Kettering Foundation is the Ford Foundation with **McGeorge Bundy** as president and among the trustees **Robert S. McNamara** and **J. Irwin Miller**, both of whom have a long history of promotion of globalist interventionist projects.

Once again we have evidence of a widespread and rather loose coalition: "approval of the highest political and financial circles was obtained," including the trustees of maybe half a dozen foundations.

We can thus conclude that the Trilateral Commission

1. Originated with **David Rockefeller**
2. Was chosen by **David Rockefeller** and a small group of four assistants, and
3. Was financed in great part by **David Rockefeller,** the Kettering Foundation, and the Ford Foundation.

Without being accused of hastiness or bias, one can reasonably conclude that **David Rockefeller** is the power behind The Trilateral Commission, and. presumably stands to gain most from its activities.

A mistake made by many analysts is to assume that because the Rockefellers exercise immense corporate power and demonstrably dominate Trilateralism and similar vehicles that they are the only holders of such power and therefore control a "conspiracy." Whether there is, or is not, a conspiracy is really irrelevant. If it is a conspiracy, it is the most open conspiracy in world history. What is important is intention. Obviously, the trustees of the Kettering Foundation and Ford Foundation, with immense resources at the ready to promote "world order," are right there with David. Analysis needs to push further into the forest than the **Rockefeller** family group.

What are the practical levers of power? Political influence is not created in a vacuum: it comes largely from financial backing. Who provides most financial backing? Who has the power to finance or not to finance? And who gains? In our society it is the major institutions such as labor unions, multinational corporations (MNCs), foundations, and international banks. Obviously, Trilateralism was not founded by labor unions or any group of ambitious academics. The first step in our analysis then is to portray the links of Trilateralists with international banking and MNCs. Such links are complex because bank interlocks are complex. Banks are interwoven into a network, controlling the U.S. economy in a large part through stock voting, debt holding, and interlocking directorships.

The diagram that follows is a highly simplified portrayal of this network (for all the criss-crossing lines) based on information released by congressional committees. It is drawn to highlight several facets of the power base:

- There is an interlock between major banks mostly oriented overseas,
- This interlock is measured by the stockholding rank that one bank holds in another, Trilateral commissioners are plotted onto the bank interlocks,
- The end result is a reflection of the political financial power network based on international banks, identifying the location of Trilateral representatives in the net-

work.

Don't be concerned about the complexity of this diagram. Focus attention on the top one-third. The two large triangles represent two potential financial power bases: the **Rockefeller** family group on the left and the Kirby-Allegheny group on the right. Why is the Kirby-Allegheny group important? Only because in terms of financial power as measured by stock voting it is right up there with the Rockefellers. Yet an interesting and fundamental comparison can be made between the two financial groups. Note the following (reading from the diagram):

- The **Rockefellers** are the Number 1 stockholder in Chase Manhattan Corporation with 591,533 votes, while Kirby-Allegheny Corporation (Number 3) has 300,000 votes. (The Number 2 stockholder is California Employees Retirement System.)

- The **Rockefeller** family group has no direct holdings in Citicorp (although Chase Manhattan Corporation is Number 11 holder with 1,001,000 votes), but Kirby-Allegheny group is Number 6 holder in Citicorp with 1,661,000 votes.

- The Kirby family group controls Investors Diversified Services with interests in numerous multinationals: Northwest Airlines; Pepsico, Inc.; Atlantic Richfield, Inc.; and so on.

Look at the diagram again, at the smaller black triangles which represent Trilateral members. The **Rockefeller**-dominated bank influence in the commission can now be followed precisely:

- Two Trilaterals are in the Rockefeller family group (**David and John D. Rockefeller IV**, governor of West Virginia,)

- The **Rockefeller** family group is Number 1 shareholder in Chase Manhattan Corporation. Six Trilaterals are on the board of Chase Manhattan Corporation.

- In turn, Chase Manhattan Corporation is Number 1 stockholder in First Chicago Corporation. Three Trilaterals are on the board of First Chicago Corporation. (The reader can trace the other influences from the diagram.)

- Seven Trilaterals are on the Chase International Advisory Board.
- The Kirby-Allegheny group has no Trilaterals at all.

What is the vital difference between the **Rockefeller** family group and the Kirby family group? There is one all-important distinction between the two financial groups. **Rockefellers** are *politicized. Kirbys* are not. *Rockefellers apparently subvert the political process to gain their objectives. Kirbys apparently* do *not.*

An interesting historical note is that (today) no families directly control J. P. Morgan and its subsidiary, Morgan Guaranty. The one-time fiefdom of J. P. Morgan and the Morgan family was the power behind the creation of the Federal Reserve System in 1913 and the power behind the throne of Woodrow Wilson. Today Number 1 stockholder in J. P. Morgan is Citibank and Number 2 stockholder is Chase Manhattan Corporation. Moreover, J. P. Morgan controls Morgan Guaranty which, in turn, is Number 1 stockholder in Citicorp.

What does this picture add up to? It is like a snake swallowing its own tail, or a nest of snakes swallowing each other's tails. The essential point to hold in mind, however, is that a global multinational corporation (Chase Manhattan) is in control of a power vehicle that controls the U.S. government. In 1976 the American voter thought he had elected **Jimmy Carter**; in fact, he has elected Chase Manhattan. And the ideology of the global corporation is entirely different from the philosophy on which the Constitution of the United States is based. For example, Citicorp Chairman Walter Wriston phrases it this way:

> *The development of the World Corporation into a truly multinational organization has produced a group of managers of many nationalities whose perception of the needs and wants of the human race know no boundaries. They really believe in One World.* [3]

These would-be global managers have rejected the United States. As Richard J. Barnet comments in *Global Reach*:

> *The global corporation is the ideal instrument for integrating the planet, the World Managers contend, because it is*

*the only human organization that has managed to free itself
from the bonds of nationalism.* [4]

The economic clout of these "World Managers" must be offset
by a tunnel vision endemic to globalists. This is not a paradox.
Global aspirations are induced by greed, the ruthless drive for
profit and power; and trampling on anyone in the way to achieve
the globalist goal is not discouraged. Their own ambitions are
openly placed above human welfare. As Wriston states:

*In this dialogue, the role of the world corporation as an agent
of change may well be even more important than its demonstrated capacity to raise living standards.* [5]

The illusions suffered by the global corporatists are strange i
deed. Bank of America President **A. W. Clauson** states:

*The expansion of our consciousness to the global level offers
mankind perhaps the last real chance to build a world order
less coercive than that offered by the nation-state.* [6]

We have to suppose **Clauson** is serious and doesn't see the hu-
mor of this statement: large corporations are notorious for their
authoritarian structures, the Bank of America not excluded. How
an authoritarian attitude can create a "less coercive" world is beyond understanding.

Walter Wriston of Citibank offers the same illusion:

*The World Corporation has become a new weight in an old
balance and must playa constructive role in moving the
world toward the freer exchange of both ideas and the means
of production so that the people of our planet may one day
enjoy the fruits of a truly global society. This is a goal worthy
of us all.* [7]

Despite the illusions and inconsistencies, the globalist would-
be World Managers, are getting ready for their revolution: changing corporate names to non-American, internationally neutral
titles. Some examples are these:

- Standard Oil of New Jersey is now EXXON neutral in
  almost any language and without the geographical attachment of "New Jersey."

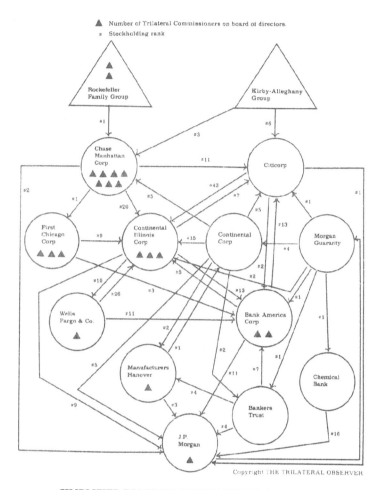

SIMPLIFIED DIAGRAM CONTRASTING TRILATERAL REPRESENTATION AND STOCKHOLDING INTEREST IN TWO FINANCIAL GROUPS

- City Bank of New York, an old-time New York bank is now, under Henry Wriston, neutral Citibank or Citicorp.
- U.S. Rubber is now Uniroyal.
- Minnesota Mining and Manufacturing is now just plain 3M.
- American Metal Climax is AMAX.

We can suppose the next move will be for the budding World

Managers to neutralize their own names: **Rockefeller** will become "Rokafela"; Clauson will become "Klorson."

One of these global corporations, Caterpillar Tractor, has no fewer than three Trilateralists (**Ingersoll**, **Morgan** and **Packard**) on its board of directors; and **David Rockefeller** tells how he was prompted to conceive the original Trilateral idea when he visited World Headquarters of Caterpillar Tractor in Peoria. Illinois. Caterpillar lives and breathes globalism. Its 1976 annual report, for instance, has a map of the world on the front cover with the Caterpillar logo superimposed: The corporate address is "World Headquarters. Peoria. Illinois." The introductory pages are full of globalist gobbledygook: "world forums," "world-wide respect" and "positive contributions of multinational business enterprise."

What these World Managers do not see is that their philosophy is pure totalitarianism, removed only infinitesimally from the Hegelian philosophies of Adolf Hitler and Josef Stalin. In practice, in their own corporations these globalists are ruthless authoritarians ‐ and outside impartial observers remain unconvinced that the expansion of the budding World Managers' corporate horizons to globalism will allow them to understand the values of individual freedom.

TOTALITARIAN TAKEOVER OF THE U.S. EXECUTIVE BRANCH

A straightforward and reasonable conclusion is that there has apparently been a covert fascist (national socialist) takeover of the United States government. By fascist we mean a corporate socialist state of the type established by socialist Mussolini in Italy in the 1920s. All forms of socialism derive from the .same philosophical bases. Mussolini was editor of a Marxist socialist newspaper before developing his own brand of corporate socialism based on Marxist ideology. Corporate socialism was later promoted in the United States by General Electric Chairman Gerard Swope and became Roosevelt's New Deal (i.e., "Swope's Plan"). Herbert Hoover described the New Deal in this way:

Among the early Roosevelt fascist measures was the National

Industry Recovery Act (NRA) of June 16, 1933. The origins of this scheme are worth repeating. These ideas were first suggested by Gerard Swope of the General Electric Company...following this they were adopted by the United States Chamber of Commerce...[8]

It is socialist revolution by stealth: rather than by blood in the streets, but revolution just the same. Trilateralism is the current operational vehicle for a corporate socialist takeover. The bitter joke is that Roosevelt and **Carter** have been mainly supported by "liberals" and "do-gooders" who would have us believe they are horrified by fascism and corporate socialism!

ENDNOTES

1. Send $1.00 to Freemen Institute, 1331 South State Street, Box G, Provo, UT 84601, for full text on the interview. Ask for vol. VI, no. 7, 15 January 1978.
2. Trustees: Harrison Scott Brown, Norman Cousins, John Sloan Dickey, George A. Gallup, Samuel B. Gould, Carroll A. Hochwalt, Frederick J. Hoover, Robert A. Kerr, Charles F. Kettering II, Richard D. Lombard, Walter Orr Roberts, Howard E. Skipper, and James M. Stewart.
3. Walter Wriston, "The World Corporation - A New Weight in an Old Balance" (address before International Industrial Conference, San Francisco, Ca., September 17-21, 1973), p.17.
4. Richard J. Barnet, Global Beach: The Power of Multinational Corporations (New York: Simon and Schuster, 1974). Barnet is an interesting character in the establishment lineup. Cofounder (with Marcus Raskin) of the Institute for Policy Studies (an Establishment think-tank/action vehicle), Barnet is pure elitist.
5. Ibid., p.16.
6. Ibid., p.56.
7. Wriston, "The World Corporation," p.19.
8. Herbert Hoover, The Memoirs of Herbert Hoover: The Great Depression, 1929- 1941 (New York: The Macmillan Company, 1952), p. 420. See also Antony C. Sutton, Wall Street and FDR (New York: Arlington House, 1975.)

Chapter Four

The Plan For World Agricuture

Whatever Trilateralists may release about their objectives, common sense suggests that any control they acquire over the daily lives of individuals means a corresponding loss of control for the individual. Power gained at the political center is power lost at the periphery. If some central body makes regulations and orders, this reduces the freedom of individuals to order their own lives. In brief, globalism means reduction of individual freedom.

One Trilateral objective is to exaggerate world problems so that Trilateral power to control and order a new world may be enhanced. Such problems have been identified according to the following criteria:

- The problem should be important from a global stand-point.
- The problem should be one that can be solved by some degree of Trilateral - Communist cooperation following
- a presumed unstated objective to merge the U.S. with a
- socialist structure.
- The venture must be one that can be pursued without undue intrusion into the internal affairs of the partici-

pating states. [1]

An important problem area that fits the criteria for selective manipulation is that of world food. Food supplies are inadequate, people need food to live, and the technological and financial abilities for food production are heavily within Trilateral countries. As Triangle Paper No. 13 puts it:

> *Prospects are somewhat more substantial for cooperation in the realm of increasing food production. Production increases require both more effective domestic agricultural policies on the part of developing countries and enlarged provision of outside capital and technology to them for agricultural development.* [2]

In particular Triangle Paper 13 claims:

> *The prospects for cooperation are more promising with regard to the third objective: the development of adequate food (particularly grain) reserves. A reserve stock policy that could keep cereal price changes within a less disruptive range than in the recent past could make a considerable contribution not only to restraining inflation in the developed and developing worlds, but also to ensuring that adequate food supplies are available to developing nations at prices that will not impose an undue drain on foreign exchange...*

In considering Trilateral targets for international food reserves and world agriculture, we need to consider what the Trilaterals say they want and compare it to what they *really* want. Fascinated by the idea of "food power" and "contrived shortages," the Trilaterals intend to use food as a weapon to bring about the New World Order. One stated objective is to create an "international system of national food reserves" by massive manipulation of recently acquired political power against private markets and initiatives. It is proposed. for example:

- To keep grain prices in a "less disruptive range,"
- Restrain inflation,
- Ensure adequate food reserves for lesser developed countries (LDC's) and
- Overcome periodic food imbalances.

Trilateral intentions for a world grain storage program are published by the Trilateral Commission and the Brookings Institution, headed by Trilateral Commissioner **Bruce K. MacLaury**. Other Trilateralists on the Brookings Board of Trustees include **Robert V. Roosa** (partner in Brown Brothers, Harriman), **Lucy Wilson Benson** (presently under secretary of state for security assistance) and **Gerard C. Smith** (ambassador at large for non-proliferation matters.) In 1976 Brookings Institution Senior Fellow **Philip H. Trezise** with the assistance of former Assistant Secretary of Agriculture **Carroll Brunthaver**, published *Rebuilding Grain Reserves: Toward An International System.* **Brunthaver** had previously been involved in a conflict of sworn testimony, investigated by the Senate Permanent Subcommittee on Investigations. (See Report, *Russian Grain Transactions,* 93rd Congress, 2nd Session, p. 33.) In the **Trezise** book, the problems for multilateral agreement on grain reserves are considered to be "formidable." Going ahead is "compelling" because of the following: upward moves in grain prices have a "pervasive influence" on all food prices; they mean more worldwide hunger; and grain stocks can be used in periods of famine. More specifically, **Trezise** proposed:

- An initial reserve of sixty million tons of grain, rising to between seventy-five and eighty million tons by 1981,

- Contributions from all industrial countries, including Argentina and South Africa,

- A program cost of $6 billion plus $640 million in annual storage costs,

- That stocks should be "national," bought at 10 percent above floor prices and sold at 10 percent below ceiling prices,

- That twenty million tons be set aside for famine reserve.

As in most Trilateral writings, **Trezise** includes only evidence *in favor* of proposed Trilateral policy. Trilaterals typically use an ideological procedure of gathering facts and opinion supporting their argument, never allowing a hint of serious counter-argument. Two glaring unstated consequences in **Trezise's** book are:

1. Any such massive stockpiling will *raise* the long-term price of grain, negating the objective of "restraining inflation;

2. The only way to stop the resulting inflation is through rigid government *price controls* and *regimented farming*.

The choice of food products as a means of reducing national sovereignty is emphasized in the following paragraph:

There are several reasons why commodities are treated differently than other products that enter into trade. Probably the most basic reason is that commodity supplies are linked to land, tying them to the concept of territory, over which nation- states exercise sovereignty. As a general proposition, the demand for, and the supply of, most commodities are rather unresponsive to changes in price over short periods of time, so that quite sharp fluctuations in price can be generated by fairly modest changes in overall market conditions. Moreover, the time required to expand supplies is often lengthy, although this property varies widely among individual commodities. Although the value of all commodity consumption represents no more than about ten percent of annual economic activity in industrialized nations, and even though substitutes exist for any particular commodity, commodities are sometimes distin- guished as "core products." [3]

The Trilateral elite, through control of the U.S. executive branch, will-be calling the shots on a world basis to reduce producer control and indirectly national sovereignty. The amount of political power possessed by world grain producers can be measured by comparing the area devoted to 1976 wheat production in Trilateral regions:

	Thousand Hectares
European Economic Community	11.232
Japan	89
United States	28,700
USSR (for comparison)	50,462

This U.S./Trilateral dominance is further reflected in world export figures of wheat plus flour for 1975-76:

	Metric Tons
United States	31,522,000
Canada	12,136,000

Australia	8,072,000
European Economic Community	7,729,000
Argentina	3,111,000
Japan	38,000

If it were possible for other countries to substantially increase their wheat production, the quickest way to do so would be to raise government   price support levels. However,   except for Argentina, the already has the *lowest* support levels among the thirty or so wheat producing countries in the world. Thus, one can see how the U.S. has acreage, yield, and production efficiency all working for it at the bargaining table.

THE TRILATERAL BIG STICK

This discussion of "food power" is not academic - it has major significance for any grain trader, farmer, firm, or individual in any way connected with grain products.

The Trilaterals propose international sanctions against any government, private firm, or producer (in or out of an association) that interferes with Trilateral objectives. These sanctions will not be applied in any principled way, but will be used pragmatically to achieve Trilateral goals. The key to this plan and associated sanctions is in Triangle Paper 10, "Seeking a New Accommodation in World Commodity Markets." Therein, the concept of "contrived shortages" is floated. A contrived shortage is any non-Trilateralist action in the market place that interferes with Trilateral objectives. For example, a farmer withholding grain from the market and waiting for a higher price, is guilty of contrived shortage. The paper further states that these contrived shortages can be informal, rather than brought about by a formal association of producers. [4]

While all offenders are to be subject to effective international investigation and action, the penalties are not to be applied equally. A non-Trilateral developed country such as Argentina or South Africa will be dealt harsher penalties (i.e., sanctions) than underdeveloped Zaire or Zambia (phrased subtly as "...in the case of non-industrialized countries, however, it is necessary to consider this issue from a broader political perspective").

Consequently, any informal or formal farmers group in the U.S. protesting price levels - and such protesting will be inevitable when Trilateral objectives surface - will be subject to penalties. When can these individual firms and non-favored governments anticipate Trilateral hostility? Probably under the following conditions:

- If they attempt to stabilize or move market prices to non- Trilateral levels,
- If they respond to market imperfections or undertake any systematic withholding of supplies from the market,
- If they make any information exchange for these purposes.

Trilaterals, are well aware that market fluctuations in agriculture are highly sensitive to supply changes, and that whoever controls the supply controls the market. [5]

In Triangle Paper 14, "Toward a Renovated International System," two additional and interesting caveats relating to international grain reserves appear:

1. That the Soviet Union can benefit from fixed prices and guaranteed sources of supply, and

2. That if the U.S.S.R. doesn't see the wisdom of joining the Trilateral plan, the Trilaterals will go it alone.

On the other hand, the paper comments:

"We have not sought ventures that would exacerbate Sino-Soviet rivalry. We have thus focused, for the most part, on projects that would involve either the USSR or China, but not both. This does not mean that cooperation with the Soviet Union and China cannot be pursued simultaneously   only that it should not focus on the same projects.

"The chances of Soviet or Chinese agreement are, of course, uncertain; our assessments are tentative, based on such limited evidence as exists. Only by seeking cooperation can its feasibility be ascertained. [6]

THE PLAN AND THE AMERICAN FARMER

A nation-wide farm strike was well underway in mid 1978, with participating farmers from all areas of agriculture. Demonstrations like "tractor cades" were common events covered on national T.V. While some farmers in wintered areas were not sure if they would be planting spring crops, others were already pressed to the wall with bankruptcy: they had no choice but to refrain from planting as long as prices remained relatively low. Once again the banks were in danger of becoming owners of real estate - farms. Since banks do not want that responsibility, every effort is being made to support shaky farms and ranches. Recently, the Federal Land Bank (where most farmers have found an easy and inexpensive source of credit for decades) announced it would not foreclose on farmers in default. The implications of this are far reaching, especially since no one knows just how many farmers are in serious trouble.

Big changes cannot be implemented only during periods of crisis. It appears the Trilateralists are pushing for a major farming crisis in the within the next year or so, one that can be manipulated for Trilateral ends. If the farming industry becomes bankrupt, the government's only choice will be to "institutionalize" the nation's food production in the same manner that Amtrak was "nationalized." On the other hand, if the government chooses to let prices rise to the point where farmers can realize a profit in 1978, it will be only with additional and far-reaching controls over the farmer. Government--induced prosperity has always resulted in a trade-off: Profits for Controls.

The current situation in the U.S. plays directly into Trilateral hands. The grain or "cereal snake" will be a foregone conclusion when the Trilaterals find themselves caught in the vice between farmers crying for higher prices and consumers demanding lower food prices. But, of course, it will have been a "contrived" crisis in the first place.

How then will a national grain reserve - keyed to the international grain plan of the Trilateral Commission affect the American farmer?

The carrot offered by the **Carter** administration, now under Trilateral control, will be stable and "high" prices. Farmers, suffering from four years of low prices, will be eager listeners. Secretary of Agriculture Bergland (a Trilateral nominee) has vowed "to even out the booms and busts" in agriculture. (To this, former Secretary of Agriculture Earl Butz responded, "...you'll notice he's going to even out the boom first.") In practice, the **Carter** grain storage program will produce the following:

- A narrow grain price snake. The government will support the floor of the snake, while whipped-up consumer pressure, through a captive media, will create a lid on the ceiling of the snake, making an ultimate government price ceiling inevitable.
- More - and more - government control.

If the government determines quantities produced and market prices, then ultimately, it will decree who plants what, and where. Farmers have yet to learn they cannot have traditional freedoms and security at the same time.

THE PLAN IS UNDERWAY

The summer of 1977 was favorable for grain farmers, due to increased yields and stocks. Today, worried over production and low prices, farmers are asking for acreage cutbacks. By August 1977, Secretary Bergland called for a 25 percent cutback in allotments. Secretary of Treasury **Blumenthal** and Secretary of State **Vance** wanted no cutbacks: they argued increased production was needed for the storage program. It is not clear if this was a dispute between Trilateralists and non-Trilateralists in the cabinet, but it is not likely. Former Minnesota Congressman Bergland is not a Trilateral member, but he was sponsored by Vice President Walter Mondale - and Bergland has a longtime image to maintain of being "the farmer's friend."

President **Carter** made a contradictory decision by calling for Congress to legislate a 20 percent acreage cutback plus adding 30 to 35 million tons of grain for the national stockpile. **Carter** is a master of such paradoxes: he also wants to achieve full employment while wiping out inflation.

TRILATERALS IN THE FAR EAST

Another effort to involve Trilateralism in world agriculture surfaced at the October 1977 Eighth Annual Trilateral Meeting in Bonn, Germany. In a Trilateral Task Force Report, *How to Double Rice Production in South and Southeast Asia*, doubling the production of rice (the staple food of 1.3 billion people) within 15 years is proposed. Such a plan will cost some $54 billion and will be financed by Trilateral governments (actually, their taxpayers), the Organization of Petroleum Exporting Companies (OPEC), and LDCs. The highlights include the following:

1. Intensification of rice production - not merely increased output,

2. Expansion of irrigated land, requiring increased water control and irrigation systems, and

3. Increased use of agricultural machinery and fertilizers.

The institutional fundamentals (i.e., transportation, financing, land tenure systems, communications, etc.), all basic to healthy economic expansion, are ignored in this plan. The emphasis is on spending $54 billion on a *Technologically Intensive* form of production, not normally used in the *labor-intensive* Far East. The reason for this is not complex: Trilateral members heavily reflect the multinational firms who will be supplying the needed technology, equipment, and supplies.

THE REAL TRILATERAL GOALS

The adage "Watch what governments do, not what they say," is the guide to Trilateral objectives.

The summer 1972 grain fiasco was also the biggest grain sale in American history. The Soviets bought over 700 million bushels of grain, including 440 million bushels of wheat - about 25 percent of the total American wheat crop. The sale wiped out U.S. reserves, disrupted shipping and grain transportation flows, created farm product shortages and forced up food prices to American consumers. Who initiated this program? The original directives came from **Henry Kissinger** (then national security advisor to President Nixon.) On 31 January 1972, **Kissinger** directed the departments of state, commerce, and agriculture

to allow the Department of Agriculture to take the lead in negotiating grain sales to the USSR. On 14 February 1972 the
Department of Agriculture was directed to develop a "negotiating scenario." The subsequent negotiating team from Washington
included Secretary of Commerce **Peter G. Peterson**, Secretary of
Agriculture Earl Butz, **Henry Kissinger**, and Peter Flanigan.

Subsequent shortages and price rises were deliberately created by Trilateralists-to-be as part of "detente" with the USSR,
to the great disadvantage of the American consumer. (See U.S.
Senate, *Russian Grain Transactions"* Permanent Subcommittee on
Investigations, 1973- 75.)

The Trilateral agriculture/food production/storage program
smacks of self-interest and manipulation. The plan will yield major beneficial advantages for Trilateralist multinationals, who are
already gearing up for it, and it will provide "crisis management"
situations for the World Planners. Doubling rice production in the
Far East by intensive methods and ignoring the institutional changes
vital for lasting economic change will require massive inputs of agricultural machinery and fertilizers.

Agricultural equipment makers without direct Trilateral connections are cutting production, while Trilateral-connected firms
are expanding production. In general, 1977 was not a good year
for agricultural equipment manufacturers. Allis-Chalmers reported a projected cutback of 15 percent for 1978. Wisconsin-
based J.R. Case says equipment conditions "have seriously declined" since early 1977 and predicts either flat or declining sales
for 1978. In Des Moines, a Massey-Ferguson spokesman stated
that the 1978 market is "a matter of great concern." And the agriculture equipment division of Chromalloy looks for a flat 1978
market. None of these firms has direct Trilateral connections.

On the other hand, those companies with direct Trilateral
connections are following a different road. Deere & Company,
the largest maker of agricultural equipment and the fifty-second
largest firm in the U.S., is in the midst of the largest capital expansion program in company' history. In 1977, Deere negotiated an
agreement with Yanmar Diesel Engine Company (Japan) to form
"an engineering company that will be jointly owned and will design future tractors in the smaller horsepower sizes." New ba-

sic machines will go into production in 1978 a crawler dozer, a crawler loader, a four-wheel- drive loader, and a new hydraulic excavator. Existing Deere plants are to be expanded, and new plants built overseas, with a total expenditure in 1977-78 of $1 *billion.* The chairman of the board of Deere & Company is **William A. Hewitt.**

Another Trilateralist, **Henry B. Schacht**, is chairman of the board of Cummins Engine Company, by far the largest truck engine manufacturer in the U.S., with 49.4 percent of the heavy-duty truck- engine market. Large numbers of Cummins engines are used in farm equipment, and Cummins is now "the power leader in the highest horsepower, four wheel drive tractor market." J. Irwin Miller, longtime internationalist, member of the Council on Foreign Relations, and trustee of the Ford Foundation (which financed Trilateralism), personally owns 19.4 percent (1,339,620) of the common stock of Cummins and participates in other large blocks of stock. In addition, Cummins former vice-president of corporate action was recently appointed by President **Carter** to be under secretary of the interior.

John Perkins is president and William A. Hewitt and Arthur M. Wood are directors of Continental Illinois National Bank and Trust Company of Chicago. Continental Illinois and its subsidiaries are operators in the agricultural industry worldwide. For example, the 1976 annual report has a half-page photograph of "a central-pivot irrigation system" financed by a subsidiary of Continental Illinois Leasing Corporation. The firm provides agricultural management services through Continental Agricultural Properties Management Division, maintaining a global banking network for agricultural operations.

John Harold Perkins is also director of the Pillsbury Company, which in 1976 agreed with Cargill, Inc., of Minneapolis to use Cargill port facilities to put Pillsbury into the grain export field. (**William R. Pearce** is vice president of Cargill.) In early 1978, the Memphis, Tennessee, firm of Cook Industries, ($500 million in annual sales) sold to Pillsbury its grain merchandising assets, including an export elevator in Louisiana, seven inland elevators, an office network, grain inventories, and contracts. In short, Pillsbury is now a major operator in the grain export business, whereas before 1976, its operations were limited to domestic merchandising and food services.

Caterpillar Tractor Company is one of the world's largest makers of tractors and earth-moving equipment. The following Trilateral commissioners are directors: **Lee L. Morgan** (president of Caterpillar); **David Packard** (of Hewlett-Packard;) and **Robert S. Ingersoll** (formerly the chairman of Borg Warner Corporation, U.S. ambassador to Japan, director of Atlantic Richfield, assistant secretary of state for East Asian and Pacific affairs, deputy secretary of state, and director of First Chicago Corporation).

All together, those agricultural equipment firms and bankers with Trilateralist representation will do very well by the Trilateral scheme for "internationalizing" food production. Firms outside the magic circle, according to their *own* corporate forecasts for 1978, do not anticipate any expansion in their business. Coincidence?

ENDNOTES

1. Collaboration with Communist Countries in Managing Global Problems: An Examination of the Options," Triangle Paper No. 13, p.2. 2. Ibid., p. 30
2. Ibid., p. 4.
3. "Seeking a New Accommodation in World Commodity Markets," Triangle Paper No. 10, p. 14.
4. The Carter administration has a penchant for stockpiles - $5 billion for oil, $6 billion for wheat and reexamination of the strategic metals stockpile program - and this raises a question mark about long-term intentions. Stockpiling of oil, wheat, and metals is a common historical prelude to aggressive warfare. The pragmatic logical apparatus of the Trilateralists is highlighted: they want an oil stockpile under *Project Independence* and a wheat storage program under the flag of New World Order *Interdependence.*
5. "Toward a Renovated International System," Triangle Paper No. 14, p. 2.)

Chapter Five

The Trilateral Energy Hoax

The Trilateralist **Carter** administration thumps a repetitive theme of a major energy crisis, threatening the very survival of the U.S. The consequences of this mighty crisis, so we are told, include:

- The dollar dilemma, brought about by our importation of oil and the subsequent bill for these imports which "wrecks" the U.S. balance of payments,
- The fact that the U.S. is too dependent on foreign oil in case of national emergency, and
- The depletion of U.S. oil and gas in the ground.

Some Trilateral commissioners have entered the energy crisis directly. For example, First Chicago Bank (Commissioners **Ingersoll, Morgan** and **Peterson** are directors) recently placed full-page ads in the *Wall Street Journal* (25 July 1978) on the energy crisis pushing the scary line, "America can't wait" and "energy isn't easy to come by anymore."

President **Carter** has announced, in the same vein, "the world is watching the United States to see if it has the will, the resolve to solve its energy problems and end its insatiable appetite for imported oil."

All of which might lead you to think we really *do* have an energy crisis.

In fact, Trilateral energy assertions are always couched in terms of crises, emergencies and wrecking." Reflect for a moment that if one wants to manage the world, "problems" and "crises" to manage are absolutely essential, or else the managers are out of a job: there is nothing to manage. Can you have an energy plan without an energy crisis? Of course not.

So let's ask an elementary question, a silly question in the light of **Carter** dogma, but we'll pose it anyway: Is there an energy crisis at all? The general belief is that the answer is obvious: of course there is an energy crisis. Washington says so. The politicians say so. The Trilateralists say so. Most of the media says *so.* Everyone (almost) says so.

On the other hand, have you seen printed in any media or in any administration statement, a list of the energy resources currently available within the United States available today for use and development?

We doubt it. So let our first simplistic (common sense is always attacked by the elite as "simplistic") question be "how much energy do we have available in the U.S. today? And "in what form?" [1]

Several basic, readily available statistics dispose of the "energy crisis" and expose its falsity.

The United States consumes about 71 quads of energy per year. (A quad is one quadrillion British thermal units or 1015.) There is available today in the United States, excluding solar sources and excluding gas and oil imports, about 150,000 quads of energy.

Put another way, this statistic means we have sufficient known usable energy resources to last us for over two thousand years. The *type* of energy we use and how we use it will, of course, change - as the type has changed before from wood to coal and from coal to electric power. But to say we have any absolute shortage of energy resources is simply a false and irresponsible statement.

This elementary statistic means that the energy crisis is a phony, a created crisis, a hoax on the American people. But if you happen to be in the business of crisis manipulation, such an energy crisis, if you can convince enough people of its reality, is a handy sort of crisis to be manipulated. One can impose rationing and price controls, plan resource uses, restrict consumption, and invent all manner of happy little projects under the name of "solving" an energy crisis.

Looking at this 150,000 quads in more detail we have approximately the following supplies available in the future:

Natural gas	At least 200 years (probably closer to 600 years)
Petroleum	At least 130 years
Oil from shale	At least 1,500 years
Coal	At least 6,000 years
Breeder reactor resources	inexhaustible

A Breeder reactor produces more fuel than is consumed. There is sufficient U238 in storage for the initial one hundred years of breeder reactor operation.

These geological estimates are conservative: Vincent McKelvey of the U.S. Geological Survey (who was recently fired for his disclosure publicly discussed a figure of six-hundred-year-reserves of natural gas. Moreover, using biomass production methods, natural gas reserves are virtually inexhaustible.

These elementary statistics must be the starting point of any rational discussion of energy "shortages."

SUPPRESSION OF INFORMATION

The previous information has been suppressed. Elitist discussion *assumes* we have a shortage of energy. The "shortage" is mythical. Check the indexes of the establishment press the *New York Times,* the *Washington Post,* the *Los Angeles Times,* the *Christian Science Monitor,* and you will find no statistics of total energy resources. Why not? Isn't the amount of energy currently available in the ground, an essential prerequisite to any reasoned discussion of shortages and crises? Does this absence of clearly relevant information imply there has been an attempt to create a synthetic belief structure for the American people. [2]

Has there been suppression of vital facts so that the crisis managers may have a juicy synthetic crisis to manage? The hidden power of elitists over the weaker and more susceptible among us was amply demonstrated in the August 1, 1978 issue of *The Ruff Times*, (Reprinted in *California Mining Journal*, September 1978). In *Ruff Times*, Howard Ruff describes what happened when he tried to question Vincent E. McKelvey, former head of the U.S. Geological Survey. Earlier this year, McKelvey, a longtime bureaucrat, made the innocent mistake of disagreeing with **Carter** and the administration line about "energy crises." McKelvey was fired because of certain revealing statements he made in a Boston speech - that we have sufficient domestic natural gas available to provide up to a six-hundred-year supply (quoted in *Wall Street Journa1*.)[3] Wrote Ruff, "When we taped the show, I had a very nervous man on my hands...he was obviously frightened of something - or somebody." What McKelvey had probably discovered was that anyone in the U.S. who promotes unwelcome news for the elite receives some unwelcome attention in return. (An IRS audit is common, or a call to visit the boss of the institution or organization where the luckless whistle blower may be working.)

In most national newspapers you just do not read about the gigantic new oil and gas finds which have made a mockery of the official party line of crisis and scarcity. For example, the following find was apparently reported nationally only in *Barrons* (13 February 1978).

In August 1977 Chevron was drilling its Walter C. Parlange Well No.1 in Point Coupee Parish, Louisiana. At 21,000 feet the drill hit a reservoir of high pressure methane and blew out. The blowout was so intense and accompanied by such an enormous flow of steam that the well was closed for eighteen days. The theory of Baton Rouge oil expert Paul Hastings Jones is that the drill entered a long-theorized geopressurized superheated water plus methane gas reservoir. If this happened, new vistas for U.S. natural gas production are now open. The U.S. uses about 20 trillion cubic feet of methane a year. The Louisiana geopressurized methane reserves alone may total 3,000 trillion cubic feet, another 150-year gas supply, and there's much, much more out in the Gulf of Mexico all of which information is a disaster for any political scare energy plan.

Furthermore, the long opposition of the **Carter** administration to breeder reactor development contrasts with the following:

- Europe is forging ahead with breeder reactor technology.
- There has never been even one fatal accident in a commercial nuclear reactor. (About three hundred men a year are killed in coal mines.) This logically disposes of the anti-nuke argument.(How about some anti-coal demonstrations at coal mines?)
- Nuclear power is cheap, much cheaper than oil and gas.

Now could it be that total profits in a nuclear-powered world will be much less than with oil and gas and this probability has created a vested interest to restrict nuclear development? Could the myth of low oil and gas reserves have been deliberately promoted so that energy price hikes will appear acceptable to the general public?

Certainly political manipulation has taken the form of restricting some energy forms and interfering with the supply of others:

- As we have noted, the **Carter** administration is against breeder reactors, the source of low-cost ample energy; and in August 1978 **Carter** agreed to breeder development only in exchange for political support for his natural gas bill.
- The natural gas bill continues political interference into basically economic and technical decisions.
- Allowing the market system to develop our ample fuel resources is never discussed in elitist energy crisis reports.

THE CRISIS CREATORS

Elitist energy reports include A *Time To Choose,* from the Ford Foundation, *Achieving Energy Independence,* from the Committee for Economic Development, and *Energy: A Plan for Action,* 1975. from the Commission for Critical Choices for Americans.

The Ford Foundation financed the Trilateral Commission, and the Ford Foundation contribution to energy crisis manipulation is A *Time To Choose. a plan which demands:*

- A massive socialist bureaucracy to plan and control all energy use.
- Ultimately. a massive reduction in energy use plus income redistribution.
- Price controls plus fuel allocations plus tax increases.

The **Carter** energy crisis is guided from the White House by the same S. David Freeman who wrote sections of this Ford Foundation report. Not unexpectedly. A *Time To Choose* unleashed a flood of criticism, even from a member of the Ford Foundation Advisory Board, president of Alcoa, John Harper, who described the Ford energy plan as one"...abhorrent to me and I am sure, to most of the people in this nation."

Similarly, the Committee for Critical Choices for Americans was financed by the Rockefeller Foundation, with Nelson Rockefeller and a host of Rockefeller appointees determining the energy future for the rest of America. In principle, *Energy: A Plan for Action* does not differ from the socialist interventionist principles in the Ford Foundation plan.

WHO CONTROLS ENERGY RESOURCES?

The **Rockefeller** financing of *Energy: A Plan for Action* and its primary association with Trilateralism through **David Rockefeller** together with the Ford Foundation's association with Trilateralism and also with energy plans poses a basic question: Who controls energy resources? Are these self-interested proposals? To answer this, we need to examine two related phenomena:

a. Who controls energy resources? and,

b. Are these controllers related to the Trilateral Commission and its lock on energy policy making?

If we can identify an interlock between the energy controllers and energy policymakers, we can reasonably presume that Trilateral energy policy is formulated with the interests of the controllers in mind.

The oil and gas world is dominated by seven major firms (the "seven sisters"). A listing of controlling ownership in these major oil and gas companies by banks with Trilateral commissioners as directors follows:

Major Oil Company	Share Ownership by Banks with Trilateral Representation	Rank
ARCO	Manufacturers Hanover	2
Exxon Corporation	Chase Manhattan	1
	Manufacturers Hanover	3
Mobile Corporation	Chase Manhattan	3
Standard Oil (Cal.)	Chase Manhattan	2
	Wells Fargo Bank	4
Standard Oil (Ind.)	First National (Chicago)	4
	Continental Illinois	3
Texaco	Continental Illinois	3

There are highly significant Trilaterally-connected bank holdings in the major oil companies where such holding places the bank among the top five shareholders; that is, the Trilateralist bank has a controlling influence. Chart 5-1 illustrates those major oil companies with Trilateral commissioners as directors.

To this picture, we can add the direct personal shareholding interest of the Rockefeller family in these major oil companies, in addition to indirect interest via the above Trilaterally connected banks:

Exxon Corporation	Rockefeller Family	6
Standard Oil	Rockefeller Family	6

Finally, we can list Trilaterally-connected bank control of *other* major energy companies as follows:

The Energy Industry – Major Oil Companies and
Trilateral
Commissioners

Other Major Energy Companies	Share Ownership by Banks with Trilateral Representation	Rank in Shareholding
American Elec. Power	Chase Manhattan	1
Columbia Gas System	Wells Fargo Bank	2
Commonwealth Edison	First National Bank, Chicago	1
Florida Power & Light	BankAmerica Corporation	2
	First National Bank, Chicago	3
Middle South Utilities	First National Bank, Chicago	2
	BankAmerica Corporation	4
Occidental Petroleum	BankAmerica Corporation	4
Pacific Gas & Elec.	BankAmerica Corporation	3
Phillips Petroleum	Manufacturers Hanover	5
Texas Utilities	First National Bank, Chicago	1
	BankAmerica Corporation	3

Trilaterally connected banks dominate the boards of many
of the largest power and utility companies in the United States.
It is interesting to note that although BankAmerica Corporation
is a powerful shareholder (No. 4) in Occidental Petroleum, the
bank has done nothing to dilute the pro-Soviet policies of Armand
Hammer, (Lenin's friend and a key capitalist) in building Soviet
military power. It is reasonable then to suppose that BankAmerica
approves of Hammer's Soviet policies.

Other Trilaterals are influential in smaller oil companies:
Kaiser has just bought into Ashland and Roth is influential in
Honolulu Oil and Barber Oil.

More startling, we find an ominously close interlock among
the "seven sisters" major oil companies. Four of the seven majors
have Trilateral commissioners as directors: **Ingersoll** at Arco,
David Rockefeller and **Jamieson** at Exxon, **David Packard** at
Standard Oil of California, and **Robert Roosa** (creator of the disastrous **Roosa** bonds) at Texaco. The interlock among major oil firm
directors is shown in the following table:

The tight interlock among the seven majors both with each other and the Commission makes for ready transference of Trilateral ideas and proposals; and oil company ideas and proposals are funneled through the TC and related "think tanks."

BANKS WITH TRILATERAL CONNECTIONS AND THEIR STOCKHOLDING RANK IN MAJOR OIL COMPANIES
Indirect Interlocks Among Major Companies
With Trilateral Commissioners

Major Oil Firm*	Atlantic	Exxon	Mobil	Shell	Standard Oil of Cal.	Standard Oil of Ind.	Texaco
Atlantic Richfield (1)		4	3	1	2	5	2
Exxon (2)	4		6	1	6	2	2
Mobil	3	6		3	3	3	4
Shell	1	1	3		1	0	0
Standard Oil Of Cal. (1)	2	6	3	1		0	0
Standard Oil of Ind.	5	2	3	0	0		0
Texaco (1)	2	2	4	0	0	0	

*Numbers in parenthesis represent Trilaterals.

A reasonable presumption is that the seven majors strongly support Trilateralist energy policy with its anti-nuke and anti-breeder reactor thrust. Nuclear energy is cheap and safe. Oil is relatively costly and dirty. So the energy crisis scenario becomes readily understandable if only as a means to increase oil company profits.

The exception to this generalization is Mobil - with no Trilateral commissioners but with substantial Chase stock holdings. Mobil is a vocal advocate of deregulation and the return of a market economy to the energy sector.

Having identified a possible reason for the nature of Trilateral energy policy, we can dispose of the superficial public relation reasons for crisis. Does the energy crisis and the need to import oil create a balance of payments crisis as the **Carter** administration argues? There are two refutations to this:

- Europe and Japan have far, far higher import ratios for oil and gas - and *they* don't have energy and currency problems;
- Bureaucratic regulation and energy policy in the U.S. have restricted energy resource development, thus artificially *expanding* oil/gas imports.

Is there a strategic energy problem? If we continue to subsidize Marxist regimes - yes, there will be a strategic energy problem. If we continue to meddle in low-level crises around the world (while ignoring the human rights horror stories, as in Cambodia) - yes, there will be a strategic problem. But remember these international crises stem from previous "solutions" which never worked, and one could justifiably suspect "crisis management" scenarios as a root cause of continuing international problems.

Do we have a "shortage" of energy resources?

No, we most emphatically do not. There is no energy crisis in absolute terms: The crisis is a synthetic belief structure created in order to provide a problem to be managed. In the management process, other goals dear to the hearts of elitism will be achieved, for example, global control and domestic resource planning.

All of which reminds us of a Trilateral retort to widespread criticism of Trilateralism and its objectives as expressed by European Trilateral **Georges Berthoin**:

One doesn't like to feel that people have a totally false impression of an organization one is associated with...there have been a number of publications from the right and left that have made these charges about undue influence. They are without foundation and I'm afraid most of the criticism is based on ignorance of the facts...

The reader is urged to compare this official Trilateral statement with the facts on energy resources and control presented above. One finds the following to be true:

- "Undue influence" in energy is more than obvious;
- Trilateralism is heavily interlocked with both energy companies and energy policy formation in the White House,
- Accusations of smear tactics "from left and right" are "standard operating procedure." They divert attention from responsible reasoned criticism with no attachment to a synthetic political spectrum (and we place the *Trilateral Observer* in this category).

Berthoin commented further that: "...if the image was the reality most of the European members, including myself would not like to be members." To which **David Rockefeller** is reported to have added, "That goes for all of us."

The truth is that the totalitarian image of Trilateralism *is* the reality: and we are long past the day when these power plays can be disguised from the American people.

David Rockefeller, Georges Berthoin and their fellow Trilateralists will not at least dispute one assertion from this editor: that in these secret elitist conclaves, a perennial topic under discussion is "how do we foster political will?" In brief, how do we get the people (the "peasants") to go along with authority (i.e., "We, the elitists?"). In some future elitist meeting, Trilaterals will do well to step back and look at themselves. *Who* gave the TC elected authority to even discuss globalist plans and new world order? The authority is self-anointed. And Trilateralists are no different from other power usurpers in history, Joseph Stalin and Adolf Hitler. The analogy will not impress Trilateralists because from this editor's observations their thought structure is utterly impervious to the concept of individual freedom. However, and more importantly, the analogy will not be lost on Americans at large.

ENDNOTES

1. Detailed back-up data is contained in a forthcoming book by this editor entitled *Energy: The Created Crisis* (Books in Focus. Inc.. 160 E. 38 Street. Suite 31B, New York. N.Y. 10016).
2. *The Wall Street Journal* and *Barrons* are prominent exceptions to this belief structure programming. Both sources have run numerous articles and editorials with this basic energy data and draw implications which parallel those of the *Trilateral Observer.*
3. *Wall Street Journal.* 27 April 1977.

CHAPTER SIX

TRILATERALS AND TAXATION

California's Proposition 13, a measure reducing property taxes by 60 percent, is still echoing around the world. The mildly socialist London Economist ran a lead article on 17 June 1978 entitled "Throwing Tax Overboard," expressing horror at the turn of events. The solidly free enterprise Northern Miner (Toronto, Canada) editorialized on 15 June 1978: "There may be hope for the Western World yet," but claimed "13" wasn't enough; we need, wrote the editor, "to finish the job by eliminating entrenched bureaucrats."

All of which bring us to examine the common principles of taxation held by both Marxists and Trilateralists. Oddly, while there are Trilateralist papers on almost every major policy issue, there are none at all on taxation. After some research, we discovered a possible reason for the silence. Taxation is not a pressing problem for Trilateralists; it is only a pressing problem for you and me. Research unearthed an interesting paradox: Trilaterals emphatically favor more taxes for the common man, but do very well avoiding taxation for themselves and their corporate vehicles.

When we were able to identify Trilateral public statements on Proposition 13, for example, they were not unexpectedly strongly against reducing California property taxes. For example,

- Bank of America (Trilaterals **Clawson** and **Wood** are

directors) contributed $25,000 to defeat Jarvis-Gann (Proposition 13).

- Governor **Thompson** of Illinois, who is making appropriate presidential noises, rejected a similar tax reduction program in Illinois.
- **Carter** said Proposition 13 is an "aberration" that will nt sweep the country.
- The Los Angeles Times (a director is Commissioner **Harold Brown**) was described by Jarvis himself as "the vindictive paranoiac, schizophrenic *Los Angeles Times*" for the vitriolic nature of its opposition to 13.

In sum, Trilaterals put their weight against Jarvis-Gann and tax reduction.

AMBIGUITY IN TRILATERAL VIEWPOINT ON TAXES

Trilateral opposition to tax reduction most emphatically did not apply to their own taxes nor to those of their corporate affiliations. Trilateral multinationals have successfully avoided paying taxes in the United States and have made some headway in tax a voidance in England and possibly elsewhere.

The United States picture was publicized recently by Congressman Charles A. Vanik (on 26 January 1978) after a congressional study of the taxes paid by major multinational corporations. Reported Congressman Vanik:

This study, covering tax year 1976, examines 168 companies. These include 108 industrial, 7 mining, 8 airline, 9 railroad, 5 trucking, 13 utility, 8 retailing, and 10 commercial bank companies. Because a few did not furnish data adequate for computation, some categories of taxes or rates could not be computed.

Where sufficient data made computations possible, the average effective U.S. tax rate on worldwide income of the corporations was approximately 13.04 percent, down significantly from the 21.3 percent rate in tax year 1975. In order to qualify for a tax rate this low, an average family of four could only have earned $20,000. The companies listed in this study had a pretax income of more than $38.7 billion.

*The figures show that 17 companies paid nothing in effective
Federal income taxes in tax year 1976 6 more than tax year
1975 despite combined total worldwide net incomes of more
than $2,594,060,000 table 1. The 17 companies accumulated
tax credits of more than $375 million. In some cases, however,
companies paid no taxes because they sustained net losses. In
other cases, some companies will claim to have "paid" Federal
taxes, but their credits exceed taxes, resulting in no effective
payment and an effective tax rate of zero.* [1]

Included in this tax avoidance group of multinationals we find
numerous corporations with Trilateral connections.

WHAT TAXES DO TRILATERALS PAY?

Having assumed the burden of deciding the future for American
society and the New World Order, one would at least expect that
Trilaterals pay their full share of the costs. We therefore examined the Vanik study from the viewpoint of identifying the taxes
paid by multinationals represented in the Trilateral Commission
by company directors.

The lowest income tax bracket for an individual U.S. taxpayer
is 14 percent. On the other hand, Chase Manhattan, Continental
Illinois, and First Chicago, the power houses behind Trilateralism,
all pay far lower rates.

In fact, Chase Manhattan Bank paid no U.S. taxes at all in 1976.

On the one hand, **David Rockefeller** (chairman of Chase and
the largest individual shareholder in Chase,) wants to decide the
future of American society and the world; on the other hand,
his bank is totally unwilling to make a contribution to the new
American society and a New World Order.

Given these facts, we have every right to be skeptical about announced Trilateral intentions and objectives. We have every right
to assume that the Trilateral Commission may be a gigantic rip-
off on American society.

The following is a list of international banks with Trilateral
commissioners on the board, and their effective U.S. tax rate on
worldwide income in 1976.

U.S. Tax Rates of Banks with Trilateral Commissioners as Directors

Trilateral Commissioner	Director of this Bank	Effective U.S. Tax Tate on Worldwide Income	
		1975	1976
Rockefeller, Coleman, Hewitt, Haggerty, Jamieson, Kissinger	6 - Chase Manhattan	3.4%	0.0%
Hewitt, Prkins, Wood	3 - Continental Illinois	33.7%	10.5%
Ingrsol, Morgan, Peterson	3 - First Chicago	n/a	6.3%
Clausen, Wood	2 - Bank of America	14.2%	14.9%
Whitman	1 - Manufacturers	0.0%	3.8%
Austin	1 - J.P. Morgan	14.2%	17.6%
Arbuckle	1 - Wells Fargo	n/a	n/a

As we all know, personal income tax rates are much higher than the rates paid by the tax-avoiding multinationals. In the U.S. the starting individual tax rate is 14 percent and the highest rate is 70 percent. In Canada the rate starts at 17 percent and ranges to 43 percent. Other European countries have even higher rates up to a confiscatory 98 percent in Britain. If you are a Trilaterally connected international bank, your effective rate in 1976 was much lower than the lowest individual bracket. In order of their success in avoiding taxes, Trilateralist banks rank as follows:

Bank	U.S. Taxes in 1976
Chase Manhattan	0.0%
Manufacturers Hanover	3.8%
First Chicago	6.4%
Continental Illinois	10.5%
Bank America	14.0%

If you will examine the chart in chapter three, note how the three linked banks in the top left (Rockefeller) corner of the chart that have remarkable success in avoiding U.S. taxes. This success in avoiding

taxation is carried abroad by these same multinationals. Take, for example, a report in the London Economist (14 January 1978) from the British viewpoint, under the scathing headline:

"No Tax Please, We're Banks"

American and other foreign banks in London could end up paying little or no British tax if their huge claims for relief which are now being examined by the inland revenue are accepted. Even the British clearing banks could have their tax bills dramatically reduced.

A deluge of claims was lodged around Christmas 1978, following rumors that one of the smaller American banks had persuaded the inland revenue (British equivalent of IRS) to grant stock appreciation relief (SAR) on its holding of foreign currency notes as well as on gold bullion, which has been allowed for some time.

DO ALL MULTINATIONALS PAY LOW TAXES?

A prominent Trilateralist, **Peter G. Peterson**, chairman of Lehman Brothers and formerly assistant to President Nixon for international economic affairs has this to say about MNCs and taxes:

...the MNC is also a source of concern to some governments, since from its wide base it is often able to circumvent national monetary, fiscal, and exchange policies. The possibility of distortions arising from intra-corporate pricing practices to take advantage of national variations in tax laws has also been cited with concern.

A check of multinational corporations and their 1976 U.S. tax rates on world income turns up some multinationals that did pay significantly high U.S. tax rates.

Company	U.S. Taxes in 1976
Getty Oil	21.14%

R.J. Reynolds	41/0%
Greyhound	46.8%
Textron	40.1%

Generally, however, those MNCs with Trilateral connections appear to pay significantly lower rates. This is only an approximation. It could be a spurious correlation, but there is sufficient evidence to warrant a closer look.

Company	1976 Tax Paid
Exxon (Controlled by **Rockefeller** interests)	8.0%
Standard Oil of California (**Rockefeller** and **Packard**)	17.1%
Eastern Airlines (controlled by **Rockefeller** interests)	0.0%
Arco (**Ingersoll**)	11.4%
Occidental Petroleum (**Armand Hammer**, one-time friend of Lenin, is chairman of the board of Occidental. In 1919, Julius Hammer, father of Armand, was secretary of the Communist Party U.S.A. Hammer has been probably the most active western capitalist in building the military power of the Soviet Union.	4.2%
Gulf Oil (Gulf provides almost $1 billion a year in oil concession revenues to the Marxist Neto regime. Gulf's Cabinda oil wells are protected by Cuban troops, thus releasing Angolans to support the SWAPO forces invading South-West Africa.	7.0%

TRILATERALISTS PROTECT THEIR OWN

We can push this argument a little further. Trilateralists in government are protecting fellow capitalists from taxation.

A recent report by the House Government Operations Committee disclosed the following:

- IRS decisions on some multinational oil firms have cost the U.S. Treasury over $7 billion since 1974. "By the early 1970's, multinational petroleum companies were operating abroad under a set of factual and legal circumstances completely at variance with those upon which the previous foreign tax credit rulings were based."
- IRS failed to audit oil company returns or require them

to provide supporting information for their expense claims. (Presumably audits are only for individual tax-payers.)

- These favorable actions stemmed from "interference" by then Secretary of State Henry Kissinger.

- More recent "improper interference" for the same purpose came from Secretary of Treasury **Blumenthal**.

The committee did not cite the U.S. oil companies involved, except to note that they operate in Saudi Arabia, Libya, and Indonesia. Aramco alone was named in one place: this company is linked with Exxon and Chase Manhattan interests.

In brief, a House committee has charged Trilateralists **Henry Kissinger** and **Michael Blumenthal** with "improper interference" with IRS to obtain benefits for certain companies. Even further,

In September 1977, at the very time that the subcommittee discovered and criticized a suggestion made by a Treasury official a year earlier to have IRS and Treasury officials "co-operate" in secret dealings with Indonesia and oil companies therein regarding foreign tax credits (a suggestion which was also admonished as being improper by other Treasury officials), the new International Affairs officials were recommending similar actions.

Don't hold your breath expecting further investigation. **Henry** has either a charmed life or personal sovereign immunity from the rule of law.

Compare this protective treatment for favored Trilateral associates with the **Carter** "energy" plan. The energy plan is a disguised tax plan aimed at the middle class. **Carter** proposes to give a few low-income energy users a small credit, and tax high-income energy users. When you total up the sum of credits and the sum of taxes, it turns out that the energy credits just disappear after a year or so and the energy taxes keep on mounting.

The disappearing **Carter** energy tax credit looks like this, in net total receipts per year:

1973	$801,000,000 credit to low income workers
1977	298,000,000 extra tax
1980	1,147,000,000 extra tax
1985	8,999,000 extra tax

This change from credits to taxes comes about because while low-income taxpayers and energy consumers qualify for credits in the early years, inflation quickly pushes these low-income groups into higher tax brackets (without credits). So by 1985 all energy users pay energy taxes and none get energy credits.

Compare this deceptive "energy plan" for taxpayers with the already cited benefits derived by Trilateralist connected firms with **Kissinger** and **Blumenthal** to run "interference" at IRS.

To emphasize the discriminatory approach of the **Carter** administration on tax matters, we can do no better than quote the congressional testimony of Philip E. Vision, supervisory revenue officer in the Chicago District Office of IRS, who in 1976 blew a small whistle on IRS procedures before the Subcommittee on Oversight of the Committee on Ways and Means. Congressmen Jones asked Vision about differing treatment of rich and poor taxpayers:

Is there pressure to seize a small business or a poor taxpayer's property in order to close the case, and pressure to perhaps settle quickly with a rich taxpayer who has plenty of accounting and legal ability to drag things, out?

To which IRS official Vision replied:

In all candor, Congressman, I must say this: You will find those branches or groups that are involved in the inner city of Chicago, the low income, the closures are highest because there is really no problem. It requires no technical skills or knowledge to prepare a levy upon the employer of an employee who is getting take-home pay of about $80. We can go in, serve the levy and take the entire $80.

Certainly a taxpayer who is earning $80 could hardly be expected to employ an expensive attorney or CPA. Usually when he comes in, in response to the levy, it is with tears in his eyes because he allocated that $80 to the gas or electric company *and because IRS took that money, his electric and gas will be shut off and also part of that money was intended to feed his family. This is a common practice.*

I am sorry to report that, but if you would look at the closures in the poor areas of Chicago, the depressed areas, you would find that the closures of the small dollar TDA's are overwhelmingly larger than they are in the affluent suburbs of Deerfield where I live.

TRILATERAL SENATOR ROTH JOINS TAX REVOLT?

Given our skepticism of the **Carter** administration policy on taxation, how do we assess Senator Roth's tax reduction proposals? Take a hard look at the Roth-Kemp Amendment for a federal tax reduction. Senator **William V. Roth Jr.**, is a Trilateralist. The proposal would cut federal taxes by 33 to 36 percent for hard-pressed (over $20,000) middle income groups. Effects for a family of four are contained in the following table:

THE IMPACT OF ROTH-KEMP AMENDMENT ON A FAMILY OF FOUR

Gross Income	Present Tax*	Proposed Tax*	Tax Cut	Percent Cut
$8,000	$120	12	108	90%
10,000	446	218	228	51%
12,500	917	539	378	41%
15,000	1,330	811	519	39%
17,500	1,745	1,092	653	37%
20,000	2,180	1,388	792	36%
25,000	3,150	2,047	1,103	35%
30,000	4,232	2,781	1,451	34%
35,000	5,464	3,589	1,875	33%
40,000	6,848	4,512	2,336	33%

* Present Tax: After average standard deductions

Are the Trilaterals getting out in front of the tax revolt? Not at all. **Roth**-Kemp just won't increase real income. The catch is that the tax reduction under this proposal will be phased in over three years and is totally insufficient to cut the fat in Washington. We are heading into a period of further major price inflation: 10 to 15 percent a year is more than probable. Where does that leave a taxpayer pushed into higher tax brackets? He will save one-third in federal taxes under **Rot**h-Kemp and lose one-third from the hidden tax of inflation! In sum, **Roth**-Kemp is a deception.

The only useful tax reform at the federal level is repeal of the Sixteenth Amendment.

THE GRADUATED INCOME TAX OF MARX AND ENGELS

To fully understand the implications of a viciously graduated income tax system aimed at the small/medium American businessman and the broad middle class and to understand as well the role of the multinationals and the international bankers who make up the power elite behind the Trilateral Commission, we need to go back to 1847 and the *Communist Manifesto* of Karl Marx and Friedrich Engels.

Of the Communist revolution, Marx and Engels wrote:

In the first instance, this can only be affected by despotic inroads upon the rights of property and by despotic interference with bourgeois methods of production; that is to say by measures which seem economically inadequate and untenable, but have far-reaching effects, and are necessary as means for revolutionizing the whole system of production.

In brief, elimination of property owners and small- and medium- sized businessmen ("bourgeois methods of production") outside the orbit of the multinationals and international banks is an essential prerequisites to socialism.

Then Marx and Engels outline the famous ten "measures" for achieving revolution in the advanced countries to bring about socialism.

These measures are described by Marx and Engels as follows:

In the most advanced countries they will, generally speaking, take the following forms:

1. *Expropriation of landed property, and the use of landrents to defray State expenditure.*

2. *A vigorously graduated income tax.*

3. Abolition of the right of inheritance.

4. Confiscation of the property of all émigrés and rebels.

5. Centralization of credit in the hands of the State, by means of a national bank with State capital and an exclusive monopoly.

6. Centralization of the means of transport in the hands of the State.

7. Increase of national factories and means of production, cultivation of uncultivated land, and improvement of cultivated land in accordance with a general plan.

8. Universal and equal obligation to work; organization of industrial armies, especially for agriculture.

9. Agriculture and urban industry to work hand-in-hand, in such a way as, by degrees, to obliterate the distinction between town and country.

10. Public and free education of all children. Abolition of factory work for children in its present form. Education and material production to be combined.

Notably, there is a parallel between Marx and Trilateral propositions: centralization of credit in IMF and the Federal Reserve System parallels Marx's measure 5. AMTRAK, federal funding of rapid transit, and persistent efforts to cut down on use of individual automobiles parallels Marx's measure 6. Finally, our Sixteenth Amendment to the Constitution, the "income tax amendment," is none other than the "vigorously graduated income tax" proposed by Marx in the Manifesto. What has this to do with Trilateral multinational avoidance of taxation? Plenty, as it turns out.

It is interesting to reread Karl Marx's Manifesto in the light of the alliance between Wall Street multinationals and the Communist imperialists, Marxists, especially, should reread Marx. The enemy of Marxist totalitarianism is not the capitalist but rather the "bourgeoisie," the middle class. Marx sees the bourgeoisie as the source of all that is evil, yet he does not include all the ruling establishment in those designated for elimination. To the contrary, when the class war is about to be fought to a finish, Karl Marx envisaged a curious event: "a small part of the ruling class breaks away to make common cause with the revolutionary class, the class which holds the future in its hands."

In sum, Marx envisaged a coalition of ruling interests of the revolutionary Marxists and a segment of the ruling class. This is precisely what history has recorded in the hundred or so years since the Manifesto was published. One of the most significant forces in modern world development has been the assistance from a relatively small yet powerful part of the ruling Western establishment to the Soviet Union channeled through such influential organizations as the Council on Foreign Relations (CFR) and today, the Trilateral Commission. In Marx's terms, are not Cyrus Eaton, Armand Hammer, **David Rockefeller** and the Trilateral Commission ruling class breakaways? Have not Marxists and the "breakaway ruling class capitalists" joined hands to eliminate the American middle class? Unfortunately, academic analysts are blind to the implications of the alliance: they read Marx with preconceptions. So let's present some evidence.

Earlier this year, the Marxist government of Angola reorganized Diamang, its diamond-producing monopoly. Now the Neto Marxist government will own 60.8 percent, and the balance will be owned by the former foreign corporate owners. It will be a mixed company. But which former owners will be expropriated to make way for the new Marxist shareholders? Not the big greedy capitalists we hear so much about in socialist literature, but, in the words of the Neto government "a large number of small shareholders." The major "foreign companies," the large multinationals, that is, the ruling capitalists, will not be affected by the takeover. In other words, the ruling class joins hands with Marxist revolutionaries against the small bourgeois owners.

Another example follows for those readers who have read Antony Sutton's *Wall Street and the Bolshevik Revolution* and who may remember that in 1918 the leading Wall Street law firm supporting the infant Bolshevik regime in Russia was Simpson, Thacher and Bartlett of New York. As one indication of their support, partner Thomas D. Thacher wrote a report which became decisive in gaining British cabinet support for the Bolsheviks. Also Thomas Lamont, Dwight Morrow, and H. P. Davison were closely involved in developing policy towards the Bolsheviks: all were partners in the J. P. Morgan firm.

While in London on 13 April 1918 Thomas D. Thacher, a member of the American Red Cross Mission to Russia, wrote to the American ambassador in London that he had received a request from H. P. Davison, a Morgan partner, "to confer with Lord Northcliffe" concerning the situation in Russia and then to go on to Paris "for other conferences." Lord Northcliffe was ill, and Thacher left a memorandum to be submitted to Northcliffe on his return to London with yet another Morgan partner, Dwight W. Morrow. This memorandum not only made explicit suggestions about Russian policy that supported the pro-Bolshevik position of William Boyce Thompson (director of Chase, now Chase Manhattan, Bank), but even stated that "the fullest assistance should be given to the Soviet government in its efforts to organize a volunteer revolutionary army."

The first three proposals in Thacher's report follow:

First of all...the Allies should discourage Japanese intervention in Siberia.

In the second place, the fullest assistance should be given to the Soviet Government in its efforts to organize a volunteer revolutionary army.

Thirdly, the Allied Governments should give their moral support to the Russian people in their efforts to work out their own political system free from the domination of any foreign power...

Was Wall Street attorney Thacher a capitalist enemy of the Bolsheviks? Of course not. Thacher was right in there, helping the revolution, as part of the "breakaway ruling class," along with capitalists from J. P. Morgan and Chase Bank.

Similar aid for Marxist revolution is taking place today in South Africa and Red China. And who is U.S. secretary of state today in charge of facilitating this aid? **Cyrus D. Vance**, who before his appointment as secretary of state was also a partner in Simpson, Thacher and Bartlett. As a final twist, do you recall that Senator Clifford P. Case was defeated in the primaries last month in New Jersey? Well, Clifford P. Case was also a member of the firm of Simpson. Thacher and Bartlett from 1928 to 1953, when he became president of the Fund for the Republic, the foundation that funded the study for a "new constitution" so desired by the elite.

Yet another memorandum from William Boyce Thompson (director of the Federal Reserve Bank of New York and Chase Bank) to Lloyd George (prime minister of Great Britain,) December 1917, supported the Bolsheviks and admitted in part:

About the overthrow of the last Kerensky government we materially aided the dissemination of the Bolshevik literature, distributing it through agents and by aeroplanes to the German army. If the suggestion is permissible, it might be well to consider whether it would not be desirable to have this same Bolshevik literature sent into Germany and Austria across the West and Italian fronts.

Does this sound as if Wall Street and the Bolsheviks were enemies? Another excellent example of the capitalist-communist alliance is Gulf Oil in Angola, the financial backer of the Neto government, while Cuban troops protect Gulf's Cabinda production facilities.

And how about Armand Hammer, chairman of Occidental-Petroleum? In the Russian edition of Lenin's Collected Works, you will find several letters from Lenin to Hammer addressed affectionately as "Dear Comrade." Capitalists, the big enemy of communists? Nonsense. They work hand-in-glove to rule the world.

The key to understanding world events is to look at the world in terms of a Marxist Ruling-Class Alliance. Then seemingly inconsistent actions and events make sense:

- The elite subsidizes Marxist regimes: they are not enemies.
- The elite abandons free enterprise allies: it wants socialism.
- The elite presses for more individual taxation. that is, the Marxist "graduated income tax."
- The elite reduces its own taxation in the same way that the Moscow elite lives it up at the expense of the Russian working class.

The textbook modern history is illusory because it is based on a mythical capitalist versus communist struggle.

Thus, when we are asked to believe that Trilateral ambitions are morally justified to build a New World Order devoted to the peace and welfare of mankind, two points strike us: (a) this end does not coincide with other interpretations of Trilateral motivations and actions, and (b) the means adopted appear authoritarian and suggest that the ends may also be authoritarian.

What are some of the practical lessons we can learn from this alliance?

- If you are a small- or medium-sized business man or banker, a professional, or part of the "middle class," you are targeted for elimination.

- If you are actively working for a multinational (among those cited in this book), you may as well work in the Kremlin: you are assisting destruction of free enterprise and the free world.

- If you are a socialist, you are deluding yourself. You are working hand in hand with the totalitarians you proclaim to despise.

- If you, as an individual, are interested in tax reform, the only acceptable tax reform is complete repeal of the Sixteenth Amendment.

ENDNOTES

1. Congressional Record - House, 26 January 1978.

CHAPTER SEVEN

TRILATERAL CENSORSHIP: THE CASE OF C. GORDON TETHER

Trilateralists by their own statements see freedom of the press as a threat to achieving their objectives, the First Amendment of the Constitution notwithstanding. In The Crisis of Democracy, Trilateral authors **Michael J. Crozier**, **Samuel P. Huntington**, and **Joji Watanuki** describe our society as drifting with a "dangerously progressed alienation." The media, it is argued by the three authors, has played a role in this alienation, and "the media have thus become an autonomous power...we now are witnessing a crucial change when the profession (the media) tends to regulate itself in such a way as to resist pressure from financial or governmental interests." [1]

Note the key phrase: "resist pressure from financial or governmental interests." We shall see later that the Gordon Tether case in England fits this mold precisely.

Trilateralists do not like resistance to special interest pressure because "the media deprive governments and to some extent also other responsible authorities of the time lag, tolerance and thrust that make it possible to innovate and to experiment responsibly." [2]

Again note the self-appointed Trilateralist role as "responsible authorities" and the threads of authoritarianism woven into this brief passage. And further: "the media become a tremendous sounding board for the difficulties and tensions of society. Movements and fashions take broader proportions. It is much more difficult to escape the whirlpool of public relations events and to concentrate on more basic problems."3 In other words, legitimate grievances can be stated and faulty government criticized, but this weakens "authority."

What do the Trilaterals propose to do about this "threat" of free expression? In *The Crisis of Democracy*, the counter action is spelled out: "...significant measures are required to restore an appropriate balance between the press, the government and other institutions in society."[4] Specifically, Trilaterals call for an interstate commerce act for the media, that is, a regulatory agency for the media, to assure to the government the right and the ability to withhold information at the source.

So here we have it. Trilaterals want a "responsible" press, that is, a captive censored press, and propose legislation to achieve this end. While waiting for appropriate legislation, Trilaterals are applying an informal censorship. There are some annoying journalists - like Gordon Tether of London - who feel a higher call than that of crass Trilateralism and - who are persecuted by Trilateralists.

In this chapter we will detail one case of Trilateral censorship in an English newspaper, and incidentally illustrate the long globalist arm of Trilateralism. Secret elitist groups always censor, or try to censor, news about their covert activities. Censorship stems from the overall need for secrecy, to conceal from the world at large. As long as Trilaterals (and Bilderbergers and other elitist groups) skulk around the world convening closed meetings in secluded corners with security guards to keep out the press then we may conclude that Trilaterals, Bilderbergers, and the rest have something to hide. For that reasonable conclusion, we shall probably be labeled "paranoid" - but the name calling is merely added emphasis of covert doings.

From an intelligence viewpoint knowledge of what such secret groups want to suppress is important – submerged "inside" information is a reliable clue to actual intentions, as opposed to public stated intentions. The case of C. Gordon Tether, a prominent London journalist, is important precisely because a Trilateral commissioner squashed Tether's articles. Tether, for his part, retained the suppressed information and has since made it available to the public.

Who is C. Gordon Tether? Tether, age sixty-three, is a very well- known London journalist. For twenty years Tether wrote as the Financial Times's "Lombard," the longest running columnist in England and listed as such in the Guinness Book of Records. After 1974 some Tether articles were not printed and some not-too-subtle hints were made by the Financial Times about rewriting others. Tether refused and was thrown out on his ear – after twenty years at the Financial Times, and only a year or so before retirement.

The managing editor who banned the articles and did the firing is German born Trilateral Commissioner M. H. (Ferdy) Fisher. Of added significance to the United States is the Financial Times's plan to enter the American market in late 1978 with a special edition printed in West Germany. Of still further significance is the Trilateral influence in the media, such as, La Stampa (Italy), Avanti (Italy), Die Zeit (Germany), Field Enterprises (U.S.) and the Kyodo News Service (Japan).

WHO READS GORDON TETHER?

What makes Gordon Tether especially damaging to Trilateral ambitions is his readership. And let's make it clear from the start that this author does not necessarily agree with all Tether's views; what is critical is the suppression of free speech and the subject matter suppressed. Tether's readers would make most of us writers downright envious. For instance, they include(d):

- King Faisal of Saudi Arabia, who had such high regard for the "Lombard articles they were translated into Arabic for Faisal's personal perusal..."
- Conservative member of Parliament Peter Tapsell, who considers Lombard articles "required reading" for someone like himself (although Tapsell disagrees on Tether's low marks for the Common Market and the value of multinationals).

- Harold Wilson (Labor prime minister) who cited Tether as "...one of the most distinguished independent writers..."

- Former *Financial Times* editor (for twenty years before **Ferdy Fisher**) Sir Gordon Newton, who testified that Tether was "amenable to suggestions from him" and that "he (Newton) would not ban a subject." Further that he (Newton) "always defended Mr. Tether's column on occasions when it was disapproved by members of the *Financial Times* board."

- Labor Minister for Overseas Development Mrs. Judith Hart, testified, "...it would be a very dangerous situation if columnists in our newspapers were to find they were not able to say what they thought."

You see why Tether's writing could be either extremely useful to Trilateral ambitions or extremely damaging?

Over twenty years Tether had built up an influential and admiring (if not always agreeable) readership. That adds up to power, although Tether is almost certainly not looking for power. Trilateralists are well aware of the crucial role of journalism in surfacing or suppressing information. **Michel Crozier**, **Huntington**, and **Watanuki** in *The Crisis of Democracy* term media "the gatekeeper":

"Their main impact is visibility. The only real event is the event that is reported and seen. Thus, journalists possess a crucial role as gatekeepers of one of the central dimensions of public life." [5]

Now there is much information that Trilaterals do not want seen by the public, that they want to remain invisible and to go unreported and suppressed as nonevents.

Unruly journalists who do not read the guidelines on the elitist gate are unwelcome: after all they have the means to sabotage the New World Order.

THE BANNED ARTICLES

Forty-six Tether articles were banned by Financial Times editor cum Trilateral Commissioner **Ferdy Fisher**, presumably because they contained information which was supposed to remain invisible.

Certainly an editor has control over the content of a newspaper or journal. That is an editor's right and responsibility. However, in Tether's case, a long-lasting twenty-year editorial relationship had been established by mutual consent - so that Fisher's censorship was a one- sided action tantamount to breach of contract. This is a vital point to hold in mind. Moreover, many of the "banned articles" were later published elsewhere, ranging from the *Spectator* (conservative) to *New Solidarity* (socialist), which makes nonsense of the *Financial Times's* plea that Tether's articles were "not up to standard."

The most objective way to get to the root of the Tether-*Financial Times* dispute is by a theme analysis. Every piece of writing has a theme. By assessing and grouping themes, one can isolate what, if anything, was annoying Commissioner **Fisher**. We extracted a random sample of nine articles (every fifth banned article) and listed their themes. (See table.) Run your eye down the list of selected banned titles. Then do the same with the theme column. There is a common theme which will hit readers like a ten ton truck.

The themes of the nine selected banned articles 6 strongly suggest what is bothering **Ferdy Fisher** (and his Trilateral cohorts). Any editor or writer in the transatlantic Establishment press who touches upon certain topics too often or in too much depth receives a polite telephone call to suggest that "perhaps you have exhausted the potential on this topic."

No fewer than five Tether articles (of the selected nine) have a common theme - a "no-no" theme of criticism of the supercapitalists, international bankers who act as if God has ordained their right to rule the world. Two articles are anti-European Economic Community (EEC), and EEC is a vital first step to the global authoritarian structure demanded by Trilaterals. Let's look briefly at each of these nine banned articles:

(1) A July 1974 article ("Need for a City Lobby") points out the one-sided nature of City (of London) propaganda and its delicate avoidance of the seamy side of the financial world. Just a

THEME ANALYSIS OF NINE TETHER ARTICLES (RANDOM SELECTION)

Title	Banned	Theme
Need For a City Lobby	5 July 1974	One-sided nature of city propaganda promotes international banker without exposing the unflattering aspects of "the city."
Spotight on the Honours System	12 Frb. 1975	Weskness of the Honours Systemis inability to get awy from class distinctions - the system needs rexamination of, not increase, in awards to business.
Silencing the Resistance	12 June 1975	Suppression of antimarket forces is first step towards a polics state.
Newsletters at Loggerheads	19 Sept. 1975	Vigorous differences among the hard money leetters.
Supercapitalists Fall Out	16 Jan. 1976	Something needs to be done about the supercapitalists (including Rckefellers) before their conflicts disturb world peace.
The Prince and the Bilderbergers	3 March 1976	"Bernhard and Bildbergers meet in secrecy. If there is nothing to hide, why so much effort to conceal?"
Mocking at the Spirit of Easter	15 April 1976	It is time that leaders of the world grow up and stop spendding $500 billion a year on armaments.
Those Toosting Chickens	10 May 1976	Anti-European Economic community.
Losing Ground in the Battle of Ideas	5 July 1976	IMF is an engine of inflation, needed to phase out key role of U.S. dollar.

week before this **Ferdy** had banned another article ("Beyond the Limits of Detente"), in which Tether attacked the supercapitalist **Kissinger** policy of subsidizing Soviet military prowess. From this author's personal experience at the Hoover Institution at Stanford University (influential Trilateralist **David Packard** is on the executive board), I can assure the reader that our subsidy of the USSR is a very touchy subject among Trilaterals - they know they are betraying the Western world but can't resist the profits.

(2) "Spotlight on the Honours System" (banned 12 February 1975 but printed ten days later in **The Spectator)** refers to the British system of awarding "Honours," that is, titles, in an annual "Honours List." Tether made a simple point: that the great disadvantage of such a system is "our inability to get away from class distinctions." Furthermore, businessmen are well rewarded monetarily for expertise and shouldn't be clamoring after such baubles. Tether suggests resentment is thereby generated and undue attention is given to "unscrupulous power-- seekers."

(3) "Silencing the Resistance" (banned, 12 June 1975) touches on the Europeanization of England, a necessary first step to a Trilateralist world government. Tether doesn't like Europeanization, nor the EEC (European Economic Community). The theme is that suppression of anti-EEC views makes England a "one party state" and could be "the first step down the path leading to a Police State."

(4) "Newsletters at Loggerheads" (banned 19 September 1975) is another "no-no" subject in the Establishment media. There are several hundred "hard money" (i.e., pro-gold) newsletters, maybe more, mostly in the United States, which over the last decade have been far more accurate in their advice than pro-Establishment financial media. Tether reports in this article on their differences, affirming that a healthy underground financial press exists. Schultz and Myers for example may have differences, but both have been more right in their prognostications over the long run than such newsletters as Greens Commodity Reports or newspaper financial columnists such as Sylvia Porter who tend to reflect the Establishment "party line." Schultz, Myers, and other pro-gold newsletter editors are "non-persons" so far as the Establishment is concerned.

(5) In "Supercapitalists Fall Out" (banned 16 January 1976) Tether comments favorably on Solzhenitsyn and argues that the rivalries among the supercapitalists can have great significance for the world. We should start to take an interest in their doings before they get us into trouble. Tether cites Woodrow Wilson's famous lines: "Some of the biggest men in the U.S. in the fields of commerce and manufacturing know that there is a power so organized, so subtle, so complete, so pervasive that they had better not speak above their breath when they speak in condemnation of it." Tether correctly records that this behind-the-scenes power still exists. Of course this is another "no-no" for the Establishment press; you won't find *this* topic investigated by the *Washington Post*, and the *New York Times*.

(6) In "The Prince and the Bilderbergers" (banned 3 March 1976) Tether hit the jackpot. Every self-respecting journalist knows that the Bilderberger secret comings and goings and meetings are just *not* to be reported in depth. But Tether actually complained, "why is it that, if there is so little to hide, so much effort is devoted to hiding it?" Tether's conclusion is logical: *the Bilderbergers have something to hide.* (The article was later published in Verdict in November 1975.)

Prince Bernhard (onetime leader of the Bilderbergers) was personally involved in the messy Lockheed kickback affair, and this supports an argument that all these groups (Trilaterals, Bilderbergers, Council on Foreign Relations and so on) use moralistic talk of peace and world order as a cover for their own profit.

(7) "Mocking at the Spirit of Easter" (banned 15 April 1976) comments critically on Citibank's proposal for a thirty year rearmament program against Soviet imperialism. One can understand Citibank sensitivity. Not only has Henry Wriston publically made known his dislike of such freewheeling commentary, but Citibank is one of the international banks responsible for the need for rearmament. These bankers financed and subsidized the Soviet Union to its present military prowess. Heaven forbid that any journalist should publicly discuss *that* story of greed and amorality.

(8) "Those Roosting Chickens" (banned 10 May 1976) continued Tether's anti-EEC commentary.

(9) The final article in our random selection, "Losing Ground in Battle of Ideas" (banned 5 July1976), the most important theme is that the IMF is an engine of world inflation and that reform of the world's monetary system must begin with phasing out the key role of the U.S. dollar.

What can we say about the overall thrust of these nine banned articles?

- All the articles in some way are critical of "the powers behind the Establishment," that quasi-secret world rarely, if ever, reported in the U.S. or European media.[7]

- Six of the nine banned articles zeroed in on the internationalist banking establishment and their power games. Tether's rather mild view is that their globalist antics may not be healthy for our world.

- Tether names names - **Rockefeller**, Citibank, **Prince Bernhard**, Bilderbergers - and it is notable that the context in which these names were reported, that is, as having met in secret conclaves, is rarely, if ever, mentioned in the U.S.

In recent years an exposure of these groups has been made by independent academics in the U.S. One of the best is a series of books by G. William Domhoff, professor of sociology at University of California, Santa Cruz. Domhoff explores the American ruling class, its operations, 8 functions, and meeting grounds in *The Higher Circles* (1970), *Who Rules America?* (1967), and *The Bohemian Grove and Other Retreats* (1974.) These books also portray the background of Trilateral Commission operations and the sensitivity of the ruling elite when its more nefarious activities are exposed to public view. That is, after Domhoff's careful exploration of the heavy drinking and prostitution in the Bohemian Grove retreat, for example, we are left with an explanation of the ineptness and lack of moral fiber displayed by the elite in international affairs. After such exposes we might accurately view the elite as a group of naughty little boys, rather than the far-sighted statesmen of their own self-portraits.

GORDON TETHER AND THE MISSING GOLD

While this surfacing of suppressed information is quite sufficient to turn Establishment heat onto Tether he may have sinned
further by refusing to accept the party line for the condition of
the U.S. gold reserves - although Tether's Fort Knox articles were
not banned.

Tether was probing the "Fort Knox gold mystery," that is,
the possibility that U.S. gold reserves are not as reported. On
11 February 1975 Tether wrote an article raising questions on
the quality and quantity of U.S. gold reserves, and he presented
his grounds for believing that a gigantic "cover-up" is in progress - that the U.S. gold (if any) is at least of inferior quality (and
Washington acts as if an inventory might reveal some unpleasant
secrets).

There is no doubt that the Establishment is sensitive on this issue. In November 1977 this author made the observation (at the
Monetary Conference in New Orleans) that four-fifths of the gold
in U.S. stocks is .85 coin melt, not acceptable for "good delivery."
Commodities Journal picked this up and asked pro-Establishment
Charles R. Stahl of Greens Commodity Reports about this statement. Stahl immediately, as if stung by a bee, responded, "This is
nonsense." Yet a telephone call to the Treasury Department will
confirm the coin melt nature of U.S. stocks. On the other hand, the
alloy-grade quality of the reserves is a fact that the elite wishes to
be kept invisible.

In brief, we know there is a knee-jerk reaction to hide two
facts:

a.   The quantity of inventoried gold in U.S. reserves,

b.   The quality of this gold, Le. 80 percent is alloy "coin melt."

The assault on Tether may well stem in part from his willingness to tackle this potentially explosive scandal.

ELITIST INFLUENCE IN BOOK PUBLISHING

This raises the question of the extent to which the book publishing industry has been dominated by elitist themes and con-

cepts. While this must be balanced by the observation that Harper & Row published The Bohemian Grove, and Hawthorn, The Plot to Seize the White House, on balance it is usually difficult to publish anti-Establishment books in the U.S.

How pervasive is Trilateral censorship in the U.S.? Potentially, there is an unhealthy penetration by Trilateralism of the book publishing industry. This may give you an idea of the scope:

1. CBS (Commissioner **Henry B. Schacht** is a director) owns Holt, Rinehart & Winston, Popular Library and Fawcet (about 15 to 20 percent of mass paperback market), plus seven monthly and 60 annual magazines

2. TIMES-MIRROR (Commissioner **H. Brown** is a director) owns: Harry N. Abrams (art publisher), New American Library (mass paperback) and Los Angeles Times

3. TIME, Inc. (Commissioner **Hedley Donovan** is editor-in-Chief and **Sol Linowitz**, is a director) owns: Little, Brown; New York Graphic Society; Time/Life Books; Book of the Month Club plus Time, Fortune, Money, and People.

In practice, elitist dominance of book publishing does not stop books from being published; however, it does inhibit widespread distribution. Book publishing has low barriers to entry: the capital and skill requirements are relatively low. The essential requirement for success is the marketing skill of obtaining distribution; and in recent decades, a flood of anti-Establishment books demonstrates that increased distribution is possible. On the other hand, there are curious events to suggest elitist intervention at some point in the book distribution channels. A personal example will make the point. In 1974 this author published *Wall Street and the Bolshevik Revolution* with a New York publishing house (Arlington House.) Given the esoteric nature of the topic, sales were quite respectable - something over 25,000 in hardback. Yet, distribution of the book through regular channels was effectively strangled.

The trade journal *Publishers Weekly* (5 August 1974) selected the book for its leading entry under "nonfiction" with a healthy four inch review. Most books receive a couple of lines and, of course, only one book leads off each section. Obviously, the reviewers at Publishers Weekly took the material at face value. The review read as follows:

NONFICTION
WALL STREET AND THE
BOLSHEVIK REVOLUTION

Anthony (Sic) C. Sutton. Arlington House, $7.95. Professor Sutton, affiliated with the Hoover Institution at Stanford and author of "National Suicide" (1973), uses State Department files, private papers of Wall Street figures and other sources (biographies, etc.) to document his astonishing thesis that Wall Street, notably the J.P. Morgan interests, played money games with both the Kerensky regime and the Bolsheviks in 1917. Among other things he notes the preponderance of U.S. financiers rather than humanitarian personnel on the American Red Cross Mission to war-torn Russia at that time; he suggests too that the American writer John Reed ("Ten Days That Shook the World") was secretly supported by the Morgan people. At least by association Sutton demonstrates an eyebrow-raising interest on the part of Wall Street powers in making hay with their archenemies some 50-odd years ago. Conservative Book Club selection. (September 3, 1974)

The above report is objective and adequate. It *appears that Publishers Weekly* plays no favorites. Then "something" happened. Not a single bookstore in the U.S. known to the author carried the book. A few ordered the book for customers by special request. Not a single review of the book was published in the Establishment press nor the left-liberal press. The book was effectively made "invisible." Sales were made through a book club and by mail order for the most part. Why? Obviously, because of the extreme sensitivity of the topic, no bookseller would stick his neck out.

Certainly, there is potential for massive intervention into freedom of expression by elitist suppression. Currently the Authors' Guild is pressing the Department of Justice to institute a Clayton Act case against publishing mammoths, fearing that authors' freedoms have already been infringed upon. Yet, the problem is much more than mere financial control of the press and publishing. A greater roadblock to public comprehension has been expressed by Trilateralists themselves:

> ...the ruling elite and the educated audience play a major role as an important screen. They constitute the primary audience of the highbrow publications, which in turn tend to structure the problems that will finally reach the broader audience. Public relations of a public figure will be conditioned by the existence of these two levels. This means that there is a very serious buffer against too immediate reactions." [9]

In brief, problems and solutions are already "structured" *before* they reach the general public.

About 1984 when the Trilaterals meet to review progress, or lack of progress, in the past decade, they will find a fundamental error in their strategy. From the start, it has been known that the Trilateral thrust is in conflict with the Constitution of the United States. Efforts have been made - by the Fund for the Republic and others – to amend the U.S. Constitution. This was an impossible objective. American citizens like the protections of the Constitution, especially protection from those ambitious persons who would rule the world. So an elitist decision was made to go it without changing the Constitution - to meet the problems as and when they arose, trusting that the cement of the New World Order would harden before enough citizens were aroused to protest the violence to the Constitutional order. This will prove to be the crowning error.

In any event, English journalist Gordon Tether may have the last laugh yet: *Financial Time's* circulation is slowly shrinking - down 7.2 percent from 1973 - and readers don't take kindly to the idea that their daily newspaper may be filtering news. Yet Gordon Tether's case is a warning to us. Tether has appealed to the London Industrial Tribunal for arbitration in the dispute; and it is already the longest such hearing in the history of the Tribunal. In England there is no constitution, only a convention to define freedom of expression. There is, on the other hand, the First Amendment in the United States. So we would do well to sharpen our awareness and be watchful for any intrusion upon freedom of the press from whatever quarter it may come.

ENDNOTES

1. Michael J. Crozier, Samuel P. Huntington. Joji Watanuki. The Crisis of Democracy (New York: University Press. 1975) p. 35.
2. Ibid.. p. 35
3. Ibid.
4. 4. Ibid.. p. 181
5. Ibid.. p. 35
6. If you believe the random selection process is unfair or biased. then purchase "The Banned Articles" and read all fifty-six. Copies may be obtained from The Trilateral Observer, Box 4775. Scottsdale, AZ 85258. Enclose $3.50 please.
7. The only English language newspaper in recent times to run an exposure series on this behind-the-scenes power has been The Citizen (Pretoria. South Africa). understandably peeved at U.S. interference in internal South African affairs. The Citizen. no doubt. decided to blow a small whistle. Reprints available from ACSA Foundation. P.O. Box 4335. Scottsdale. AZ 85258.
8. On this. see G William Domhoff's The Bohemian Grove and Other Retreats. (New York: Harper & Row. 1974).
9. Michael J. Crozier et al.. Crisis of Democracy. p. 36

Chapter Eight

Trilateral Hatred Of Gold

Trilaterals hate gold because it is a restriction, and an insurmountable restriction, on the fulfillment of their global ambitions. An "elastic" currency controlled by the Federal Reserve System gives power to control the broad direction of the financial structure and the economy. Gold, however, gives sovereignty to individuals and removes them from the center of authority. No totalitarian system can be operated on gold: both Hitler and Stalin are proof of this point. Similarly, Trilaterals need to remove gold from the world monetary system before their globalist ambitions can be achieved.

Triangle Paper 1, *Towards a Renovated World Monetary System*, contains the blueprint for world monetary arrangements. Naturally, gold, the challenge to the world order authority, is treated with disdain in the New World Order central bank; and it is proposed that

- Reserves will be held *only* as Bancor, an artificial "goldless" money,
- National currencies *will not* be counted in reserves, and
- Gold will have no role at all in the new international money system.

The Trilateral Commission has its hands squarely on the U.S. gold policy faucet: any decision to sell U.S. official gold reserves will be made by Commissioner **W. Michael Blumenthal** (Secretary of the Treasury) and **Anthony Solomon** (Under Secretary of the

Treasury for Monetary Affairs). However, *Triangle Paper 1* also reflects enough realism to agree that this goldless artificial money world is "some time away." The authors, therefore, propose certain market actions to reduce the international monetary role of gold. "We believe in action consonant with our long-run objectives and at the same time advancing the interim aim of calming markets would be the coordinated and joint sale of official gold into private markets." [1]

The stated intent in *Paper 1* is to depress the price of gold "greatly" and "interject much uncertainty into the market place." An earlier Trilateral proposal to use gold sales to raise funds for the LDCs has already been adopted, and Trilaterals have the political clout in IMF and the treasury to carry out such policies in the immediate future. For example, a recent letter (dated 19 July 1978) from assistant secretary for legislative affairs at the treasury to Congressman J. Kennet Robinson even went so far as to reject the national security role of the U.S. gold reserves:

> *The Treasury program of monthly public sales of gold does not affect the ability of the United States to meet strategic or domestic gold mines which exceeds that required for defense-related uses. Moreover, our existing stocks are extremely large in relation to such uses for the foreseeable future. Gold is not an important medium of payment, and the relatively small amounts which might be useful in unusual circumstances can readily be provided. We have seen no practical need, therefore, to regard any specific portion of our stocks as a contingency reserve.*

Trilateral gold policy reveals a long-run intent to impose a world dictatorship through control of money but also an uncomfortable awareness that gold is a fundamental challenge to these objectives. In contrast to this wariness, the Trilateral gold proposals will not solve their problem. The war on gold is age old. It didn't start with current New World Order dreams. No political power has ever defeated gold - because it is portable sovereignty. Those individuals who dislike or distrust Trilateral intentions will simply buy and hold onto gold. Gold is *their* lifeline to a sane world, and it will be the Achilles' heel of the Trilaterals.

What the Trilaterals do not understand is the vital necessity of gold for any nation. Maybe the Trilaterals dream of a goldless one-world dictatorship, but they need gold to attain this dream. History is replete with instances of the usefulness of gold. The U.S. financed and won World Wars I and II with gold. In 1941 we had almost two-thirds of the world's gold stock and a national debt of only $40 billion, short term obligations to foreigners of only $3 to 4 billion, a favorable balance of payments, and a money supply of only $42 billion covered by $24 billion in gold, a ratio better than 1:2. In 1943, when it looked as if Rommel were defeating our forces at Kasserine Pass, General Mark Clark had to pay for military supplies in gold: suppliers would not accept paper dollars. The same happened in the Pacific following defeat at Pear I Harbor. French monetary expert, Jacques Rueff, de Gaulle's financial adviser stated: "I am not sure that your military people, for reasons of national security in case of emergency want to be left with so little gold." [2]

Proponents of a goldless world speculate that the value of the dollar - its purchasing power abroad - depends on a country's productivity without the gold cover.

Under the guidance of academic monetary experts, Trilaterals have been assured that gold can safely be removed from the world monetary system. For instance, Charles Kindleberger, professor of economics at MIT made the following statement to Congress in 1968:

> *My inclination is to stabilize the ratio of gold to dollars as long as our gold stocks hold out - and I predict that this will be a very long time - and then to move, not to gold, but to dollars as an international medium of exchange, as it now is, and store of value, as it is in part - dollars managed by an internationally determined monetary policy, to be sure, but dollars.*

> *An analogy between language and money suggests that the dollar is the equivalent of English, which is the world's lingua franca for communication, especially in business and science; the French proposal to return to gold is like trying to restore the world to the use of Latin, the language of world intellectuals in the Middle Ages.* [3]

This statement is ridiculous in the face of history. No fiat currency has ever survived. Yet in spite of history, the Trilateral commissioners have a concerted action plan to implement a sell-gold policy.

Commissioner **John H. Perkins** (chairman of the Continental Illinois Bank and Trust Company) has discontinued sales of all gold coins at his bank (Krugerrands, Mexican pesos, and Austrian coronas), reportedly because gold coin sales weren't producing profit for the bank. More likely, however, the move was in line with overall Trilateral objectives. Paradoxically, **Perkins** wrote in *Trialogue* (Spring 1976) that "it will be little benefit to anyone if there is a repetition of the policies which led to the devastating world wide inflation and subsequent recession experienced during the first half of the 1970s." [4]

In another action, Commissioner **Harold Brown** (Secretary of Defense) has ordered the Department of Defense (DOD) to dispose of the emergency store of 15,000 gold sovereigns and gold napoleons used in the "escape kits" carried by air crew members over hostile territory. From now on, USAF crew members crash landing in enemy territory will presumably offer paper dollars or computer blip Special Drawing Rights (SDRs) to hostile inhabitants.

Commissioner **Blumenthal** has blocked the effort of the President's Commission on Olympic Sports to mint a gold commemorative coin or medal. The committee estimates a gold coin would generate $300 to 500 million for the Olympics. Unknown to the committee, its gold program is unwelcome to the Trilaterals - it would put gold in the hands of individuals.

Moreover, a bill to strike gold medallions from the U.S. gold stock (SB 2843) introduced by Senator Jesse Helms has come under bitter attack from **Blumenthal** and the treasury. **Blumenthal** has stated publicly that he fears the medallion will be used as a coin:

I do not believe it is in the public interest for the U.S. Government to take an action which would encourage our citizens to use gold as a substitute for U.S. legal tender as a medium of exchange; moreover, the issuance of such gold medallions could lead those who favor the return to a gold--

based domestic monetary system to seek to make such me-
dallions legal tender as the next step in a continuing process
to restore the monetary role of gold. [5]

This statement flies in the face of history: people, not governments, decide ultimately what will be used as a means of exchange.

But, the Trilateralists are skating on thin ice in attacking gold; to attack from strength, they need gold in the vaults. Perhaps Trilaterals actually believe that the United States has the world's largest above- ground gold stock. Not only Establishment media but well informed foreign sources assume that the U.S. has $11.5 billion of good delivery gold in Fort *Knox* which, if placed on the market, would collapse the price. [6]

We know Trilaterals want to sell gold and that **W. Michael Blumenthal** and **Anthony Solomon** will make the decision to sell gold. The question is, Does the U.S. really have the gold to sell?

Although the official gold reserve statistics are recorded as "Gold stock - $11.719 (billions)," the United States doesn't have that much good delivery gold in the vaults. We assume that the "gold" referred to in official statistics is good delivery bullion, valued at the "official price" of $42.22 an ounce, as established on 21 September 1973. This is not so. The bulk of U.S. gold reserves consist of unmarketable gold alloy of .85 fineness and less, not good delivery bullion of .995 fineness and above in 400 ounce bars.

The official published statistics are grossly misleading. The latest unpublished U.S. Treasury inventory of "good delivery gold bars," the quality called for in world markets, is as follows (as of 1 November 1977, compared to 1973 to indicate changes):

INVENTORY OF U.S. TREASURY GOOD DELIVERY GOLD BARS (1973 and 1977) Total Weight of Bars in Ounces

Weight of Single Bar	November 1973	November 1977	Change (Minus)
5	2,650	2,450	(200)
10	48,850	6,470	(42,380)
15	270	0	(270)

20	260	0	(260)
25	142,350	23,075	(119,275)
30	1,140	0	(1,140)
50	398,250	0	(532,750)
400	47,350,800	48,016,800	660,000
1000	-	280,000	280,000
Total	48,477,320	48,333,145	(144,175)

* Source: U.S. Bureau of the Mint.

NOTE: At the "official" price of $42.22 per ounce, the U.S. gold stocks should be recorded as: 48,333,145 fine ounces times $42.22 equals $2,040,625,381, or roughly $2 billion, compared to the official published figure of $11.5 billion), assuming this gold is in the vaults. No physical inventory has been taken. While there were audits of the seals in 1953 and 1976, audits of seals are not inventories of gold bars. Readers interested in the possibility of "missing gold" should send a self addressed business size envelope

The balance of the gold stock is "gold alloy" of .85 fineness or less, mostly coin melt (i.e., the coins seized for FDR in 1933). It cannot be sold as good delivery.

Compare this 48 million ounces of good delivery gold to the European stocks:

Country	Approximate Ounces
West Germany	115,0001000
France	97,000,000*
Italy	80,000,000
Switzerland	80,000,000
Netherlands	53,000,000
Belgium	40,000,000
Great Britain	23,000,000
Austria	21,000,000

* Plus 100,000,000 ounces privately held.

Perhaps more importantly one should compare the notable increases in these European gold stocks from 1971, when the U.S. went off gold, to 1978:

Country	Increase
West Germany	16%
France	15%
Italy	15%
Switzerland	14%
Netherlands	14%
Belgium	10%
Great Britain	15%
Austria	15%

Why not melt the large treasury stock of gold alloy and recast into good delivery bars? To a very limited extent, the treasury has done just this. Comparison of the U.S. Bureau of the Mint inventory of gold bars between November 1973 and November 1977 shows that the mint has re-melted its stock of "Hershey bars" (i.e., end-of-melt pourings) of good delivery fineness into good delivery weights. In the earlier 1973 inventory list, the mint showed numerous bars with weights less than 400 ounces (Le., 5-, 10-, 15-,20-,25-,30-,50-, and 250-ounce bars) not acceptable in the international market. By 1977 many of these bars had been re-melted. The 1977 inventory discloses no bars with weights of 15, 20, 30, and 250 ounces, a marked reduction in bars with weights of 5, 10, 25, and 50 ounces, and an increase of 1,665 bars of 400 ounces good delivery weight. The total inventory of good delivery gold is a little less - a reduction of 144,175 ounces to 48,333,145 ounces (compared to 48,477,320 ounces in 1973). A significant change is 280 additional bars of 1,000 ounce weight.

TOTAL NUMBER OF BARS

Weight of Single Bar	November 1973	November 1977	Change (Minus)
5	530	490	(40)
10	41,885	647	(41,238)

15	18	647	(18)
20	13	0	(13)
25	5,694	923	(4,771
30	38	0	(38)
50	7,965	87	(7,878)
250	2,131	0	(2,131)
400	118,377	120,042	1,665
1000	-	280	280
Total	139,651	122,469	(17,182)

* Source: U.S. Bureau of the Mint.

The question remains, what can the mint do with the coin melt bars? Considering that the U.S. has a total gold refining capacity of about 2 million ounces per year, it would take seventy-five years to convert the 150 million or so ounces of coin melt. Although up-to-date statistics on world gold refining capacity do not exist, it would surely take many years to refine 150 million ounces of gold. Moreover, the treasury has protested about the unacceptable work burden of just counting the bars for a complete physical inventory. Finally, a re-melt program would raise some awkward public questions, such as what happened to the original $24 billion of the U.S. gold stocks?

Of course, the United States could always revalue its good delivery gold at the market price giving us 48,333,145 ounces times $176.00 (7 February 1978) equals $8,506,633,520. But, this is an impossible approach for Trilaterals, as it would mean abandoning the "gold is dead" theme. It is critical for the U.S. Treasury to maintain the statistical fiction of $11.5 billion of good delivery bullion in reserve because when the time comes to sell U.S. gold against a rising gold price, the treasury wants to create the picture of a vast supply overhang crashing down into the market place. This supply overhang simply does not exist: $2 billion of good delivery gold of .995 fineness is far, far less than is needed, even for a bare minimum strategic reserve.

Now you see why in March 1965 Congress removed the requirement that Federal Reserve Banks keep a 25 percent reserve in gold certificates against members' deposits, and why on 18 March 1968, they removed the 35 percent reserve requirement against Federal Reserve notes; and why on 15 August 1973 the U.S. closed the gold window and suspended convertibility. And remember this removal of the gold cover was done over the vehement protest of organizations such as the Independent Bankers Association of America, which warned:

> *The lesson of history clearly reminds us that no nation has been able to survive the deliberate removal of the gold backing from its currency. The likelihood is that if this universally recognized basis were eliminated, gold would rapidly flow out of this country.*
>
> *The Association fears that depriving the United States currency of its gold backing would do irreparable harm to the nation's economy in the years ahead.*

Will Trilaterals seize American gold?

On April 5, 1933, Franklin D. Roosevelt, who had entered the White House only a few days before, issued an executive order requiring American citizens to surrender gold coins, gold bullion, and gold certificates to the nearest Federal Reserve Bank. The treasury offered to pay any cost of transportation, and it is interesting to note the gold was ordered to the nearest Federal Reserve Bank, a private organization, not to the nearest United States mint or depository.

Later in 1933, the Federal Reserve System turned over the surrendered gold to United States mints. In exchange, the Fed received Series 1934 gold certificates each with a nominal value of $100,000, and issued only to the Federal Reserve System by the U.S. Treasury. Most appropriately, these non-circulating notes bear the face of Woodrow Wilson, who signed the Federal Reserve Act into law a few days before Christmas in 1913.

Series 1934 gold certificates are in effect a claim on seized citizens' gold by a private money monopoly which we know as the Federal Reserve System. The certificates bear the following statement on the obverse:

> *"This is to certify that there is on deposit in the Treasury of the United States one hundred thousand dollars in gold payable to bearer on demand as authorized by law."*

This seizure precedent must be viewed in light of a highly significant statistic: how much of the circulating gold coin was surrendered in response to the executive order? Only 49 percent of gold coins in circulation were actually surrendered, the balance of the $287 million of gold coins were kept under mattresses and buried in backyards. This unaccounted-for balance has been written off, or as Milton Friedman puts it, "the $287 million was retained illegally in private hands."

For a year the federal government huffed and puffed and threatened to sue these Americans who had decided to keep their own coins. Only one lawsuit was ever filed and that one objection was by an angry citizen against the federal government to protest seizure of his gold. The seized gold coins, Double Eagles and Liberty's, irreplaceable segments of America's artistic heritage, were melted down by the mint to plain gold alloy bars and today form part of the bulk of our gold reserves.

Gold owners of 1978 area different breed from those of 1933. There is no likelihood that 49 percent, 15 percent, or even 5 percent of the citizenry would turn over 1978 gold holdings, and this is evidenced by the rapidly growing markets for concealment devices, (safes and vaults).

Will Trilaterals ban gold imports?

A Trilateral ban on gold imports is much more likely than another attempted seizure of citizens' gold. The excuse for the ban could be a balance of payments crisis, an energy crisis, or one of several other created crisis scenarios: the real unstated reason will be elitist fear of a mass dumping of nonconvertible paper dollars into gold. Thus the timing of any future gold ban is much more likely to be determined by a monetary crisis than by an energy or balance of payments crisis.

A gold import ban would of course generate a temporary premium on gold bullion and coins, as was the case in France and England. However, if we follow historical precedent, the premium will decline as new gold supplies are smuggled across the Mexican and Canadian borders and lengthy shorelines, all relatively unguarded.

A ban on gold imports will be required at some point to fulfill Trilateral monetary objectives, and the risk of public alienation will be weighed against the long-run objectives. Historically speaking, the Trilaterals will find that gold bans serve only to create more anti- Establishment groups.

ENDNOTES

1. "Towards a Renovated World Monetary system," Triangle Paper No.1, p.30.
2. Jacques Rueff, The Monetary Sin of the West (New York: Macmillan Co., 1972), p. 72.
3. "Removal of Gold Cover," (Statement to Congress, 1978), p.171.
4. "Looking Forward," Trialogue (Spring 1976), p. 3.
5. See for example, The Economist. (London), 4 - 10 February 1978, p.113/4.
6. Today these certificates are recorded on the Federal Reserve "Statement of Condition" as assets. (See, for example, FRS H. 4) (a) 19 January 1978, p. 2. Gold Certificate Account $11.719 million dollars.

CHAPTER NINE

TRILATERAL PAPER MONEY SCHEMES

Trilaterals by their own words are interested in political power: all objectives are subordinate to the political power needed to order the world as the Trilateralists see fit. So you will not find rational consideration of alternatives, or the weighing of options in Trilateral dogma. You can, however, expect an irrational drive, come what may, to control the world in the name of globalism and New World Order.

Therefore, you must hold a key fundamental proposition in mind: Trilaterals are not interested in what monetary system works best, or most equitably, or whether gold is a more effective monetary device than paper, or what monetary system will support a higher standard of living for the world's poor. The overriding drive for Trilaterals is to manage the world economy, manage being a euphemism for control. This control is exercised through so called coordination of macroeconomic policy, in spite of the dismal results from attempted macroeconomic direction. It is argued that the prime *desideratum* for this control device is to keep world peace. Nowhere is there any recognition of the historical fact that such control has always led to conflict: that denying national and ethnic independence is a sure road to strife and bloodshed.

Triangle Paper 14, *Towards a Renovated International System,* concludes that the 1944 Bretton Woods system has already "come under increasing strain," and events have forced traumatic changes, that is, the periodic assault on the dollar and floating exchange rates. The current Trilateral objective is to build an international system, a world order based on cooperation and focusing on two aspects which require such *cooperation:*

• International lending, and

• The creation of international reserves.

The Trilateral proposal is to involve five to ten leading *core countries* in establishing the new system. The rest of the world will have to go along as best it can. Some ideas to this end have already been implemented: for example, a new, man-made artificial international money, the Special Drawing Rights (SDRS) has been created for central banks. As the SDR is introduced, gold will (supposedly) be phased out of the international reserve system.

The task ahead for the Trilateral Commission world managers is to integrate these ideas into the world monetary system and make them work. The immediate and most compelling task is to operate the floating rate system to dampen erratic movements in exchange rates, which are, of course, damaging to international trade. Such erratic movements do not occur in fixed rates tied to gold. However, gold moves the world away from the "cooperative" international arrangements needed by Trilaterals, and gold, therefore, is a bigger problem than floating rate disorder. Following this is the task of world reserve management. The Trilaterals want "wider cooperation since the key to world reserve management is restraint in the additions to central bank holdings of gold and of course currencies such as the U.S. Dollar, the German Mark, the British Pound and the French Franc." 1

The sinking dollar is also a problem, and an unforeseen one, particularly as it inevitably leads to lesser use of dollars as a world reserve unit. Trilaterals with their vague views on gold were not able to foresee that the 1971 suspension of gold convertibility would be a millstone around the neck of the dollar and "international cooperation." The following diagram illustrates far better than words the decline in value of the fiat dollar in relation to both gold and currencies tied to gold and thus the decline in the ability of Trilaterals to create a workable fiat reserve dollar world system.

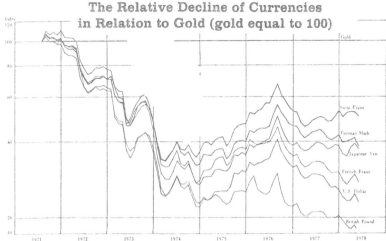

Source: Adapted from Gold Standard Corporation (1127 West 41st Street. Kansas City. MO 64111) News Briefs. June 1978.

The out-of-date views on gold held by the U.S. Treasury, un-under Trilateral control, are well exemplified by a recent letter from Gene E. Godley, Assistant Secretary for Legislative Affairs at the treasury to Congressman J. Kenneth Robinson - a letter which incidentally illustrates clearly why the treasury has been able to lose billions of dollars for the U.S. taxpayer.

There is, moreover, a high degree of uncertainty about the usefulness of gold as money. Its monetary role has greatly diminished in recent years, and its market price has varied widely. Thus, our gold stocks no longer represent an assured source of financing for our imports.

The U.S. Treasury and Trilaterals would do well to ponder the above chart, and the nonsense it makes of official anti-gold statements. Using 1971 as a base of 100, all fiat currencies have declined in value compared to gold, and the U.S. dollar has declined the most (except for the pound sterling). The Swiss franc and other currencies tied to gold have declined least. The treasury, under Trilateralist direction, has assumed facts directly contrary to the chart.

Trilaterals do recognize that as long as countries build reserves with national currencies and gold, then the SDR and global fiat systems will take second place. The IMF is the vehicle to achieve the twin objectives, and the IMF is supposed to evolve into a "central bank for national central banks." At the moment, the IMF does not have the reserve resources for this: the Trilaterals propose to artificially create the necessary reserves out of thin air. The IMF is also supposedly the forum for "coordination of macroeconomic policies."

How are our Trilateral friends faring with their plans? To answer this, we have to go back to Bretton Woods and the Keynes-White schemes for Bancor and Unitas. After we identify the differences in these schemes and why Bretton Woods failed, we can assess the road ahead for the Trilaterals.

JOHN MAYNARD KEYNES AND HARRY DEXTER WHITE IN 1944

Keynes was not the originator of the 1944 Bancor scheme, nor are the Trilaterals the originators of the 1978 Bancor scheme, their global monetary unit. In 1892 a German economist, Julius Wolf, came up with the idea of an international gold reserve deposited in a neutral country with international bank notes issued on the basis of this gold reserve - very much the Keynesian concept reflected in Bretton Woods and the IMF. The major differences between 1978 Trilateral plans and the Anglo-American Keynes-White proposals of 1944 are these:

- Keynes wanted a "consciousness of consent" from the general public; Keynes argued the arrangements would not succeed if hatched in secret.
- The system was to be linked to gold.

Trilaterals have *no* "consciousness of consent," and they have abandoned gold: these are critical differences.

The principal objective in 1944 was much narrower than current proposals: the system was to be one of multilateral clearing, a universal currency valid for trade transactions throughout the world. According to Keynes:

It is not necessary in order to attain these ends that we

should dispossess gold from its traditional use. It is enough to supplement and regulate the total supply of gold and of the new money taken together. The new money must not be freely convertible into gold, for that would require that gold reserves should be held against it, and we should be back where we were, but there is no reason why the new money should not be purchasable for gold." [2]

When it came to christening this new money, Keynes said, "What shall we call the new money? Bancor? Unitas? Both of them in my opinion are bad names, but we racked our brains without success to find a better." Even "Bezant" was proposed, interestingly the name of the last international coin (a gold coin) that circulated throughout the then known world for eight hundred years because it was a *gold* coin and never debased.

Actually the two proposals, Bancor (British) and Unitas (United States), had different features. The adopted American plan, Unitas, deposited part of the U.S. gold reserves with the IMF together with a specific amount of domestic currency but created no international currency. By contrast, the Keynesian plan, Bancor, provided an international currency with overdraft facilities at the clearing union. In other words, today the Trilaterals have taken us back to the Keynesian Bancor plan rejected in 1944.

A comparison of the two monetary schemes clarifies their major differences:

Keynes Bancor Scheme (not adopted in 1944)	Trilateral-modified Bancor scheme of 1978
Universal money – Bancor	Universal money – SDR's (Special Drawing Rights)
Gold accepted as a reserve	Gold not accepted as reserve
No gold convertibility	No gold convertibility
National currencies not held as reserves	National currencies not held as reserves
Public approval necessary	Public approval not necessary

Bancor was not adopted in 1944. It's now a matter of history that the related Harry Dexter White Unitas plan which was adopted led the U.S. into bankruptcy: the dollar weaknesses of today are directly traceable to the Bretton Woods Unitas plan.

Today's Trilaterals are political animals, with New World Order objectives, not interested in orderly world trade but in a specific future world structure under their control. The question is not to design a workable system to facilitate trade and improve human welfare, but to design a system that will enhance and preserve power for the Trilaterals. The Trilateral answer is to reinvent the system not used in 1944, the Keynesian Bancor, but modified this time as a universal currency divorced completely from gold and national currencies.

The extent of insider willingness to disregard, and even distort, widely held pro-gold views of others is exemplified by an extraordinary statement in Robert Solomon's book, which is aptly subtitled An *Insider's View*. This is Solomon's interpretation of the motivation of gold oriented economists:

> *Those who are worshipful of gold (gold bugs or, more politely, chrysophilites) are usually motivated by one or more of these concerns: particular economic theories now held by a small minority of economists, distrust of government, international political objectives (there is discernible among non-Americans a correlation, far from complete though it is, between attachment to gold and anti-Americanism), and, last but not least, hope of personal pecuniary gain.* [3]

Each of Solomon's so-called motivations is in error. It may be that a majority of American economists dislike gold, but certainly not a majority in the world at large. Anti-goldism is an American preoccupation. It is not distrust of government per se that motivates gold holding but distrust of "insiders" who manipulate government for their own ends. Gold holding is not related to anti-Americanism, but it may be related to anti-imperialism, a different aspect altogether. Neither is gold holding related to pecuniary gain: it is related to protection of wealth from marauding insiders.

COOPERATION, COORDINATION OR PIGHEADEDNESS

Trilaterals are failing to achieve the wished-for coordination of macroeconomic policies among the core countries. In early February 1978 these core country finance ministers, vital to the success of the revived and modified Bancor, met in Europe — a supposedly secret meeting that became public knowledge. There is no concealing the cold reception for the Trilateral scheme from Europeans. U.S. Secretary of the Treasury **Blumenthal** tried to arm-twist Germany into a "locomotive" role; that is, Germany should reflate, spur its economy in good Keynesian fashion, and hopefully, pull lagging economies onto a higher plane of economic activity. This is presumably the "coordination of macroeconomic policies" planned. The Germans welcomed the Keynesian loco-motive no more in February 1978 than in previous years. German Economics Minister **Count Otto Lambsdorff** commented, I am surprised by American stubbornness," and Chancellor Helmut Schmidt indicated zero chance of a stimulative (i.e., inflationary) German policy.

This rather crude Trilateral attempt to strong-arm Europe into reflation can be compared to the publicly announced method of achieving cooperation through consultation. To quote Robert Solomon again:

> *Just as there is a need in each country for economic policies aimed at high employment and price stability, there is a need, at the international level, for a similar effort to make the policies of individual countries compatible with the wellbe-ing of the world economy. Since there exists no international authority that can directly perform this function, it can be done only by means of consultation and cooperation among representatives of independent nations meeting together in established international form.* [4]

This European episode and the later creation of the European Currency Unit (ECU) exemplifies the Trilateral weakness in his-torical precedent. Why did the Germans refuse to go along with Keynesian demand stimulation? Because two factors are locked into the German psyche and ignored by American planners. First, the unparalleled rise of the German economy from the ashes of 1946 was due to plain old laissez faire free enterprise, not artifi-cial Keynesian locomotives. Second, Germany has had two recent devastating price inflations (1923 and 1946), and both times the Mark went to zero. Germans *know* the consequences of inflation and Keynesian-type stimulation.

Michael Blumenthal was born in Germany and lived in Shanghai until 1947. He must have some remembrances of the postwar Chinese currency inflation and the 1946 collapse of the mark. Unfortunately, **Blumenthal** was not in Germany during the years of German economic revival.

In sum, a combination of factors - German refusal to adopt Keynesian stimulation, the French political scene, and the collapse in the leading indicators (signaling a depression in 1979) - has reduced international cooperation and coordination.

One can perceive in the background a central reason why the Trilaterals, essentially the big New York banking powers, must move ahead with Bancor...why they must develop the so-called Witteveen facility...why they must create elastic international reserves, to be expanded at the push of a computer key.

The central unstated propellant for global fiat money is that the international monetary system is on a precarious merry-go-round: borrow - generate a deficit - be unable to repay - reschedule - borrow some more. The world debt balloon must be kept inflated. If the balloon goes bust, so do the New York banks (remember Chase receives 78 percent of its earnings from abroad). If one of the world players decides he's had enough, if a New York bank says no to Zaire, if Turkey or anyone of a dozen other LDCs default, the whole pack of monetary cards will come tumbling down. Trilaterals push for an international monetary system based on Bancor-created money simply because their banker necks are already in the wringer; the gold solution is no longer available because the U.S. long ago shipped out its good delivery gold.

At this stage, Keynesian dogma is useless. Keynes left no guidance to his followers for the contemporary world mess. Although he was personally aware of the role of gold, he did not anticipate that the greed of his followers might exceed their good sense.

INTERNATIONAL BANKERS AND BANCOR

The benefits of Bancor will accrue to international bankers more tl1,an to anyone else. The interlock between New York international bankers, the Trilateral Commission, and thus, Trilateral proposals in Bancor can be traced precisely.

The earnings that major banks receive from overseas is a matter of public record and is a measure of the division between their domestic interests in the United States and a global economy. The degree of domestic control over the economy by international banks has been identified in a report published by the late Senator Lee Metcalf, "Voting Rights in Major Corporations."[5] Also a matter of public record are the names of international bankers who are Trilateral Commissioners. When we integrate these three statistics, (a) source of bank earnings, (b) control of domestic companies, and (c) Trilateral membership, we identify a highly significant interlock between international banks and the Trilateral push for a global economy.

Table 9-1 ranks twelve international banks in order of their 1976 earnings from overseas; that is the bank with the highest percentage of its earnings from overseas is ranked Number 1, and the bank with the least percentage from overseas is ranked Number 12 (columns 1 and 2). This percentage is compared with the equivalent 1970 figures to demonstrate that foreign earnings have ballooned over the past five years or so (columns 3 and 4). Column 5 is the Metcalf Index of domestic control by these same bankers, defined as the number of the 122 companies examined by a congressional committee in which the bank is among the top five shareholders. Column 6 lists Trilateral commissioners who are also directors of these banks.

Chase Manhattan is the bank with the highest percentage of earnings from abroad: a remarkable 78 percent compared to 22 percent in 1970. In brief, **David Rockefeller's** international merchandising has made Chase a global bank, not an American bank, and we might call David a de facto world citizen, not an American citizen. At the same time, Chase has a very low rating on the Metcalf Index. The bank is among the largest five stockholders in only eight of the 122 companies studied by the sub committee (compared to Citibank's 25 and J. P. Morgan's 56.)

No fewer than six Chase Manhattan directors **(Kissinger** is on the Chase International Advisory Board) are represented on the Trilateral Commission. In sum, Chase is heavily, almost totally, oriented outside the United States. Its pecuniary interest in promoting a New World Order is slightly more than obvious.

Contrast Chase to J.P. Morgan where 53 percent of income is from overseas (up from 25 percent in 1970) with only one Trilateral representative. Banks like Charter New York (formerly Irving Trust) and Chemical Bank do not appear on the Metcalf Index at all and have no Trilateral representation, that is, they are not apparently involved in creating a New World Order.

This pattern is dramatized if we rearrange the data in table 9-1 with highest Trilateral representation first.

INTERNATIONAL BANKS AND THE TRILATERAL COMMISSION

Rank in 1976 Foreign Earnings	International Banks	Percent of Earnings from International Operations		Numer of TC Members as Directors
		1970	1976	
1	Chase Manhattan	22	78	6
2	Citicorp	40	72	0
3	First National Bank of Boston	8	65	0
4	Banker's Trust	14	64	0
5	Charter New York	12	58	0
6	Manufacturers Hanover	13	56	1
7	J.P. Morgan	25	53	1
8	Chemical Bank	10	44	0
9	Bank of America	15	40	2
10	Continental Illinois	0	23	3
11	First Chicago	2	17	3
12	Wells Fargo	9	12	1

BANKS WITH TRILATERAL REPRESENTATION

In a few words: the Trilateral Commission is dominated by a very few international banks, essentially Chase Manhattan, and is an institution focused outside the United States. At the same time, the Trilateral Commission has taken over the United States executive branch. We have *not* been taken over by communists or Russians or Martians but by a group which wants to "revise" the Constitution (to organize more political power) but is without majority financial and economic ties to the United States.

A REALISTIC VIEW OF THE MONETARY WORLD

A rational international monetary system now evolving could brush the IMF and the Trilateral fiat "coordinated" monetary arrangements into the dust. Whatever foreign finance ministers may say to **W. Michael Blumenthal** face to face, a new monetary system is slowly emerging with its roots in gold, fixed exchange rates, and rejection of Keynesian demand stimulation techniques.

Pointers to this hard money, gold-based system include:

- Jacques Rueff, de Gaulle's chief financial advisor, author of *The Monetary Sin* of *the West,* unabashedly gold oriented, was advising French and Japanese governments, prior to his death in 1978.

- The European attitude to American financial policy is noticeably hardening: witness

Blumenthal's February trip to Paris brought hostile European reaction, and more importantly, the creation of the European Currency Unit (ECU)

- Japanese citizens may now hold gold deposits outside Japan, and there are internal efforts to develop the use of gold. Soviets are interested in a gold-based international monetary system.

- Arabs are skeptical about exchanging scarce crude oil for ever-depreciating paper dollars and are searching for a reliable monetary medium.

- South Africa has awakened to U.S. imperial designs in Africa ("strangling with finesse" as Prime Minister Vorster phrases it).

- At home billions more are scheduled for boondoggles (Humphrey-Hawkins), which will backfire and push even more Americans into the hard money camp.

Project the above facts to their logical conclusions and we conclude:

- Floating rates will be rejected as too costly. Contrast this to the Trilateral proposal "learning to live with floating rates." Fixed rates will return at some point.

- Reintroduction of gold into the world system will pull

the rug from under Trilateral international monetary arrangements based on Bancor.[6]

- If the United States, under Trilateral guidance, cannot sell the core countries on its international monetary arrangements, it will never sell the other hundred or so countries in the world.

- Unless the U.S. gets its monetary house in order, it will notably lose world prestige and influence; it will skirt revolution at home and endure major social consequences.

ENDNOTES

1. Motoo Kaji. Richard N. Cooper. Claudia Segre. "Towards a Renovated World Monetary System," Trilateral Commission TaskForce Report No.1 (New York. 1973). p. 19.
2. John Maynard Keynes. Essays in Persuasion (London: Hart-Davis. 1952). p. 209.
3. Robert Soloman. The International Monetary System, 1945-1976: An Insider's View (New York: Harper & Row. 1977), p. 333.4. Ibid.. p. 336.
4. Referred to as the Metcalf Index.
5. This was written in mid-1978, before the gold-based ECU was announced.

CAPTER TEN

THE COMING FINANCIAL PANIC

The repeated monetary crises that have plagued the United States since the early 1960s have not been solved. Washington and New York have merely applied temporary propaganda palliatives. No effort has been applied to the fundamental dilemma. To a decade of mismanagement we can now add Trilateralist ambitions to rule a world economy in their own image. Consequently, the day of reckoning will be all the more costly.

The coming financial panic will be a logical consequence of these repeated financial crises, themselves symptoms of a deep malaise, the politization of economic activities.

The late Jacques Rueff, that penetrating French financial expert, once commented that the American financial problem "was the outcome of an unbelievable collective mistake which, when people become aware of it, will be viewed by history as an object of astonishment and scandal." [1]

The "unbelievable collective mistake" made by the New York-Washington elite, now continued by Trilateral ideology, is the replacement of a free market system by a fiat money managed system. We suggest that as ordinary American citizens react and become aware of what Rueff called "an object of astonishment and scandal," a financial panic is likely to be fomented. The *realizers* will hasten to protect their threatened assets, and the rush to the exits will be awe inspiring.

The realizers, a term coined back in the first decades of the

Woodrow Wilson administration when *elastic* currency was being debated, are those investors who understand the hollow character of a politicized monetary system. Their key attribute is an ability to think beyond and never move with the herd: the herd instinct is suicidal. When gold markets are quiet, the realizes is quietly transferring assets from paper to gold; in fact, many have been doing just that for a decade. When gold markets are hectic the realizer may lighten up, knowing that all markets react. But when the day of panic arrives, the realizer's only problem will be to protect his store of wealth.

The responsibility for the "collective mistake," seen only by the relatively few realizers lies heavily with members of the Trilateralist elite. Chapter eight concluded with three observations:

- Fixed exchange rates tied to gold will be reintroduced, contrary to the Trilateral goal to "learn to live with" floating exchange rates by international monetary management.

- Reintroduction of gold into the world money arena will pull the rug from under Trilateral goldless IMF proposals and Bancor, and the European Currency Unit (ECU) is a first step in this direction.

- Unless the U.S. gets its financial house in order, we shall witness social upheavals and monetary panic exceeding anything in American history.

We can now (November 1978) see the outline of these observations reflected in world events:

- The U.S. has embarked on its fiat money, anti-gold crusade, stifling its Western friends and subsidizing its Marxist enemies.

- U.S. Establishment-oriented economists predict that the shocks of 1973 to 1975 can never reoccur and that *this* time their forecasts will be right. These predictions were broadcast even while a minor flight from the dollar demonstrated their inaccuracy.

- By contrast, major European governments, led by West Germany and France, are moving with extraordinary and unparalleled rapidity to protect Europe from the coming financial holocaust.

While American representatives are jetting around the globe muttering clichés about "management of interdependence," "intensive interactions," "New World Order," and similar nonentities, the real monetary economic world is disintegrating around our ears. And now Europe has said to the United States, "We have watched you play the fool long enough; our patience is exhausted."

EUROPE MOVES TO PROTECT ITSELF FROM A COLLAPSING DOLLAR

The new European Currency Unit (ECU) introduced in mid-1978 by Chancellor Helmut Schmidt and President Valery Giscard d'Estaing as a European Community unit of account is a clear warning to the U.S. that there is financial chaos ahead. If the U.S. will not act responsibly with the dollar, then Europe is prepared to go it alone. Neither Giscard nor Schmidt, the joint architects of ECU are Trilaterals, and it is worthy of note that both Schmidt and Giscard are former finance ministers of their respective countries. Furthermore, there is a report that European bankers had muffled, but still audible, reservations about the Giscard-Schmidt plan. European Trilaterals include powerful European bankers: **Baron Leon Lambert**, **Alwin Munchmeyer** (German Banking Federation), **Baron Edmond de Rothschild, Anthony Tuke** (Barclays International), and **Luc Wauters** (Kredietbank, Brussels.) Also, prominent European Trilaterals **Raymond Barre** (prime minister of France) and **Count Otto Lambsdorff** (minister of economics, Germany) are not prominent in the ECU plan: the ECU plan appears to be a non-Trilateralist, Schmidt-Giscard creation.

The ECU system, scheduled for operation by January 1979, will link major European currencies to the German D-Mark. ECU is more than a broader "snake" and currency defense scheme: its members are required to place 20 percent of their dollars and *their gold* into a pool along with an equal amount of national currencies. *The ECU system is gold based.* It reinforces the use of *gold* as *money.* It reintroduces *the monetary role* of *gold.*

The object? To defend European currencies against speculation. What kind of speculation? Obviously a future flight from fiat dollars.

ECU places the United States and the European Community in opposite camps, and two competitive world reserve assets will ultimately emerge: a European gold-based currency (the forthcoming ECU is only for interbank transfers) and the U.S. dollar based on the printing press and Washington elitist hot air. In fact, a European currency, tentatively called EUROPA, has been under study for some time at European Economic Community Headquarters in Brussels, and the gold-backed Europa could well be the world's replacement for the declining fiat dollar and the almost worthless fiat ruble.

NATURE OF THE COMING FINANCIAL PANIC

The nature and scope of the forthcoming financial panic can be delineated from historical precedent but not — as yet - the precise timing of the panic.

Timing of monetary panics usually depends on random events which trigger underlying distortions, and these events are not always in themselves major events. The 1907 financial panic, by way of example, was triggered by failure of the third largest trust company, Knickerbocker Trust. The August 1978 run up in the gold price from

$180 to $215 in U.S. currency was a minor flight from the dollar triggered by the U.S. refusal to face its balance of payments deficits and domestic price inflation. It was not the full-scale flight from the dollar which has yet to come.

The United States has major structural defects which guarantee an ultimate monetary panic. These defects are either not recognized by the elitists running the U.S. or they do not want to recognize them. Let's examine these defects.

THE FIRST INGREDIENT FOR FINANCIAL PANIC: DEFICITS

One ingredient making for ultimate financial panic is the manner in which Washington finances federal budget deficits. Three basic deficit financing methods are available to the federal government: (a) raising taxes. (b) borrowing the deficit and thus channeling funds from productive private investment to largely unproductive public boondoggles. or (c) creating more dollars. thus reducing the value of all existing dollars (Le.. price inflation). Although the preferred financing method is (c) when stealing from the value of the dollar becomes a visible process, dollar holders will dump dollars for more stable wealth-holding vehicles.

The cumulative U.S. budget deficit from 1962 to 1977, excluding off-budget accounts is $292.219.242.817 almost 300 billion dollars, generated under *both* political parties, Democrats and Republicans - the only two political parties subsidized by law from public funds.

Budget Year	Budget Deficit
1962	$ 7,136,988,565
1963	4,750,889,740
1964	5,921,855,327
1965	1,596,321,595
1966	3,795,959,063
1967	8,701,851,561
1968	25,161,232,923
1969	3,236,294,206
1970	2,844,534,843
1971	23,033,168,126
1972	23,372,529,351
1973	14,848,573,651
1974	4,687,858,607
1975	45,107,821,495
1976	66,477,795,275
1977	45,035,045,016
Est. 1978	51,100,000,000
Est. 1980	30,000,000,000

There is not a whit of practical difference between Republicans and Democrats in the basic question of fiscal probity. Rhetoric doesn't reduce deficits. Periodically, Congress acts out a charade extending the "temporary debt ceiling." As of 31 March 1978, the federal debt was $798 billion, with a "permanent" ceiling of $398 billion. The totally dishonest practice of "temporary ceilings" allows Congress to avoid facing the issue of the federal deficit. The academic world, for its part, explains the almost $800 billion debt with the cliché that "we owe it to ourselves," although precisely how this vacuous expression bears on the topic of fiscal prudence is unknown.

The crux of the federal deficit is that sooner or later, voluntarily or involuntarily, this debt monument has to be repaid or the dollar depreciated to zero value; that is a fraud must be perpetrated on the debt holders. The former process is politically impossible.

THE SECOND INGREDIENT FOR FINANCIAL PANIC: DEBT

Another guarantee of ultimate financial panic is a mountain of state, city, and unfunded private debt - a paper mountain almost staggering comprehension. The current surplus position of non-federal institutions is a deception. (As a whole, state and local governments had a $29 billion surplus in 1977, for the tenth year running.) Remember that although $68 billion a year flows from Washington to local governments, Proposition 13-type legislation will reduce the surplus to zero by 1980.

Within this mountain, the really dangerous trigger for panic is New York City debts held by New York banks. The 954 banks holding New York obligations have over 20 percent of their equity capital in New York obligations. *About* 70 *banks hold more than* 50 *percent* of *their capital in New York securities.* While default may not result in total loss of investment, it is doubtful if the psychological tidal wave unleashed by a New York default could avoid national panic.

You are probably safe *until* 1982. The big New York banks unloaded New York securities onto small holders. This poses a very real question of fraudulent misrepresentation on their part, now under investigation by New York State officials. The state investigation has questioned numerous "small" holders of New York City securities and found they were misled by major New York banks. The following is an extract from the official assembly report:

The individual investor responses indicate that the majority had never invested in municipal securities before, and 90 percent responded that a factor in their investment was their belief that an investment in City securities was "safe and secure." The survey also found that, at the time they made their investments:

78 percent of the investors believed the City's bookkeeping and accounting practices to be excellent or good; and

79 percent of the investors believed that the City was in good or excellent financial condition.

Additional comments volunteered by a number of these individual investors concerning their experiences with these investments were overwhelmingly negative, and indicated quite clearly that, in their purchase of City securities, they had been "misled." [2]

The year 1982 is a key date to hold in mind because the statute of limitations on such misrepresentations runs out then. You can be sure Congress will oblige New York City with interim financing until this critical date.

And it will be a miracle if the New York State investigation progresses to the point of indictments.

THE THIRD INGREDIENT FOR FINANCIAL PANIC: OVERSEAS DEBT

Another debt mountain consists of dollar and foreign currency denominated obligations and stateless currencies held overseas in a variety of forms. private and public:

- The giant multinational banks generate an uncontrolled
- $400 billion plus market in Eurocurrencies, a global transnational money market outside the control of governments and central banks. These funds could be used to collapse the dollar either deliberately, by sheer weight of transfers or by simple miscalculation.

- The U.S. Treasury owes more than $86 billion in dollar denominated Treasury securities to foreign central banks and the Organization of Petroleum Exporting Countries (OPEC).
- More importantly, the U.S. Treasury owes substantial amounts in *Swiss franc* denominated bonds (more below).

THE FOURTH INGREDIENT FOR FINANCIAL PANIC: NO GOLD

The European Currency Unit will be based on *European gold reserves.* At this time Europe has about *twice the gold reserves* of *the United States.*

Moreover, the U.S. does not have $11 billion of good delivery gold as suggested in the establishment financial media. The U.S. gold stock, as we noted in chapter eight, is as follows:

- Forty-eight million ounces of good delivery valued at $2 billion officially and $9.6 billion in the market place;
- The balance in coin melt.

Whether this gold belongs in fact to the U.S. Treasury or even exists, has been disputed.

U.S. gold reserves have not been inventoried since 1933. The treasury persists in conducting *audits* (i.e., checks of the vault seals) when only *inventories* (counting, assaying, and weighing) will answer the critics.

The skimpy checks are reportedly due to the cost of inventories. Yet, Washington will, for example, spend $46 million on a lavish memorial to FDR who seized citizens' gold in 1933 - and $122 million on a third Senate office building - a fraction of which expenditures would provide the amount needed for an inventory of the U.S. gold stock. If reluctance to *inventory* reserves continues, we may have reason to assume that even the 48 million ounces of good delivery is not there. Furthermore, the U.S. has sufficient other hard money debts that we can state the

U.S. is technically "bust."

The fact that 80 percent of U.S. gold reserves is coin melt, not salable on the world market, is not realized even at highest elitist levels. For example, the July 1978 issue of *Foreign Affairs* (published by the Council on Foreign Relations) has an article by Jahangir Amuzegar, executive director of the IMF and ambassador-at-large for Iran. Amuzegar's article, "OPEC and the Dollar Dilemma," records gold stocks at 277 million ounces valued at "near $50 billion." This over-valuation assumes the stock is good delivery. It is not. If OPEC is unaware of the true quality of U.S. gold stocks, the impact of the awakening has yet to be felt.

THE GOLD ROAD AHEAD

With this massive debt mountain, a fiat (paper) currency and a miniscule stock of good delivery gold, the U.S. is in a precarious position - far more precarious than generally realized. While ECU is a unit of account and does not circulate, ECU is a forerunner of a gold- based European currency which will be a circulating medium; and a European gold-based circulating currency will come within five years.

In brief: By 1984 the United States will have to face squarely a *global contest between* a *fiat dollar* and *gold-backed European money.* Fiat money has never won this battle. Fiat money cannot win.

The United States will then be faced with two choices:

  a. Either allow the present fiat dollar to depreciate to zero value, or

  b. Replace the fiat dollar with a gold-backed dollar at a ratio of 10 for 1, or 10,000 for 1.

Quietly, while proclaiming the health of the mighty fiat mini-dollar, Washington has prepared for these eventualities: duplicate dollar currency is already printed and stored away at the Culpepper, Virginia, facility of the Federal Reserve and at Mount Weather in Virginia.

According to Carl Mintz, on the staff of the House Banking Committee, "I believe it's in the billions of dollars, and it's buried in lots of places." This duplicate currency will remain buried, unissued, and virtually unknown until confidence in the present fiat dollar is completely shattered.

Another available option is discussed in the July 1978 newsletter of the Johannesburg Chamber of Mines:

It has become increasingly obvious now that at this time of widespread currency instability, political and economic uncertainty, spiraling inflationary expectations and increasing protectionism, the struggle to eliminate one of the major monetary reserve assets from the international monetary system, has been a futile exercise. It would make more sense to recognize the advantages of gold and to acknowledge its role as a stabilizer in the system and to concentrate instead on underpinning the dollar to avoid its further depreciation against other major currencies.

In brief, the Chamber of Mines proposes the U.S. return to gold and abandon its anti-gold crusade.

As holders of fiat dollars grasp the gold versus paper picture, a common picture in monetary history, the flight from the dollar will begin - at first slowly as in early August 1978, then picking up speed, to culminate in panic. Because of media brainwashing, it is unlikely that most American investors will become realizers (i.e., learn the true nature of the con game) until after the dust of monetary panic has finally settled.

In the period immediately ahead, fiat dollars are going to be exchanged by the realizers in increasing quantities, initially for gold and silver, then for gold-based currencies (such as the coming European currency) and in the final phase, *anything* which represents scarce resources.

Will the United States ban imports of gold in the coming struggle in an attempt to force its edict of fiat dollars? One school of thought suggests the treasury will allow gold imports as long as possible, as long as anyone wants to exchange gold for paper dollars. Another school suggests that on the contrary, the treasury will clamp down on gold imports.

The policy of gold imports which is finally adopted may well depend on the time frame in question. Remember, the treasury bureaucrats do not *recognize* gold; they do not *understand* gold. Truly, these people believe that gold is a "barbarous" relic. Absurd as it may seem to you and me, the academics involved in the so-called demonetization of gold have a mindset that gold will have no meaning in the New World Order. While the experts in charge retain this mindset, it is improbable that gold imports will continue freely in the years ahead. The treasury is likely to clamp down on imports, and- this will send the price of gold soaring. However, at some time, pressure of circumstances or politics or new ideas will emerge and then the ban will again be lifted.

TREASURY CONFESSES TO STUPIDITY AND SHORTSIGHTEDNESS

A prime contemporary example of the cost of the treasury mindset to the American taxpayer was revealed earlier this year. On 19 April 1978 Anthony M. Solomon, Trilateral commissioner and Under Secretary of the Treasury for Monetary Affairs went cap-in-hand before the House Subcommittee on International Trade Investment and Monetary Policy, to confess to what Solomon called "some fairly important developments;" that is, the treasury had lost its shirt gambling in Swiss francs since 1961. In brief, the Treasury Exchange Stabilization Fund has been selling Swiss franc denominated U.S. Treasury notes while the franc moved from 22 cents to over 50 cents. The story goes like this...

Back in the 1960s and early 1970s, the treasury, under the guidance of three Trilateralists, **Robert Roosa**, (Deputy Under Secretary for Monetary Affairs, **Bruce MacLaury**, (now president of the Trilateral think-tank Brookings Institution), and **Paul A. Volcker,** (Federal Reserve Bank of New York), held to a superstitious notion that the price of gold should be precisely $35.00 (later $40.00) per troy ounce, a magic figure which originated over President Roosevelt's breakfast table in the 1930s. To preserve an artificial gold price of $35.00, the treasury under **Roosa** lost most of the U.S. gold stockpile. The stock went from $25 billion in 1949 to $11 billion in 1974. In 1960 gold was moving out' of the U.S. too rapidly even for the treasury, and **Roosa** hit on the idea of issuing non-marketable certificates and treasury notes to foreign, creditors and *denominated in foreign currencies.*

In the past decade the U.S. Treasury with its anti gold mind set has lost the U.S. taxpayer billions of dollars betting these foreign denominated securities against gold and the Swiss franc. As of June 1978, $901,000,000 is outstanding in securities denominated in Swiss francs and issued by the U.S. Treasury to the Swiss National Bank (the **Roosa** bonds). In fact, new Swiss-franc denominated securities are still being issued as well as redeemed by the U.S. Treasury: the latest known at time of writing being $75 million issued 9 June 1978, due 29 October 1979 with an interest rate of 7.9 percent, payable in Swiss francs. The position for 1977 is contained in table 101.

In brief, the treasury has gotten itself in debt up to its neck in Swiss francs. Even worse, the total losses to the U.S. taxpayer from treasury speculation in Swiss francs may well total $1 billion, when the chips are counted. [3]

The treasury covers its shame by arguing that this gambling in Swiss francs meant the U.S. was able to retain 36 million ounces of gold. On the other hand, the treasury also tells us that gold is a valueless, barbarous commodity!

Table 10-1

Changes in Public Debt Issues, Fiscal Year 1977
Foreign Currency Denominated Treasury Notes

Foreign Currency Series Issues of:	Outstanding 30 September 1976	Issues During Year	Redemptions During Year	Transferred to Matured Debt	Outstanding 30 September 1977
5.25%	--	$ 137,047,123	--	--	$ 137,047,123
5.60%	--	159,838,997	--	--	159,838,977
5.80%	--	50,319,678	--	--	50,319,678
5.90%	--	49,733,602	--	--	49,733,602
5.95%	--	38,479,754	--	--	38,479,754
6.08%	$ 63,839,593	--	$ 63,839,593	--	--
6.10%	127,279,185	359,927,776	26,047,833	--	461,159,129
6.20%	147,999,053	--	--	--	147,999,053
6.35%	73,703,528	--	38,183,756	--	35,519,773
6.39%	170,198,911	--	170,198,911	--	--
6.40%	38,479,754	25,455,837	38,479,754	--	25,455,837
6.50%	32,559,792	--	--	--	32,559,792
6.60%	--	22,495,856	--	--	22,495,856
6.70%	66,599,754	--	--	--	66,599,574
6.75%	29,599,811	--	--	--	29,599,811
6.95%	400,183,519	--	400,183,519	--	--
7.05%	32,559,792	--	--	--	32,559,792
7.15%	38,479,754	--	38,479,754	--	--
7.25%	170,198,911	--	170,198,911	--	--
7.35%	50,319,678	--	50,319,678	--	--
7.70%	28,711,816	--	28,711,816	--	--
7.75%	128,759,176	--	128,759,176	--	--
Total	$ 1,599,271,845	$ 843,298,603	$ 1,153,202,899	--	$ 1,289,367,748

Source: Report of the Secretary of the Treasury 1977

WHO IS RESPONSIBLE?

Many are responsible for monetary chaos, but Trilaterals in key treasury slots stand out. And one man stands out above all others: Trilateral Commissioner and former Under Secretary of the Treasury, **Robert Roosa**. In August 1967 the business journal Fortune described **Roosa's** handling of that particular year's monetary crises as follows:

> *No man has done more than Roosa did in this year at Treasury to try to make the existing monetary system continue to work. The famous "twist" in interest rates, the "Roosa" bonds, the many "swap" and other emergency credit arrangements all stand as monuments to his ingenuity.* [4]

Roosa's stopgap measures also stand as monuments to the utter lack of principle and ability among the self-perpetuated elite. Their ingenuity has been to dig a bigger monetary grave for the United States. Ingenuity has been used to stave off the ultimate day of reckoning for another decade and thus make it ultimately worse for the American people.

THE COMING FINANCIAL PANIC

The coming financial panic will, of course, be a traumatic experience. It will be far deeper than the panic of 1907, when no credit at all was available at any price, and more pervasive than the depression of 1930.

Yet, such a panic is not to be feared by those who are prepared by those we call the realizers. A panic is symptomatic. A panic is the economic system purging itself of excesses. The panic will be deep and more pervasive than any previous monetary crisis because the excesses committed in the name of a "welfare state," "interdependence" and "globalism" have been deeper and more pervasive than in the past.

Panic need be feared only by those dependent on the hand of the state to feed them or keep them in luxury or by those who use the power of the state for personal vested interests. These groups will be losers. The storm can be weathered by those who have taken precautions to protect themselves, by those who are self-sufficient, and certainly by those who do not depend on the politicians' whims and on bureaucratic regulation.

Timing? The leading indicators are flashing the seventh postwar recession. The political manipulators may try to postpone this recession, to convert it into what is called a growth recession;

or incoming overseas funds induced by the recent "benign neglect" of the dollar may well give an aura of false prosperity come election time. If left alone, the seventh post-war recession will go deeper than other recessions. Recovery from the sixth recession has been incomplete because the Keynesian demand stimulation locomotive is running down and the economy is strangled by statist intervention. Subsequent recovery will be weaker, the eighth post-war recession, deeper; and the roller coaster is now in a secular down trend.

The final flight from the fiat dollar is not, however, necessarily related to any phase of the economic cycle. Panic can be triggered by a random event which catches public fancy and snowballs as successive waves of investors dump paper dollar-denominated assets. Financial panics always need a trigger event. Some event, usually unforeseen, trips off the cumulative spiral and the subsequent panic to protect wealth before all is lost.

Although a likely trigger for financial panic in 1979-80 is price inflation and a liquidity crisis. the probabilities are against major panic in the next twelve to twenty-four months. While prices are stable or increase smoothly, holders of fiat dollars have no doubt of liquidity, that is, that dollars can be used to purchase goods and services. In brief, under these conditions dollars are still a store of value.

During periods of price inflation, some holders will seek alternative means of wealth storage. In prolonged periods of price increases or- during sudden upward price spurts, contagion sets in; and the relatively few seekers of safe storage vehicles become many. The search for gold, silver, and diamonds becomes contagious. In brief, there is a flight from paper - a flight from fiat money which is now illiquid because it will not command goods and services. *Illiquidity is a sure sign that panic is approaching.*

The monetary die was cast back in the early 1960s by men who (strangely) now occupy a key segment of the Trilateral Commission: **Roosa, MacLaury, Volcker, Parsky, Ball, McCracken, Peterson, Solomon** and **Rockefeller**.

A flight from paper cannot ultimately be controlled by this Trilateral establishment. Their recourse will be to adopt Hitlerian

or Stalinist measures: a Schachtian economy or a Soviet economy
- if they can.

ENDNOTES

1. Jacques Rueff, The Monetary Sin of the West (New York: Macmillan, 1972),
    p.24.
2. "The Bank and the Municipal Crisis: Public Responsibility and Private
    Profit," State Assembly of New York Special Report (New York, 15
    November 1976).
3. Interested readers are referred to Annual Report for 1977 of Exchange
    Stabilization Fund (Department of the Treasury).
4. "How Paper Gold Could Work," Fortune (August 1967)

THE TRILATERAL COMMISSION MEMBERSHIP LIST

As of October 15, 1978

Georges Berthoin, European Chairman
David Rockefeller, North American Chairman
Takeshi Watanabe, Japanese Chairman
Egidio Ortona, European Deputy Chairman
Mitchell Sharp, North American Deputy Chairman
George S. Franklin, Coordinator
Hanns W. Maull, European Secretary
Charles B. Heck, North American Secretary
Tadashi Yamamoto, Japanese Secretary

North American Members

*I.W. Abel, Former President, United Steelworkers of America

David M. Abshire, Chairman, Georgetown University Center for Strategic and International Studies

Gardner Ackley, Henry Carter Adams University Professor of Political Economy, University of Michigan

Graham Allison, Dean, John F. Kennedy School of Government, Harvard University

Doris Anderson, Former Editor, Chantelaine Magazine

John B. Anderson, House of Representatives

Anne Armstrong, Former U.S. Ambassador to Great Britain

J. Paul Austin, Chairman, The Coca-Cola Company

George W. Ball, Senior Partner, Lehman Brothers

Michel Belanger, President, Provincial Bank of Canada

*Robert W. Bonner, Q.C. Chairman, British Columbia Hydro

John Brademas, House of Representatives

Andrew Brimmer, President, Brimmer & Company, Inc.

William E. Brock, III, Chairman, Republican National Committee

Arthur F. Burns, Senior Adviser, Lazard Freres & Co.; former Chairman of Board of Governors, U.S. Federal Reserve Board

Hugh Calkins, Partner, Jones, Day, Reavis & Pogue

Claude Castonguay, President, Fonds Laurentien; Chairman of the Board, Imperial Life Assurance Company; former Minister in the Quebec Government

Sol Chaikin, President, International Ladies Garment Workers Union

William S. Cohen, House of Representatives

*William T. Coleman, Jr., Senior Partner, O'Melveny & Myers; former Secretary of Transportation

Barber B. Conable, Jr., House of Representatives

John Cowles, Jr., Chairman, Minneapolis Star & Tribune Co.

Alan Cranston, United States Senate

John C. Culver, United States Senate

Gerald L. Curtis, Director, East Asian Institute, Columbia University

Lloyd N. Cutler, Partner, Wilmer, Cutler, and Pickering

Louis A. Desrochers, Partner, McCuaig and Desrochers, Edmonton

Peter Dobell, Director, Parliamentary Centre for Foreign Affairs and Foreign Trade, Ottawa

Hedley Donovan, Editor-in-Chief, Time, Inc.

Claude A. Edwards, Member, Public Service Staff Relations Board; former President, Public Service Alliance of Canada

Daniel J. Evans, President, The Evergreen State College; former Governor of Washington

Gordon Fairweather, Chief Commissioner, Canadian Human Rights Commission

Thomas S. Foley, House of Representatives

George S. Franklin, Coordinator, The Trilateral Commission; former Executive Director, Council on Foreign Relations

Donald M. Fraser, House of Representatives

John Allen Fraser, Member of Parliament, Ottawa

John H. Glenn, Jr., United States Senate

Donald Southam Harvie, Deputy Chairman, Petro Canada

Philip M. Hawley, President Cater Hawley Hale Stores, Inc.

Walter W. Heller, Regents' Professor of Economics, University of Minnesota

William A. Hewitt, Chairman, Deere and Company

Carla A. Hills, Senior Resident Partner, Latham, Walkins & Hills; former U.S. Secretary of Housing and Urban Development

Alan Hockin, Executive Vice-President, Toronto-Dominion Bank

James F. Hoge, Jr., Chief Editor, Chicago Sun Times

Hendrik S. Houthakker, Henry Lee Professor of Economics, Harvard University

Thomas L. Hughes, President, Carnegie Endowment for International Peace

*Robert S. Ingersoll, Deputy Chairman of the Board of Trustees, The University of Chicago; former Deputy Secretary of State

D. Gale Johnson, Provost, The University of Chicago

Edgar F. Kaiser, Jr., President and Chief Executive Officer, Kaiser Resources Ltd.

Michael Kirby, President, Institute for Research on Public Policy, Montreal

Lane Kirkland, Secretary-Treasurer, AFL-CIO

*Henry A. Kissinger, Former Secretary of State

Sol M. Linowitz, Senior Partner, Coudert Brothers; former Ambassador to the Organization of American States

Winston Lord, President, Council on Foreign Relations

Donald S. Macdonald, Former Canadian Minister of Finance

*Bruce K. MacLaury, President, The Brookings Institution

Paul W. McCracken, Edmund Ezra Day Professor of Business Administration, University of Michigan

Arjay Miller, Dean, Graduate School of Business, Stanford University

Lee L. Morgan, President, Caterpillar Tractor Company

Kenneth D. Naden, President, National Council of Farmer Cooperatives

David Packard, Chairman, Hewlett-Packard Company

Gerald L. Parsky, Partner, Gibson, Dunn & Crutcher; former Assistant Secretary of the Treasury for International Affairs

William R. Pearce, Vice President, Cargill Incorporated

Peter G. Peterson, Chairman, Lehman Brothers

Edwin O. Reischauer, University Professor and Director of Japan Institute, Harvard University; former U.S. Ambassador to Japan

*Charles W. Robinson, Vice Chairman, Blyth Eastman Dillon & Co.; former Deputy Secretary of State

*David Rockefeller, Chairman, The Chase Manhattan Bank, N.A.

John D. Rockefeller, IV, Governor of West Virginia

Robert V. Roosa, Partner, Brown Bros., Harriman & Company

*William M. Roth, Roth Properties

William V. Roth, Jr., United States Senate

John C. Sawhill, President, New York University; former Administrator, Federal Energy Administration

Henry B. Schacht, Chairman, Cummins Engine Inc.

*William W. Scranton, Former Governor of Pennsylvania; former U.S. Ambassador to the United Nations

*Mitchell Sharp, Member of Parliament; former Minister of External Affairs

Mark Shepherd, Jr., Chairman, Texas Instruments Incorporated

Edson W. Spencer, President and Chief Executive Officer, Honeywell Inc.

Robert Taft, Jr., Partner, Taft, Stettinius & Hollister

Arthur R. Taylor

James R. Thompson, Governor of Illinois

Russell E. Train, Former Administrator, U.S. Environmental Protection Agency

Philip H. Trezise, Former Assistant Secretary of State for Economic Affairs

Paul A. Volcker, President, Federal Reserve Bank of New York

Martha R. Wallace, Executive Director, The Henry Luce Foundation, Inc.

Martin J. Ward, President, United Association of Journeymen and Apprentices of the Plumbing and Pipe Fitting Industry of the United States and Canada

Glenn E. Watts, President, Communications Workers of America

Caspar W. Weinerger, Vice President and General Counsel, Bechtel Corporation

George Weyerhaeuser, President and Chief Executive Officer, Weyerhaeuser Company

Marina von N. Whitman, Distinguished Public Service Professor of Economics, University of Pittsburgh

Carroll L. Wilson, Mitsui Professor in Problems of Contemporary Technology, Alfred P. Sloan School of Management; Director, Workshop on Alternative Energy Strategies, MIT

T. A. Wilson, Chairman of the Board, The Boeing Company

Former Members in Public Service

Lucy Wilson Benson, U.S. Under Secretary of State for Security Assistance

W. Michael Blumenthal, U.S. Secretary of the Treasury

Robert R. Bowie, U.S. Deputy to the Director of Central Intelligence for National Intelligence

Harold Brown, U.S. Secretary of Defense

Zbigniew Brzezinski, U.S. Assistant to the President for National Security Affairs

Jimmy Carter, President of the United States

Warren Christopher, U.S. Deputy Secretary of State

Richard N. Cooper, U.S. Under Secretary of State for Economic Affairs

Richard N. Gardner, U.S. Ambassador to Italy

Richard Holbrooke, U.S. Assistant Secretary of State for East Asian and Pacific Affairs

Walter F. Mondale, Vice President of the United States

Henry Owen, Special Representative of the President for Economic Summits; U.S. Ambassador at Large

Jean-Luc Pepin, P.C., Cochairman, Task Force on Canadian Unity

Elliot L. Richardson, U.S. Ambassador at Large with Responsibility for UN Law of the Sea Conference

Gerard C. Smith, U.S. Ambassador at Large for Non-Proliferation Matters

Anthony M. Solomon, U.S. Under Secretary of the Treasury for Monetary Affairs

Cyrus R. Vance, U.S. Secretary of State

Paul C. Warnke, Director, U.S. Arms Control and Disarmament Agency; Chief Disarmament Negotiator

Andrew Young, U.S. Ambassador to the United Nations

European Members

*Giovanni Agnelli, President, FIAT, Ltd.

*P. Nyboe Andersen, Chief General Manager, Andelsbanken A/S; former Danish Minister for Economic Affairs and Trade

Piero Bassetti, Chamber of Deputies, Rome

*Georges Berthoin, President, European Movement

Kurt H. Biedenkopf, Deputy Chairman, Christian Democratic Union, Federal Republic of Germany

*Kurt Birrenbach, President, German Foreign Policy Association; President, Thyssen Stiftung

*Henrik N. Boon, Former Dutch Ambassador to NATO and Italy

Guido Carli, President, Confindustria; former Governor, Bank of Italy

Lord Carrington, House of Lords, London

Jean-Claude Casanova, Professor of Political Science, Institute of Political Studies, Paris

Willy de Clercq, Chairman, Party for Freedom and Progress, Belgium

Umberto Colombo, Director-General, Research & Development Division, Montedison

Francesco Compagna, Chamber of Deputies, Rome

The Earl of Cromer, Advisor to Baring Bros. & Co., Ltd.; former British Ambassador to the United States

Antoinette Danis-Spaak, Member of Chamber of Representatives, Brussels

Michel Debatisse, Chairman of the French National Farmers Union

*Paul Delouvrier, Chairman, French Electricity Board

Barry Desmond, Member of Irish Parliament and Labour Party Whip

Jean Dromer, President Directeur General, Banque Internationale pour l'Afrique Occidentale

Francois Duchene, Director, Sussex European Research Centre, University of Sussex

G. Eastwood, General Secretary, Association of Patternmakers & Allied Craftsmen, London

*Horst Ehmke, Deputy Chairman, Parliamentary Fraction of Social

Democratic Party, Federal Republic of Germany; former Minister of Justice

Pieerre Esteva, Administrateur Directeur General, Union des Assurances de Paris

K. Fibbe, Chairman of the Board, Overseas Gas and Electricity Company, Rotterdam

M. H. Fisher, Editor, Financial Times

Garret Fitzgerald, Member of Irish Parliament and Leader of Fine Gael Party; former Foreign Minister of Ireland

Rene Foch, Delegue National aux Questions Internationales du Parti des Republicains Independants

Francesco Forte, President, Tescon, S.p.A., Rome

*Michel Gaudet, President, Federation Francaise des Societes d'Assurances

Sir Reay Geddes, Chairman, Dunlop Holdings, Ltd.

Giuseppe Glisenti, President La Rinascente

Ronald Grierson, Director, General Electric Co., Ltd.

Lord Harlech, Chairman, Harlech Television; former British Ambassador to the United States

Hans Hartwig, Chairman, German Association for Wholesale and Foreign Trade

Bernard Hayhoe, Member of British Parliament

Jozef P. Houthuys, Chairman, Belgian Confederation of Christian Trade Unions

Ludwig Huber, President, Bayerische Landesbank

Horst K. Jannott, Chairman, Board of Directors, Munich Reinsurance Society

Daniel E. Janssen, Administrateur Delegue et Directeur General, Belgian Chemical Union

Hans-Jurgen Junghans, Member of the Bundestag

Karl Kaiser, Director, Research Institute of the German Society for Foreign Policy

Sir Kenneth Keith, Chairman, Rolls Royce Ltd.

Henry Keswick, Chairman, Matheson & Company, Ltd.

Michael Killeen, Managing Director, Industrial Development Authority of the Irish Republic

Sir Arthur Knight, Chairman, Courtaulds, Ltd.

*Max Kohnstamm, Principal, European University Institute, Florence

Erwin Kristoffersen, Director, International Division, German Federation of Trade Unions

*Baron Leon Lambert, President du Groupe Bruxelles Lambert, S.A.

Arrigo Levi, La Stampa, Turin

Mark Littman, Deputy Chairman, British Steel Corporation

Richard Lowenthal, Professor Emeritus, Free University of Berlin

*Roderick MacFarquhar, Member of British Parliament

Giorgio La Malfa, Chamber of Deputies, Rome

Robert Marjolin, Former Vice President of the Commission of the European Communities

Roger Martin, President, Compagnie Saint-Gobain Pont-a-Mousson

Reginald Maudling, Member of British Parliament; former Cabinet Minister

Cesare Merlini, Director, Institute of International Affairs, Rome

Thierry de Montbrial, Professor of Economics, Ecole Polytechnique, Paris

Alwin Munchmeyer, Chairman of the Board, Bank Schroder, Munchmeyer, Hengst & Co.

Preben Munthe, Professor of Economics, Oslo University; Official Chief Negotiator in Negotiations between Labor Unions and Industry

Dan Murphy, Secretary-General of the Civil Service Executive Union, Dublin

Karl-Heinz Narjes, Member of the Bundestag

Friedrich A. Neuman, Chairman, State Association, Industrial Employers Societies, North-Rhine Westphalia

*Egidio Ortona, President, Honeywell Information Systems, Italia; former Italian Ambassador to the United States

Bernard Pagezy, President Directeur General, Societes d'Assurances du Groupe de Paris

Sir John Pilcher, Former British Ambassador to Japan

Jean Rey, Ministre d'Etat; former President of the Commission of the European Communities

Julian Ridsdale, Member of British Parliament; Chairman, Anglo-Japanese Parliamentary Group

Sir Frank Roberts, Advisory Director, Unilever Ltd.; former British Ambassador to Germany and the Soviet Union

*Mary T. W. Robinson, Member of Senate, Irish Republiac

Lord Roll, Executive Director, S.G. Warburg and Co., Ltd.

John Roper, Member of British Parliament

Francois de Rose, Ambassadeur de France; President Directeur General, Societe Nouvelle Pathe Cinema

Edmond de Rothschild, President, Compagnie Financiere Holding, Paris

Ivo Samkalden, Former Mayor of Amsterdam

John C. Sanness, director, Norwegian Institute of International Affairs

W. E. Scherpenhuijsen Rom, Chairman, Board of Directors, Nederlandsche Middenstandsbank, N. V.

Erik Ib Schmidt, Permament Undersecretary of State; Chairman, Riso National Laboratory

Th. M. Scholten, Chairman of the Board, Robeco Investment Group, Rotterdam

Gerhard Schroder, Member of the Bundestag; former Foreign Minister of the Federal Republic of Germany

Erik Seidenfaden, Directeur de la Fondation Danoise, Institut Universitaire International de Paris

Federico Sensi, ambassador of Italy; former Italian Ambassador to the Soviet Union

Roger Seydoux, Ambassadeur de France; President, Banque de Madagascar et des Comores; President, Fondation de France

Lord Shackleton, Deputy Chairman, Rio Tinto-Zinc Corporation Ltd., London

Sir Andrew Shonfield, Professor of Economics, European University Institute, Florence; former Director, Royal Institute of International Affairs

J. H. Smith, Deputy Chairman, British Gas Corporation

Hans-Gunther Sohl, Chairman of the Board, August Thyssen Hutte A. G.

Theo Sommer, Editor-in-Chief, Die Zeit

Myles Staunton, Member of Senate, Irish Republic

G. R. Storry, St. Antony's College, Oxford (Far East Centre)

John A. Swire, Chairman, John Swire and Sons, Ltd.

*Otto Grieg Tidemand, Shipowner; former Norwegian Minister of Defense and Minister of Economic Affairs

A. F. Tuke, Chairman, Barclays Bank International Ltd.

Heinz-Oskar Vetter, Chairman, German Federation of Trade Unions

Paolo Vittorelli, Member of Italian Parliament

Sir Frederick Warner, Director, Guinness Peat Group Ltd.; former British Ambassador to Japan

Luc Wauters, Chairman, Kredietbank, Brussels

Edmund Wellenstein, Former Director General for External Affairs, Commission of the European Communities

Kenneth Whitaker, Member of Senate, Irish Republic; former Governor of the Central Bank of Ireland

Alan Lee Williams, Member of British Parliament

Otto Wolff von Amerongen, President, Otto Wolff A.G.; President, German Federation of Trade and Industry

Michael Woods, Member of Irish Parliament

*Sir Philip de Zulueta, Chairman, Anthony Gibbs Holdings Ltd.

Former Members in Public Service

Svend Auken, Minister of Labor, Denmark

Raymond Barre, Prime Minister and Finance Minister, French Republic

Herbert Ehrenberg, Minister of Labor and Social Affairs, Federal Republic of Germany

Marc Eyskens, Belgian State Secretary for Budget and Flemish Regional Economy

Otto Graf Lambsdorff, Minister of Economics, Federal Republic of Germany

Jean-Philippe Lecat, Minister of Culture and Communications, French Republic

Evan Luard, Parliamentary Under Secretary of State for the British Foreign Office

Ivar Norgaard, Danish Minister of Commerce

Michael O'Kennedy, Minister for Foreign Affairs, Irish Republic

Henri Simonet, Foreign Minister of Belgium

Thorvald Stoltenberg, Secretary of State, Norwegian Ministry of Foreign Affairs

Olaf Sund, Senator for Labor and Social Affairs, Land Government of Berlin

Japanese Members

Isao Amagi, President, Japan Society for the Promotion of Science; former Vice-Minister of Education

Yoshiya Ariyoshi, Counsellor, Nippon Yusen, K.K.

Shizuo Asada, President, Japan Air Lines Company, Ltd.

Yoshishige Ashihara, Chairman, Kansai Electric Power Company, Inc.

Toshio Doko, President, Japan Federation of Economic Organizations (Keidanren)

Jun Eto, Professor, Tokyo Institute of Technology

Shinkichi Eto, Professor of International Relations, Tokyo University

*Chujiro Fujino, Chairman, Mitsubishi Corporation

Shintaro Fukushima, President, Kyodo News Service

Noboru Gotoh, President, TOKYU Corporation

Toru Hagiwara, Advisor to the Minister of Foreign Affairs; former Ambassador to France

Nihachiro Hanamura, Vice President, Japan Federation of Economic Organizations (Keidanren)

Sumio Hara, Executive Advisor, Bank of Tokyo, Ltd.

*Yukitaka Haraguchi, Chairman, Central Executive Committee, All Japan Federation of Metal Mine Labor Unions

Norishige Hasegawa, Chairman, Sumitomo Chemical Company, Ltd.

Teru Hidaka, Chairman, Yamaichi Securities Company, Ltd.

Gen Hirose, President, Nihon Insurance Co., Ltd.

Hideo Hori, President, The Association for Employment Promotion of the Handicapped

*Takashi Hosomi, Advisor, Industrial Bank of Japan, Ltd.

Shozo Hotta, Honorary Chairman, Sumitomo Bank, Ltd.

Hosai Hyuga, Chairman, Sumitomo Metal Industries, Ltd.

Shinichi Ichimura, Professor of Economics, Kyoto University

Yoshizo Ikeda, President, Mitsui & Co., Ltd.

Yoshihiro Inayama, Chairman, Nippon Steel Corporation

Kaoru Inoue, Honorary Chairman, Dai-Ichi Kangyo Bank, Ltd.

Rokuro Ishikawa, President, Kajima Corporation

Tadao Ishikawa, President, Keio University

Joji Itakura, President, The Mitsui Bank, Ltd.

Yoshizane Iwasa, Chairman, Japan-U.S. Economic Council

Motoo Kaji, Professor of Economics, Tokyo University

Fuji Kamiya, Professor of International Relations, Keio University

*Yusuke Kashiwagi, President, Bank of Tokyo, Ltd.; former Special Advisor to the Minister of Finance

Koichi Kato, Member of the Diet

Ryoichi Kawai, President, Komatsu, Ltd.

Katsuji Kawamata, Chairman, Nissan Motor Company, Ltd.

Kiichiro Kitaura, President, Nomura Securities Company, Ltd.

Koji Kobayashi, Chairman, Nippon Electric Company, Ltd.

Kenichiro Komai, Chairman, Hitachi, Ltd.

Shinichi Kondo, Advisor, Mitsubishi Corporation; former Ambassador to Canada

Fumihiko Kono, Counsellor, Mitsubishi Heavy Industries, Ltd.

Masataka Kosaka, Professor, Faculty of Law, Kyoto University

Fumihiko Maki, Principal Partner, Maki and Associates, Design, Planning and Development

Shigeharu Matsumoto, Chairman, International House of Japan, Inc.

Daigo Miyado, Chairman, The Sanwa Bank, Ltd.

Akio Morita, Chairman, SONY Corporation

Takashi Mukaibo, President, Tokyo University

Norihiko Nagai, President, Mitsui O.S.K. Lines

Yonosuke Nagai, Professor of Political Science, Tokyo Institute of Technology

Shigeo Nagano, President, Japan Chamber of Commerce and Industry

Eiichi Nagasue, Member of the Diet

Nobuyuki Nakahara, Managing Director, Toa Nenryo Kogyo, K.K.

Toshio Nakamura, Chairman, Mitsubishi Bank, Ltd.

Ichiro Nakayama, President Japan Institute of Labor

Sohei Nakayama, Counsellor, Industrial Bank of Japan, Ltd.

Akira Ogata, Chief News Commentator, Japan Broadcasting Corporation (NHK)

Yoshihisa Ohjimi, President, Arabian Oil Company, Ltd.; former Vice Minister of International Trade and Industry

*Saburo Okita, Chairman, Japan Economic Research Center

*Kiichi Saeki, President, Nomura Research Institute

Kunihiko Sasaki, Chairman, Fuji Bank, Ltd.

Yukio Shibayama, Chairman, Sumitomo Shoji Kaisha, K.K.

Masahide Shibusawa, Director, East-West Seminar

Yoshihito Shimada, President, Takahashi Foundation; former President, Japan Petroleum Development Corporation

Tatsuo Shoda, Chairman, The Nippon Credit Bank, Ltd.

Binsuke Sugiura, Chairman, The Long Term Credit Bank of Japan, Ltd.

*Ryuji Takeuchi, Advisor to the Minister for Foreign Affairs; former Ambassador to the United States

Eiji Toyoda, President, Toyota Motor Company, Ltd.

Seiki Tozaki, President, C. Itoh & Co., Ltd.

Seiji Tsutsumi, Chairman, Seibu Department Store, Inc.

Tadao Umesao, Director, National Museum of Ethnology

Shogo Watanabe, Chairman, Nikko Securities Company, Ltd.

Takeshi Watanabe, Former President, Asian Development Bank

Kizo Yasui, Chairman, Toray Industries, Inc.

*Executive Committee

Former Members in Public Service
Kiichi Miyazawa, Minister of Economic Planning

Nobuhiko Ushiba, Minister of External Economic Affairs

TRILATERALS OVER WASHINGTON

VOLUME II

PREFACE

"We have councils of Vocations, Councils of Eugenics, every possible kind of Council, including a World Council - and if these do not as yet hold total power over us, is it from lack of intention?

"Some might think - though I don't - that nine years ago there was some excuse for men not to see the direction in which the world was going. Today, the evidence is so blatant that no excuse can be claimed by anyone any longer. Those who refuse to see it now are neither blind nor innocent."

Author's Foreword, *Anthem*
Ayn Rand, 1946

In the two years since Volume I of *Trilaterals Over Washington*, the "sleeping giant" has barely awakened to yawn before going back to sleep. While then hardly anybody in the U.S. had heard of the Trilateral Commission, now somewhere around 10 per cent are aware of its existence.

In spite of this increased awareness, as this Volume II will demonstrate, little has been done to curtail or forestall the rise of Trilateralism.

The authors' view of Trilateralism and of many Trilateral Commission members has "mellowed" considerably since Volume I was written. More research, many personal contacts with members of the Commission and extensive travel have all contributed to this change.

A certain percentage of members are indeed sincere in their quest for Trilateralism, albeit sincerely wrong (in the authors' estimation). Others are not so innocent, and are quietly deceptive and misleading about their motives in creating a New Economic World Order.

We find that the Trilateral Commission, per se, is not attempting to create a world government - *that* is nonchalantly left to other forums and organizations, in which one finds many individual Trilateral Commissioners, but not the Trilateral Commission itself.

The Commission is dedicated to creating a *New Economic World Order* as opposed to a Political World Order. They cannot be directly or fairly criticized for the latter. Indirectly, of course, there are many close connections.

Neither is the Trilateral Commission a "conspiracy." The authors have been able to secure information about the Commission without undue hardship - this book proves it. The authors do not pass judgment on the legality of any specific act of this alleged "conspiracy"; that should be left for a court or a Congressional investigation.

In short, in order to properly expose the details and plans of Trilateralism it is not necessary or desirable to argue over what one *doesn't* know. The Trilateral elite is operating in full daylight, but few are willing to say "Halt!"

Meanwhile, America continues to live in a state of fantasy, unable to discern reality amidst a myriad of surrealistic stimuli. America continues to be literally brainwashed by the electronic media, but not that it was all intended that way - to a large extent, Americans are getting exactly what they asked for!

Is America calming down to the serious business of saving the world from itself by embracing atheistic Humanism? Hardly. Americans spend more than $2.3 billion per year on tranquilizers. Of the $3.34 billion per year on the thirteen most popular medications sold, eighteen percent ($600 million) is for the tranquilizer *Valium.* $1.2 billion (another 36 per cent) goes for ulcer and high blood pressure medicine.

Psychiatrists and psychologists are booked solid and different types of therapy cults are springing up all over. Families are being dissolved at an unprecedented rate, suicides are up and the still rising crime rate cannot be slowed.

Where is the world really headed? If you don't at least have an opinion after reading this book, you are in serious trouble.

How can you protect yourself? Consider this 3,000 year old masterpiece of wisdom:

> *"Do not say, 'why is it that the former days were better than these?' For it is not from wisdom that you ask about this. Wisdom along with an inheritance is good and an advantage to those who see the sun. For wisdom is protection just as money is protection. But the advantage is that wisdom preserves the lives of its possessors. Consider the work of God, for who is able to straighten what He has bent? In the day of adversity*
>
> *consider - God has made the one as well as the other so that man may not discover anything that will be after him. "*

King Solomon *Ecclesiastes* Ch. 7, v. 10 - 14

ENDNOTES

1.   Ayn Rand, *Anthem*, p. 12.
2.   *Ecclesiastes,* Chapter 7, verses 10-14, New American Standard Bible.

CHAPTER ONE

INTRODUCTION

Trilaterals Over Washington - Volume II, is the continuation from *Volume I* of the saga of the Trilateral elite. The areas of focus in Volume II are essentially different: we delve into the philosophy of "Globalism," new major economic developments, foreign policy and European Trilateralism.

One of the outstanding characteristics of the Trilateral **Carter** Administration was its pragmatic use of human rights for international elitist objectives. While Trilateral writing on human rights is scant, the Administration proclaimed to the world that it had deep concern for human rights around the world and that this concern was a basic premise of U.S. policy.

We have described in some detail how the Trilateral position on human rights is two-faced. On the one hand we present the plight of Russian Christians seeking refuge in the American Embassy in Moscow and attempts to have them returned to the dictatorship from which they were fleeing: their return will mean lengthy imprisonment as payment for their efforts to obtain human rights. On the other hand we point out the double standard with events in South Africa and Communist Hungary. Specific examples of Henry Kissinger's use of human rights as a so-called "gambling chip" are cited.

We have clearly set forth in Chapter Two the operating "philosophy" of Trilateralism, that is, *Humanism.* According to the Humanist Manifesto[1] (the "constitution" of Humanism), "No deity will save us: we must save ourselves." Pointedly atheistic, Humanism-Trilateralism is spewing out "saviors" who are implementing their own self-righteous programs while thinking they are doing us a favor by preparing a brighter future for mankind. But is it so innocent? You may not think so after seeing how Humanism and Communism both were spawned from the same group in the early 1900's. That the Trilaterals and Marxist countries can and do work together comfortably is no surprise.

Another area of concern to many Americans is the movement in schools across the country to create "global citizens" out of America's youth, paving the way for easy and painless implementation of "interdependence." This re-education of America is being funded by the same foundations that fund the Trilateral Commission. This is brought out in Chapter Three.

Chapters Four and Five take a look at the manner in which Trilateralism transcends political systems, particularly in the context of the historically erroneous theme of Capitalism versus Marxism. The broadly held idea that Capitalists are the enemies of Marxists misses the mark. The Trilateral Commission is continuing and indeed emphasizing a long-run cooperation between a segment of capitalist elitists and the emerging Marxist world. We cite, for example, former Secretary of State Cyrus Vance, a member of the law firm, Simpson, Thacher and Bartlett; this is the same law firm that in October 1918 prevailed upon Woodrow Wilson to recognize the then-new Soviet regime in Russia.

Chapter Five also points out some history behind groups that have dominated foreign policy since at least 1921- the latest of which is the Trilateral Commission. Historically, the most important of these is the Council on Foreign Relations (CFR) founded in 1920. But we should not ignore the Foreign Policy Association, the Atlantic Council and the Rockefeller Commission on Critical Choices for Americans. We show the extraordinary interlock between these organizations; for example, more than 24 percent of Trilaterals are also CFR members.

In Chapter Six we compare two examples of Trilateral foreign policy and human rights. First the case of Communist China and second the case of the Panama Canal Treaty. The Trilateral agreements with Communist China were concluded in the face of the murder of over one hundred million Chinese by the Communist regime.[2]

While China has possibly the worst record of genocide in history, it was overlooked for a reason similar to that in the early 1920's when Wall Street and the European financial elite built up the USSR - *profit.*

Normalization of relations with China will dramatically change the economic structure of the world within a few short years as the Trilateral process exploits slave labor in China at the expense of free labor forces in the US and abroad.

The Panama Canal debacle is another case of hypocrisy and double standards. That the Panama Canal had been bought and fully paid for many years ago by the U.S. was not discussed at the Congressional hearings that led to the giving away of the Canal. Would Texans squawk if the administration unilaterally gave Texas - undisputed U.S. territory - back to Mexico?

Understatement aside, we found that of the 30 or so banks that had made rather shaky loans to Panama, one half of them had at least one Trilateral on their board of directors. Had Panama defaulted on these loans, some major international banks would have faced financial ruin - a scheme had to be implemented to restructure Panama's debts.

So **Sol Linowitz**, director of Marine Midland Bank, was dispatched as "temporary" treaty negotiator (that is, his appointment did not require Senate approval). Again, profit or the fear of loss of profit - dictated a solution clearly against the majority wishes of the US public, and against its security interests. The Panama Canal Treaty was conflict of interest at its utmost.

Chapter Seven details a new and major development as a direct result of normalization with China: economic trade among countries around the Pacific Ocean has dramatically outstripped its Atlantic counterpart. The Pacific Basin Institute, a think tank to monitor this booming trade and to offer policy "suggestions," is to be located near Scottsdale, Arizona. Away from the hustle and bustle of the West Coast, PBI was proposed by Arizona Governor

Bruce Babbitt and Roger Lyon, president of Valley National Bank of Arizona and formerly a top executive with Chase Manhattan Bank in New York. This chapter is certainly the first critique of PBI, but was possible only because one of the authors of this book also lives in Scottsdale, Arizona and happened to see a reference to it in a local newspaper article.

The next to last chapter probes behind the 1980 presidential election. The evidence declares that Trilaterals were active in all three major campaigns. On the Democratic ticket, **James Carter** and **Walter Mondale** were both members of the Commission. Independent **John Anderson** was also a member. While Republican victor Ronald Reagan was not a member of the Trilateral Commission, many of his top advisors were, like **Casper Weinberger**, **David Packard**, **George Weyerhaeuser**, **Bill Brock**, **Anne Armstrong** and others. Two of these received major appointments.

In short, a victory for Reagan is certainly remote from a defeat for Trilateralism. Au contraire, Trilateralism will advance by leaps and bounds under a Reagan administration while a scarce few understand what is really going on.

The last chapter lightly covers European Trilateralism. While this topic could easily take several volumes in itself, we felt it was time to describe and analyze the European counterparts of Trilateralism. We show the link to the European Common Market, central banks and One Europe, and briefly describe Trilateral distribution among the different European countries.

As you may have already noticed, current and former members of the Trilateral Commission appear in bold type throughout this book.

ENDNOTES

1.   John Dewey and et.al., *Humanist Manifesto I and II*, p. 16.
2.   *Chinese Communist Document,* reproduced in L'Express, November I, 1980.

CHAPTER TWO

HUMANISM: THE GLOBAL IDEOLOGY

The word *Humanism* is often confused with the concept of *humane-ism.* In fact, however, Humanism is a secular, non-theistic (atheistic) religion that believes man is capable of self-fulfillment, ethical conduct and salvation without supernatural intervention.

Roots of modern-day Humanism go back to at least fifth century to the Greek philosopher Protagoras who said, "Man is the measure of all things."[1] During the period of the Enlightenment, philosophers such as Jean Jacques Rousseau (1712-1778), Immanuel Kant (1724-1804), Georg Hegel (1770-1831) and slightly later Karl Marx (1818-1883), developed humanistic doctrines that have worked their way into the 20th century in the form of Humanism, Marxism, Socialism, Communism, Collectivism and Rationalism.

Rousseau wrote in *Emile,* "Only through the individual's participation in the 'common unity' can full personal maturity become possible... nature is still the norm, but one that has to be recreated, as it were, at a higher level, conferring on man a new rational unity which replaces the purely instinctive unity of the primitive state."[2] In *Du Contrat Social* he proposed a sort of civil religion or civic profession of faith to which every citizen after giving his free assent - must remain obedient under pain of death.[3]

Hegel coined the idea, "Freedom is not something merely opposed to constraint; on the contrary, it presupposes and requires restraint."[4] Like Rousseau, he contended that the individual could be "free" even when he is being coerced into it, and even though he would not like being forced, he must follow the "public will."

Karl Marx hated Christianity, Judaism and religion in general. He stated: "Criticism of religion is the foundation of all criticism."[5] Even in his own lifetime Marx was known as a militant atheist. All of his writings were directed toward destroying the middle "bourgeois" class by means of the working class, which was to result in a classless society.

At the turn of the century, Humanism was represented in the US by the American Ethical Union (The American Civil Liberties Union - ACLU - was the legal arm of the AEU.) In 1933 *Humanist Manifesto I* was published in *The New Humanist,* Vol. VI, No.3, and in 1973 *Humanist Manifesto II* appeared in *The Humanist,* Vol. XXXIII, No. 5.[6]

The following selected quotes from *Humanist Manifesto II* will give you a general idea of its content:

"As in 1933, Humanists still believe that traditional theism, especially faith in the prayer-hearing God, assumed to love and care for persons, to hear and understand their prayers, and to be able to do something about them, is an unproved and outmoded faith... Reasonable minds look to other means for survival... False 'theologies of hope' and messianic ideologies, substituting new dogmas for old, cannot cope with existing world realities... No deity will save us, we must save ourselves".

"Ethics is autonomous and situational, needing no theological or ideological sanction."[7] [Authors' Note: This gave birth to the phrase, "if it feels good, do it."]

"In the area of sexuality, we believe that intolerant attitudes, often cultivated by orthodox religions and puritanical cultures unduly repress sexual conduct".[8]

"We deplore the division of humankind on nationalistic

grounds. We have reached a turning point in human history where the best option is to transcend the limits of national sovereignty and to move toward the building of a world community in which all sectors of the human family can participate. "

"We believe in the peaceful adjudication of differences by international courts and by the development of the arts of negotiation and compromise. War is obsolete. So is the use of nuclear, biological and chemical weapons. "

"The problems of economic growth and development can no longer be resolved by one nation alone; they are worldwide in scope."

'Technology is the vital key to human progress and development. "

"We urge that parochial loyalties and inflexible moral and religious ideologies be transcended. Destructive ideologicaldifferences among communism, capitalism, socialism, conservatism, liberalism, and radicalism should be overcome."

'[Humanism]... transcends the narrow allegiances of church, state, party, class or race in moving toward a wider vision of human potentiality. What more daring a goal for humankind than for each person to become, in ideal as well as practice, a citizen of a world community. "[9]

Corliss Lamont is one of the most prolific writers on Humanism, and is literally "Mr. Humanism" in regard to awards, mentions, etc. in humanistic circles. Lamont authored *The Philosophy of Humanism* (1977) and noted "A truly Humanist civilization must be a world civilization."[10] He further wrote:

"Humanism is not only a philosophy with a world ideal, but is an ideal philosophy for the world... surmounting all national and sectional provincialisms, provides a concrete opportunity for overcoming the age-long cleavage between East and West.

It is the philosophic counterpart of world patriotism"[11]

"The principle around which the United Nations and the International Court of Justice are organized is that the scope

of national sovereignty must be curtailed and that nations must be willing to accept, as against what they conceived to be their own self-interest, the democratically arrived at decisions of the world community. [12]

There is an extraordinary parallelism between Humanists and Marxists. Among the more obvious are:

- rejection of traditional Christianity and religion
- the necessity for subordination of the individual to state and the community
- catchwords of both Humanism and Marxism are "democracy, peace and high standard of living"
- individual rights and beliefs are non-existent
- collectivism is supreme.

CORLISS LAMONT AND THE MORGAN FINANCIAL GROUP

Corliss Lamont (previously quoted as a prime source of humanist philosophy) is the son of Thomas W. Lamont.

Let's to back to the First World War.

Thomas W. Lamont (1870-1948) was one of the original organizers of the Round Table group cited by Quigley in *Tragedy and Hope.* [13]

Lamont's autobiography is appropriately entitled *Across World Frontiers.* He was not only a senior partner in J.P. Morgan & Co., but was also a director of Guaranty Trust Company, International Harvester Co. (with its Trilateral directors today) and the law firm of Lamont Corliss & Co. Thomas Lamont was a key figure in the Morgan financial group. (For further information and extensive documentation on the links between J.P. Morgan and the development of the early Soviet Union, see *Wall Street and the Bolshevik Revolution* by Antony Sutton.)

Mrs. Thomas Lamont was a member of several unusual organizations:

- Federal Union
- American-Russian Institute (on the Attorney General's subversive list)
- National Council of American-Soviet Friendship

- American Committee for Friendship with the Soviet Union... and numerous others. (See above citation for full list.)

In short, the Lamont family epitomizes the links between:

- Humanism
- Communism
- New York financial interests

THE ASPEN INSTITUTE FOR HUMANISTIC STUDIES

Humanism today is being "taught" throughout the business world by the Aspen Institute, particularly to the multinational corporation community. The major financiers of Aspen also are the major financiers of Trilateralism, and no less than seven members of the Trilateral Commission also serve at the Aspen Institute.

The Aspen Institute was founded in 1949 by Professor Giuseppe Borgese, Chancellor Robert M. Hutchins (both of University of Chicago) and Walter Paepcke, a Chicago businessman. In 1957, Robert

Anderson became chairman, and has been its guiding force . ever since. In 1969, chairmanship switched to Joseph E. Slater, a member of the Council on Foreign Relations and formerly of the Ford Foundation.

In the past the editors have reported the connections between the **Rockefeller** Family and the University of Chicago and also between the Ford Foundation and the Trilateral Commission.

The two leading foundations contributing to Aspen are Atlantic-Richfield (ARCO) and the Rockefeller Foundation.

Moreover, the largest single institutional shareholder in ARCO is Chase Manhattan (4.5%) and the largest individual shareholder is Robert O. Anderson, who is also on the board of directors of Chase Manhattan Bank.

FUNDING OF ASPEN INSTITUTE FOR HUMANISTIC STUDIES - 1979 COLORADO		
Atlantic Richfield Foundation	$900,000	Long term support
Atlantic Richfield Foundation	250,000	Humanities & Arts Program
Atlantic Richfield Foundation	35,250	Environmental Program
Weyerhaeuser Foundation	15,000	To underwrite planning for project "Consequences of a hypothetical world climate change"
Rockefeller Foundation	150,000	To "bring together integrated and emerging leaders from all sectors of society to discuss and help shape policy by recommendations on contemporary issues."
Rockefeller Foundation	15,000	"Cost of executive seminar on women and men in a changing society."
Rockefeller Foundation	148,000	"Arms control and international security."
SEPTEMBER 1, 1980 – WASHINGTON D.C.		
Carnegie Corporation	$15,000	Seminar series of Committee for the Third Sector"
Prudential Foundation	$10,000	

The Markle Foundation (a substantial Aspen backer) is less well known but leads us back to New York banks - in this case to the Morgan Guaranty group. Markle Foundation chairman is Charles F. Biddle, also chairman of the credit policy group of Morgan Guaranty Trust. Walter H. Page is president of Morgan Guaranty Trust and president of J.P. Morgan. Another director, William M. Rees, is a director of First National City Bank.

In short, it seems the private financing for the Aspen Institute comes from the international banks in New York City, and more specifically, from foundations controlled by **Rockefeller** and Morgan interests. *Donors support activities which reflect their objectives.*

NEW YORK

Ford Foundation	24,395	Conference on student aid policies
Ford Foundation	5,000	Comparative study of state judicial systems
Markle Foundation	220,000	"To provide forum for investigation and discussion of communication in modern society, specifically to investigate relationship between choice in programming content and increasing number of distribution channels for communications"
Rockefeller Brothers Fund	30,000	"Islamic Middle East program"
Kettering Foundation	28,000	"Developing the CEO: educating the integrative leader"

In short, it seems the private financing for the Aspen Institute comes from the international banks in New York City, and more specifically, from foundations controlled by **Rockefeller** and Morgan interests. *Donors support activities which reflect their objectives.*

PUBLIC FINANCING OF ASPEN

In **Brzezinski's** book, *Between Two Ages: America's Role in the Technetronic Era,* he wrote in reference to a proposed constitutional convention, "The needed change is more likely to develop incrementally and less overtly... in keeping with the American tradition of blurring distinctions between public and private institutions."[14] A prime Trilateral objective is to blur the distinction between "private" and "public" operations so as to divert public funds into private projects set up by Trilaterals to achieve Trilateral objectives.

A Freedom of Information Act request for information on public financing granted to Aspen was submitted to the National Endowment for the Humanities. We received the following list of NEH grants:

Ad-20009-80-1434
PI: Stephen P. Strickland
Title: Aspen Institute/ United Way Bicentennial Project
Amount: $350,000 G&M (to date $90,000)

AP-00132-79-1297
PI: Robert B. McKay
Title: Development of the Justice Program Amount:
$15,000 outright
Grant Period: 11-1-76 to 6-30-80
CA-28286-77-0616
PI: Stephen Strickland/Aspen Institute
Title: Challenge Grant
Amount: $645,000
Grant Period: 11-1-76 to 6-30-80[15]

SUMMARY OF ASPEN INSTITUTE FUNDING

In brief, Aspen Institute has been funded from the following sources, taking 1979 as a representative year:

U.S. Taxpayer (via National Endowment for the Humanities)	$1,010,000
Atlantic Richfield Foundation	1,186,250
Rockefeller Foundation	343,000
Markle Foundation (Morgan financial interests)	220,000
Other Foundations	97,000

The key point to note is the heavy representation of donations that have also financed Trilateralism: these include **Weyerhaeuser**, **Rockefeller**, Ford and Kettering.

THE ASPEN EXECUTIVE SEMINAR PROGRAM

While central offices of Aspen are in New York City, it has "centers of activity" (i.e. seminar and housing facilities) in Washington, D.C., Cambridge, Princeton, New Haven, Boulder, Hawaii, Tokyo and Berlin.

According to an Aspen publication:

"The idea behind the Aspen Institute has three essential ingredients: to gather thoughtful men and women around the table, not across the table; to explore the power of ideas in great literature stretching from ancient to contemporary

time, and to translate ideas into policies and actions that meet the challenge of our age.

"In view of the rapidly increasing worldwide activities of the Institute, its international Board of Trustees and key staff act on the Institute's long-standing principle to maintain absolute control over the selection of individual participants and their mix in all its meetings, the locations at which its meetings are held, as well as the subjects to be discussed. "[16]

At these meetings, a hotchpotch of corporate executives, military people, intellectuals and media personages "mingle" and become "educated," typically for a period of two weeks at a time. This subtle form of brainwashing on global affairs is coupled with the breaking down of hard line principled positions through peer pressure. As Wilbur Mills once said, "To get along you have to go along."

This is quite successful. For example, *Newsweek* reports that Bill Moyers (a special adviser to Aspen Institute) has drawn more than ten of his Public Broadcasting Service programs from contacts and ideas developed at Aspen.[17] PBS is supported by many of the same foundations that support the Aspen Institute and Trilateralism in addition to large amounts of *public money* (Corporation for Public Broadcasting, etc.). Once again we observe a "blurring" of institutions where elitists combine their money with public financing to achieve their own ends and spread their global propaganda.

THE FUND FOR GOVERNANCE

According to the Institute's *A Brief Overview:*

"...the Institute is undertaking a sustained examination of crucial issues of Governance: how societies and their governments and institutions, public and private, national and international, can better respond to the often conflicting pressures for social justice, fairness, efficiency and individual freedom. Under this broad theme of Governance, the Institute focuses on such subjects as Financing the Future; Human Rights; The Corporation and Society; Energy; A Challenge to Governance; Tradition and Modernization; The First 20 Years of Life;

Ethics; Religion and Governance; Work, Industrial Policy and Society; and Structures for Peace.

While these issues of Governance will be pursued throughout the year and around the globe, the preeminent setting for the dealing with Governance questions is the Institute's newly acquired Wye Plantation outside of Washington, D. C. "[18]

Why should the Aspen Institute undertake this program? It merely quotes from Edmund Burke, "The only thing necessary for the triumph of evil is for good men to do nothing."[19] Apparently the Institute equates itself with the "good men."

The Institute proposes to raise about $15 million for operating capital for this project. An annual budget of at least $1.2 million will provide a staff of senior fellows and consultants (about $450,000 per year) with workshops, seminars and consultative sessions and publications costing about $600,000 a year.

The Atlantic Richfield Company provided the first grant of $1 million and it is anticipated that another $3 million will be raised from corporations and foundations. As much as $6 million could come from *public* funds - either congressional appropriations or through the National Endowment for the Humanities grants.

Some of the participants in this program will not surprise you: Harlan Cleveland, John Gardner, Trilateral **Henry Kissinger,** Marion Doenhoff and Pehr Gyllenhammar.

Without question, this Aspen program is a well-funded attack on Constitutional America.

CONCLUSIONS

- Humanism is a man-centered, atheistic religion inconsistent with and indeed utterly opposed to traditional Christianity, Biblical theology or Orthodox Judaism.
- The philosophy has been nurtured and promoted by the same group of globalists that nurtures and supports communism.

- Humanism is intimately connected with Trilateralism, and calls for the elimination of nationalism and nationalistic boundaries.

- Trilateral-style Humanism is procreated primarily by The Aspen Institute, and is funded by taxpayers' money as well as by private foundation and corporate funds.

ENDNOTES

1. Protagoras, *Protagoras IV,* 51.
2. J.J. Rousseau, *Emile.*
3. ---, *Du Contrat Social.*
4. Paul Edwards, *Encyclopedia of Philosophy.*
5. Ibid.,
6. Both of these Manifestos are available from Prometheus Books, 923 Kensington Avenue, Buffalo, New York 14215.
7. John Dewey et al, *Humanist Manifesto I and II,* p. 14-16. 8. Ibid., p. 17, 18.
8. 9. Ibid., p. 21-23.
9. 10. Corliss Lamont, *The Philosophy of Humanism,* p. 281. 11. Ibid., p. 282, 283.
10. 12. Ibid., p. 257, 258.
11. Ibid.
12. Zbigniew Brzezinski, *Between Two Ages: America's Role in the Technetronic Era,*
13. p. 259.
14. *Report of Financing Granted to Aspen Institute,* National Endowment for the Humanities, 14th report (1979).
15. *The Aspen Institute: a Brief Overview,* Aspen Institute.
16. Eric Gelman, *The Great American Salon,* Newsweek XCVI (July 14, 1980), p. 66.
17. Aspen Institute, Op. Cit.
18. Edmund Burke, *Letter to William Smith,* January 9, 1795.

CHAPTER THREE

GLOBAL SCHOOLING: THE RE-EDUCATION OF AMERICA

"National security today involves more than military preparation. Global education is one of the essential new dimensions.

"The globalization of the human condition is interweaving the destinies of all nations and peoples at an accelerating rate and affecting many aspects of life. Global education involves multidisciplinary perspectives about the extended human family, the existing condition of mankind and the planet, and foreseeable consequences of present trends and alternative choices."[1]

Note that the above was written by Robert Leestma of the U.S. Office of Education, a contributor to the 1979 book, *Schooling for a Global Age*.

While the previous chapter detailed the religion of Humanism and its thrust behind Trilateralism, this chapter seeks to document a massive re-education program of American school age children - and unwilling parents, who remain a major obstacle to a smooth transition to a global society.

On the back dust cover of the above quoted book, it is noted:

"This book is one of a series of three books on issues and prac-

tices in schooling. The other two books deal with the arts and education and with school-community relations. The series was commissioned to provide background information for A Study of Schooling in the United States, the results of which will be published subsequently. "[2]

Also noted are the financial backers of the studies:

The Danforth Foundation
The John D. Rockefeller III Fund
Martha Holden Jennings Foundation
Charles F. Kettering Foundation
Charles Stewart Mott Foundation
The Needmor Fund
The Rockefeller Foundation
The Spencer Foundation
U.S. Office of Education National Institute of Education[3]

Emphasis is added to note two things: first, the Rockefeller and Kettering foundations originally funded the Trilateral Commission. Second, public funds are intermixed with private funds to facilitate and implement a non-public supported or authorized endeavor.

We have chosen to analyze *Schooling for a Global Age* because of its authority of scholarship, financial backing and impact. It is not an *"official"* US government publication, but government officials are quoted and substantial government funds were provided so the study could be undertaken.

In light of this, we can be sure the book typifies the thinking of the National Education Association (NEA), the Department of Education, the various foundations listed and most importantly, the thinking of David Rockefeller et al.

A PHILOSOPHY OF EDUCATION FOR WORLD CITIZENSHIP

Keeping in mind the last chapter dealing with Humanism, the following *"purpose statement"* exemplifies the Humanist philosophy on global education:

- "To develop student understanding of themselves as individuals.

- 'To *develop student understanding of themselves as members of the human species.*

- "To develop student understanding of themselves as inhabitants and dependents of planet Earth.

- "To develop student understanding of themselves as participants in global society.

- "To develop within students the competencies required to live intelligently and responsibly as individuals, human beings, earthlings, and members of global society.

"...We endeavor to create in world-centered schools the kind of social order, the organizational climate, the physical

environment, and the formal curriculum that support and further the purposes of global education."[4]

"Identities, loyalties, and competencies as well as rights, duties, obligations, and privileges are associated with each of these goals. For example, students might explore the issues involved and discuss the rights one has by virtue of being a member of the human species. The Universal Declaration of Human Rights, the Humanist Manifesto, and UNICEF and the Rights of the Child are among many documents and other ma- terials which can be used in considering this question. "[5]

According to Irving H. Buchen, the student *"...will be capable of sustaining many allegiances, without contradiction, on both a national and international scale, and be closer to being, especially through the concept of global perspectives, a world citizen."[6]*

The Aspen Institute for Humanistic Studies paper, *American Education and Global Interdependence,* states:

"The educational enterprise has a vital role to play in preparing present and future generations of Americans to cope with inter-dependence. Universities contain intellectual skills needed to develop the knowledge base about global interdependence; developing a more secure knowledge base should facilitate greatly the building of political consensus on what we should do about global interdependence.

The mass media by their very nature are event-centered, imposing on schools and colleges an obligation to provide

students with the continuity and depth of understanding de-
manded by complex long-term interdependence issues.

Schools, furthermore, have the golden opportunity, if they will
but use it, of shaping the world views of future generations of
Americans along lines more compatible with the realities of
global interdependence before these views become hardened
through maturation along other less compatible lines. "[7]

Global education requires the conversion of existing local educational systems - primarily those at the elementary and second-
ary school levels - to produce students who see themselves not as
Americans but as participants in a world society.

Why? Because *"nationalism"* and *"individualism"* are lumped in
with the" *other less compatible lines."*

Society must be planned, they say, in overt and covert ways;
individual ethnic, cultural and intellectual differences will be subordinated to some predetermined set of characteristics set forth
by the elitist group preparing us for global interdependence.

AN ACTION PLAN

The Aspen Institute study noted, *"The task of bringing about*
the kind of transformation which will make education a better
instrument for coping with interdependence is formidable."[8] To
achieve their plan, global educators propose to identify and concentrate action upon what they call *"critical leverage points"* in
our present educational system.

The plan is to subvert and change these critical points into
a program to achieve global goals. When analyzed, Aspen's six
point plan of action is nothing less than cultural genocide:

"Point 1: Revise curricula, the content of teacher training and
community education toward global education. It is proposed
to use the U.S. Department of Education as well as indepen-
dent foundations and local school systems for this purpose.

"Point 2: To obtain support from political and educational
leaders at both national and local levels, particularly from
boards of trustees and professional or organizations, to mold
public support for global education.

"Point 3: To use universities and research institutions to develop a "knowledge base" on interdependence in order to help build the political consensus necessary for global policies.

"Point 4: To shape existing world outlooks within American popular culture.

"Point 5: To reach outward to the world through educational institutes, particularly through the United Nations.

"Point 6: To influence mass media to these ends, particularly through the use of internships that are part of professional training in mass communications."[9]

(Authors' note: there are many college-age students who have been raised in prototype *"global schools"* who think in global terms and can be *"interned"* in strategic places within the media.)

Aspen makes it clear that this is an *activist* plan: *"Achieving the educational transformation, which the future demands will require all of the spirit of conquest and aspiration which we possess."[10]*

CENTRALIZED, GOVERNMENT-CONTROLLED EDUCATION REQUIRED

Globalists recognize that American education is essentially de-centralized and that public education has historically played a role in the teaching of American history and government. Thus, one objective is to heavily reduce the amount of time devoted to the study of these subjects now required in the curricula of most states. These America- oriented curricula will be replaced with ones concentrating on world history and politics.

They describe the current educational system as a *"constitutional incongruity."* Certain constitutional conflicts do exist which cannot be overcome as long as education remains in the hands of local and state governments. A major answer to this was the creation of the Department of Education, which was heavily lobbied by the global- minded National Education Association (NEA).

The Aspen study also cited Roger Ulrich's *The Control of Human Behavior.* According to Ulrich, conditioning is supposed to start at the age of two years.[11] It is recognized within the global education community that the critical years for the establishment of values and ideas is around seven to twelve. Consequently, it is planned to subject students to a curricula which employs behavioral techniques involving so-called *"values clarification"* and situational ethics.

This manipulates students into an artificial belief structure. Who picks the values they will be taught? Which set of ethics will be used?

These techniques are close to those of Goebbels' in Nazi Germany, or Soviet and Chinese propagandists of today. These are programs for human behavioristic manipulation, not education!

THE PLAN IS UNDERWAY

Don't make the mistake of underestimating the forces behind global schooling. This is not some passive, *"pie-in-the-sky"* ideological exercise of academia - it is highly organized, completely funded and well staffed. It is sweeping the country.

The following *"timetable"* is quoted *exactly* from pages 240-241 of *Schooling for a Global Age.*

"PHASE 1, PREPARATORY PERIOD - BY 1980:
- *Every state education department and most school systems and teacher education programs would have a collection of some basic references on global education and would have provided opportunities for selected staff members to become aware of the global education concept, some relevant research, successful programs elsewhere, and local possibilities.*
- *In-service education programs would be available in every region of the country to begin to acquaint teachers and others with the global education concept.*
- *A survey of the role of the world in the community, region, or state and vice versa would have been conducted, planned, or under consideration in a majority of states.*

"PHASE 2 - BY THE MID-1980s:
- *Study groups would be at work in a sizeable proportion*

of state education departments, local school systems, and teacher education institutions to analyze and enrich existing curricula, requirements, and materials from a global perspective.

- *In-service education opportunities would be available in the majority of states, including through teacher centers.*
- *Pre-service education programs would be offering some orientation to global education, at least as an option.*
- *Initial research agendas would be established and studies and surveys begun.*
- *A national baseline survey of the knowledge and attitudes of students, teachers, administrators, parents, and community leaders on global education concerns would be completed.*
- *Every state education department and a sizeable proportion of school districts would become involved in an international educational exchange program for students and/ or staff*
- *State and local school board policy statements would be giving explicit support to global education.*
- *National public awareness and local community support would be growing, in part, because of increased attention to global problems and issues in the mass media, particularly television, and in the schools.*

"PHASE 3 - BY 1990:

- *Teachers in every state would have access to in-service education programs for global education, at least at the awareness level.*
- *Good case-study material on the initiation or improvement of global education programs in a variety of school and community situations would be becoming widely available.*
- *All school districts, state education departments, and pre- service teacher-education programs would have*

access to information clearinghouses and resource centers on global perspectives in education.

- *Teacher certification requirements in a sizeable number of states would begin to reflect global education concerns.*
- *State curriculum requirements in a sizeable number of states would begin to reflect global education objectives.*
- *School accreditation requirements would begin to reflect attention to global education.*
- *Local, state, and national assessments of educational progress would include attention to global educational concerns.*
- *Textbooks and other educational materials would increasingly provide more adequate treatment of global issues and perspectives.* "[12]

PARENTS NEED TO BE EDUCATED ALSO

John I. Goodlad wrote in *Schooling for a Global Age:*

"Parents and the general public must be reached also. Otherwise, children and youth enrolled in globally oriented programs may find themselves in conflict with values assumed in the home. And then the educational institution frequently comes under scrutiny and must pull back. "[13]

The question basically boils down to this: *"Are your values good enough for your children, or not?"* We have passed through the UN-sponsored "International Year of the Child" which preached children's rights. In Sweden it is now against the law to spank your own child - who could report *you* to the authorities for *"maltreatment."*

This thought is expanded:

"Parents should understand that developing independent individuals is not a goal of government education,- and this becomes apparent only with an understanding of the educator's view of an individual: 'The emerging modern individual places his confidence not in society's norms, not religion's rules, nor parents' dictates, but in his own changing experi-

ence. He is, in a very deep sense, his own highest authority. He chooses his own way.' [14]

The greatest obstacle to the implementing of global schooling is not lack of funding, trained teachers or global textbooks - it is the *parent* who is skeptical about the federal government (with its blurred distinctions between private and public institutions) being better qualified to say how his child should be raised and educated.

"Rebel" parents who have chosen to educate their children at home have become *"examples"* to globalists who drag the parents into court on civil and criminal charges of negligence.

Private schools across the country have continuously fought an onslaught of legislation that would destroy them, if passed. Whenever a student is transferred to a private school, the public school he or she attended loses state and federal budget funds for the following year. In many cases, the formula for determining funding is disproportionate to the total number of students in attendance; thus, if 40% of the students withdrew to private schools, those schools could lose 70 or 80% of its funding. This is intolerable to public educators, and pressure is put on the parent to re-enroll the student in public school.

One of the key activist groups that deals with parent as well as student problems is the National Education Association (NEA); possibly it is the most powerful special interest group in operation today. The NEA sent more delegates to the Democratic National Convention in 1980 than *any* other interest group including trade unions.

The NEA worked closely with the Trilaterally oriented Carter administration in setting up the long sought after Federal Department of Education to centralize US education.

A national movement was recently underway to pass legislation allowing tuition tax credits for parents of students enrolled in private schools. This is not surprising in that they are paying for two educations at the same time - private *and* public. If passed, it would have dealt a fatal blow to global educators because it would have encouraged parents to seek better, private education for their children; in turn, public schools would have their funding automatically chopped. The National Education Association was successful at blocking this legislation.

HOW GLOBAL EDUCATION IS BEING FINANCED

We noted earlier that the Aspen Institute for Humanistic Studies is funded primarily by Atlantic Richfield, Rockefeller, Kettering, Weyerhaeuser, Ford and the Markle Foundations. In addition, we saw that almost 40% of Aspen's funding came from the National Endowment for the Humanities (NEH).

NEH granted a whopping total of $185.3 million in 1979 to many different Humanistic and globalist endeavors, including Aspen Institute. While the US taxpayer contributes about 80% of NEH's annual funding, the remaining 20% comes from Lilly Endowment, the Ford Foundation and the Andrew W. Mellon and Alfred P. Sloan Foundations.

Watchers of the Public Broadcasting System will see many global- oriented shows sponsored by Ford Foundation.

The Kettering Foundation, a main backer of the Trilateral Commission, has as its purpose statement: *"To strengthen the mechanisms for citizen participation in public policy formation and implementation, and to support the forces for world order and peace. It supports only innovative, high-risk programs which do not receive sufficient attention from other sources.* "[15]

The following table gives you an idea of what Kettering considers *"innovative, high risk."*

SELECTED CHARLES F. KETTERING FOUNDATION

Action For a Better Community ($9,300) Rochester, NY. 2/ 15/79. For handbook, *How to Develop an Insurance Cooperative.* and to identify settings in which cooperative development would provide alternative to disruptive market forces at the neighborhood level.	*National League of Cities* ($100,000) DC. 12/15/78. For program with U.S. Civil Service Commission Bureau of Intergovernmental Personnel Programs to improve *group skills and policy management systems* of municipal policy makers in selected demonstrations cities, and *to develop national network of trainers of elected officials.*

Aspen Institute for Humanistic Studies ($28,000) NYC, NY. 1/15/78. 2-year grant. To cosponsor studies and seminars on economic modernization in the People's Republic of China.	*Policy Sciences Center* ($40,000) NYC, NY. 2/13/78. To develop process for *direct unofficial discussion* between multinational corporations and less developed countries' leaders.
Cornell University ($24,000) Department of Human Development and Family Studies, Ithaca, NY. 11/15/78. For project Ecology of Human Development, studying *child development* in relation to child care, education, and family support system policies and practices.	*Stanford University* ($29,376) U.S. China Relations Program, Stan-ford, CA. 9/1/78. To continue project, Technology Policy and Development in People's Republic of China, focusing on areas of research and development for food production and telecommunications in China.[16]

We noted earlier that Kettering was a supporter of *Schooling for a Global Age.* That book also states, *"Sub-study on the teaching of global education in schools [is] supported by an additional grant from the Charles F. Kettering Foundation."*[17] (Emphasis added.)

Among the Kettering directorship, we find two notable Humanists: George Gallup and Norman Cousins. Cousins is a director of National Educational Television and the U.N. Association of the U.S. Gallup surveys, which are supposed to be so "unbiased," are usually called for when globalists want to "prove" their case to the public by doing a public opinion survey.

While the authors have not done an exhaustive tabulation on the amount of money distributed by public and private institutions for globalist ends, it is estimated that well over $1 billion per year is sunk into "high risk" programs that would otherwise find no support.

MASS MEDIA AND THE MARKLE FOUNDATION

The Markle Foundation was identified as a prime contributor to the Aspen Institute and ties to the Morgan banking establishment were noted in the previous chapter.

Markle's statement of purpose reads: *"The goal of the current program is to strengthen educational uses of the mass media and communications technology."*[18]

This foundation deserves extra space as a prime purveyor of global education. The president of Markle Foundation is Lloyd N. Morrisett. Over ten years ago, when Morrisett was a vice-president of Carnegie Corporation, he and Joan Cooney (wife of Trilateralist **Peter G. Peterson**) originated the idea for *Sesame Street.* He is currently chairman of the board of trustees at *Children's Television Workshop,* which produces Sesame Street.

According to the 1978 Annual Report of the Markle Foundation:

"In its first operating year, 1969-1970, the Workshop had 36 employees and a budget of $6.8 million. Almost all this money came from three sources: The Office of Education, the Carnegie Corporation of New York, and the Ford Foundation. The Workshop itself was able to provide only $119,000 from its own income. "[19]

It later stated that:

"CTW has established its status as a public charity under the Tax Reform Act of 1969. The value of the public charity classification to an organization such as CTW is that it allows the receipt of individual or corporate contributions on a fully tax deductible basis for the donor. It also facilitates philanthropic donations by foundations. "[20]

Which foundations contribute to support Sesame Street so it can stay on the air? Surprisingly, not Markle Foundation, even though they are closely linked, Markle spends its funds on more *"high risk"* ventures just starting out (see Table II).

What is interesting to see is that these ventures, like Sesame Street, were persistently bailed out financially, year after year, because they could not make their own way. Further, major funds to this end came from *your* taxes, as well as various foundations.

CONCLUSIONS:

- A main tenet of Humanism is to institute global education to create a generation of "global citizens."
- Global education is being financed by the same foun-

dations that finance Humanism and the Trilateral Commission.

- Massive amounts of public funds are also being used to these ends.
- There is a plan, a timetable, sufficient personnel and funds to carry out the plan.
- Global education ideology is in direct conflict with the Constitution of the United States.

TABLE II

1975

65,213 to Cable Arts Foundation. For development of arts programming on cable television.

$35,000 to Rand Corporation, Communications Policy Program. For beginning research to identify and measure the size of special interest audiences for public television.

$112,000 to University of California, School of Medicine, Laboratory for the Study of Human Interaction & Conflict, Psychiatric Department.
For field study of the effects of television on children.

$92,298 to University of Minnesota, School of Journalism and Mass communication, Communication Research Division. To pursue research on ways in which children are influenced by pro-social television content.

1976

$2,500 to The Rand Corporation. Support of the publication and distribution of a study on new evaluation methods for "Sesame Street" and "Electric Company."

$29,000 to the University of Wisconsin, Mass Communications Research Center. Support of a study of the influence of mass communications on young voters.

1977

$14,189 to American Assembly. To sponsor an American Assembly to discuss the ways the mass media in the United States shapes the politics of Presidential selection.

$170,000 to Aspen Institute. Support of Aspen Program on Communications and Society.

$19,425 to Cultural Council foundation. Support for Independent Cinema Artists and Producers to act as a distributor with pay television systems for independent film and video artists.

$70,887 to Harvard University. Two studies to examine how children come to understand the television medium and the steps where they learn to make distinction between fantasy and reality[21]

ENDNOTES

1.   I. Robert Leestma, *Schooling for a Global Age,* ed. James M. Becker, p. 233.
2.   Ibid., Dust cover.
3.   Ibid., Dust cover.
4.   Lee and Charlotte Anderson, Op. cit., pg. 8.
5.   James Becker, Op. cit., pg. 41.
6.   Irving Buche, *Learning for Tomorrow,* ed. Alvin Toffler, p.137.
7.   *American Education and Global Interdependence,* Aspen Institute.
8.   Ibid.
9.   Ibid.
10.   Ibid.
11.   Roger Ulrich, *Control of Human Behavior.*
12.   Robert Leestman, Op. cit., p. .240, 241.
13.   John I. Goodlad, Ibid., 17.
14.   Carl Rogers, *Courses by Newspaper.*
15.   *Charles F. Kettering Foundation Annual Report,* 1979.
16.   16. Ibid., p. 36.
17.   James Becker, Op. cit., p. vii.
18.   *Markle Foundation Annual Report* (1977), p. 4.
19.   Ibid., p. 8.
20.   20. Ibid., p. 17.
21.   21. Ibid., p. 58-{j5.

CHAPTER FOUR

TRANSCENDING POLITICAL SYSTEMS: CAPITALISTS VS. MARXISTS

One of the most pervasive - but downright erroneous themes in modem textbook history is that of a competition between Capitalist and Marxist systems. In fact, given objective examination of all facts nothing could be further from the truth. The two political power groups cooperate with each other, nurture each other and in general are jointly responsible for much of the pain and suffering of the average man on the street in this world.

Much of the confusion stems from an unwillingness to define monopoly capitalism for what it is: a political power system that is much like state socialism. State socialism, as in the Soviet Union, is also remarkably akin in its operations to that of a monopoly. Thus, a Brezhnev and a Rockefeller have much in common. Both are monopolists and both thrive on use of political power to retain their monopoly.

With this parallel in mind, let's summarize the facts on the almost continuous involvement of American elitist capitalists in the buildup of Soviet military power over the past 63 years. It has been a deliberate policy. That it was done shortsightedly for financial gain is rather obvious. No one - not even a multinational businessman - commits suicide knowingly, but it is not unheard of for avarice to overcome common sense.

Apparently only one US institution has been clear-sighted on the buildup of Soviet power. *From the early 1920's until recently only one institution has spoken out.* That institution is the AFL-CIO. From Samuel Gompers in 1920 down to George Meany, major unions consistently protested the trade policies that built the Soviet military power. Why? Because workers in Russia lost their freedom with the Bolshevik Revolution, and the products used to expedite the killing of union members in Korea and Vietnam were made with the help of American elitist controlled multinational company technology. *But today Trilateral Commissioner* **Kirkland** *rules the AFL-CIO and the protest is muted.*

THE BOLSHEVIK REVOLUTION (1917)

The March, 1917, Russian Revolution overthrew the regime of the Romanov Czars and installed a free, constitutional government. In November the fledgling republic was destroyed by the totalitarian Bolsheviks and the Russian hope for freedom evaporated. The powerful American elite was involved because *Wall Street financiers* and attorneys intervened in support of the Bolsheviks. A few examples of this support are:

- Key Wall Streeters assisting the Bolsheviks included William Boyce Thompson (director of Chase National, forerunner of Chase Manhattan), Albert H. Wiggin (president of Chase Bank), establishment attorneys and Morgan bankers.

- The Wall Street bankers pressured the US and British governments to support Bolsheviks, much as **Rockefeller** and **Kissinger** pressured **Carter** into admitting the Shah of Iran into the US in 1979. *The Wall Street pressures were to assist Bolshevik propaganda, encourage formation of a Soviet army and supply arms to the Bolsheviks.*

- Some statements by American elitist businessmen on the early Soviets include the following letter from William Saunders, chairman of Ingersoll-Rand Corporation, to President Wilson, on October 17, 1918: "Dear Mr. President: I am in sympathy with the Soviet form of government as that best suited for the Russian people."[1]

- And another from Thomas D. Thacher, Wall Street attorney and member of the establishment law firm Simpson, Thacher & Bartlett (former Secretary of State **Vance** is today a member of this same firm): ". . .The fullest assistance should be given to the Soviet government in its efforts to organize a volunteer revolutionary army."[2]

Wall Street bankers, including Chase National bankers, aided the Bolshevik Revolution by intervention with the United States and British governments and were crucial to its success.

THE EARLY YEARS OF SOVIET RUSSIA

Wall Street then came to the aid of the newborn Soviet government. Armand Hammer (now chairman of the Occidental Petroleum Corporation) received the first concession contract in 1920 because his father, Julius Hammer, was then Secretary of the Communist Party in the US. However, the Rockefellers were not far behind. Under the guidance of Reeve Schley (a Chase VP) the American-Russian Chamber of Commerce was formed in partnership with Russian agents to break the U.S. government ban on trade with the Soviets.

What could not be done legally was done illegally - even to the export of military aircraft engines. *By the late 1920's Wall Street and German bankers had put the infant Soviet Russia on its feet.*

In 1925, a complete program to finance imports of Soviet raw material to the United States and to export vital machinery and technology to the Soviets was agreed upon by Chase National and Prombank (a German bank).

At the same time - even though a government ban still existed on all trade with the Soviet Union - Chase National was trying to arrange for export of Liberty motors for military planes. Years later, when writing *Western Technology and Soviet Economic*

Development, the co-author (Sutton) found the evidence in State Department files and learned that the Department of Justice was one step ahead of Chase National and intervened to stop illegal exports.

Along with Equitable Trust, Chase National was in the forefront of financing Soviet economic and military development in the 1920's. When acceptance of gold was halted by the State Department, the Chase-Soviet business was arranged on the basis of platinum credits.

Above all, the formation of the American-Russian Chamber of Commerce, with Chase VP Reeve Schley as its president, was the major factor in circumventing the ban on US technology for the Soviet Union. The Chamber was active in pressing the need for "cooperation" and "peaceful trade." The Chamber representative in Moscow was none other than Charles Haddell Smith, previously in Soviet employ and a member of the Soviet Peasant International.

By the late 1920's, Chase was even attempting to raise loans for the Soviets in the US, the first being a $30 million deal with principal and interest, payable in dollars - flatly prohibited by State Department regulations.

We also find in State Department files, letters from Chase refusing to break off the illegal relationship when instructed to do so. Public comment at that time was more caustic than in today's tame media.

Chase was called - among the more delicate descriptions - "an international fence," "a disgrace to America... They will go to any lengths for a few dollars profit."[3]

This intimate link between Chase National (which became Chase Manhattan in the 1950's) and the Soviets is unbroken throughout six decades.   .

THE FIRST FIVE YEAR PLANS (1930-45)

In 1930, Chase National was one of four American banks that financed construction of the Five-Year Plans (master plans devised to expedite economic expansion through rapid industrialization of the once largely agricultural society) and, according to

State Department files, its advisor was Soviet agent Alexander Ginsberg. In 1930, according to the U.S. Treasury, *all* Soviet accounts were with the Chase National Bank. Today the principal Chase Manhattan correspondent bank in Russia is Narodny Bank.

The Five-Year Plans have been hailed in the history books as a triumph of Soviet engineering. In fact, the Plans were entirely packaged and implemented by non-Russian companies mostly American - for the profit of Wall Street. **Rockefeller** interests received a large portion of the money that flowed from this initial effort to modernize the Soviet Union. This included its war industries, ammunition, modern aircraft, tanks and warships.

WORLD WAR II

Lend Lease (the US program offering assistance to the Allies during World War II) provided the means for the Soviets to resist Nazi aggression. The Soviet Union was the recipient of the latest in US military technology during World War II - once again for the profit of large US multinationals.

POST WORLD WAR II

The buildup of Soviet economic and military power has continued from 1945 down to the present day under the guise of peaceful trade.

A good example is the truck industry: any truck plant that produces civilian trucks can also produce military trucks. All Soviet automobile, truck and engine technology comes from the West, and chiefly from the United States. The Soviet military has over 300,000 trucks - the bulk of which came from these US-built plants.

Up to 1968 the largest motor vehicle plant in the USSR was at Gorki and it was built by the Ford Motor Company and the Austin Company as a part of so-called "peaceful trade." The Gorki plant produced many of the trucks American pilots saw on the Ho Chi Minh Trail. The chassis for the GAZ-69 rocket launcher used against Israel was also produced there, along with the Soviet jeep and half a dozen other military vehicles.

In 1968, while the Gorki plant was building vehicles to be used in Vietnam and against Israel, further equipment for the plant was ordered and shipped from the US.

Also in 1968 there was the so-called "Fiat deal" - a plan to build a plant at Volgograd three times bigger than the one at Gorki. Dean Rusk and Walter Rostow told Congress and the American public this was "peaceful trade," that the Fiat plant could not produce military vehicles. However, as previously stated, *any* automobile manufacturing plant can produce military vehicles. The main design contract for the Volgograd plant was held by Fiat, whose chairman was soon-to-be Trilateral **Giovanni Agnelli.** **Agnelli** is also on the International Advisory Committee of Chase Manhattan Bank. (The IAC chairman is **Henry Kissinger**).

Fiat in Italy doesn't make automobile manufacturing equipment; they use U.S. manufactured equipment. Fiat did send 1,000 men to Russia for the erection of the plant - but over half of the equipment came from the United States, namely Gleason Works, TRW Inc. of Cleveland,

U.S. Industries, Inc. and New Britain Machine Co.

So in the middle of a war that killed 46,000 Americans and countless Vietnamese with Soviet weapons and supplies, Trilaterals doubled Soviet auto output.

In 1972, the Soviets received equipment and technology from the West to build the largest heavy truck plant in the world the Kama plant - to produce 100,000 ten-ton trucks per year - more than produced by *all* US manufacturers put together. It is also the largest plant in the world, covering over 36 square miles.

Does the Kama truck plant have military potential? The Soviets themselves answered this one. The Kama-produced truck is rated 60 per cent higher than the ZIL-130 truck, and the ZIL series trucks are standard Soviet army trucks used in Vietnam, the Middle East and Afghanistan.

In the opening paragraphs of this chapter we quoted the support from William Saunders, chairman of Ingersoll-Rand, for the Bolsheviks in 1918. Today we find the same firm Ingersoll-Rand aiding the military buildup of the Soviet Union for military equipment in use by the Soviets. According to *Business Week:*

> *"Meanwhile, a smaller but politically still more in- flammatory shipment is also rolling - toward Russia's Kama River*

*truck plant. New Jersey's Ingersoll-Rand Co. expects to com-
plete by late this year an $8.8 million order of automated
production-line equipment used to make diesel engines at
the Soviet manufacturing which produced trucks used in the
invasion of Afghanistan. The shipments are authorized under
the Commerce Department's general licenses, not yet under
strict controls."[4]*

The pro-Soviet stance of American businessmen today, as well
as in 1918, is well typified by Dresser Industries. The company is
now finishing a drill bit plant worth $146 million at Kuibyshev.
The Soviets need high-quality drill bits to step up oil exploration,
and oil is needed to fuel its overseas expansion program.

Dresser has not only continued to press ahead with the plant,
but is attempting to keep its Soviet role quiet to avoid public back-
lash in the US. To quote Dresser's senior vice-president Edward
R. Luter:

*"Dresser is keeping a low profile on the plant. We're not look-
ing for any publicity, because we're afraid if our name comes
up, and the project is called to people's attention, they might
remember that they wanted to do something to stop it. We
hope we can let sleeping dogs lie, and let things continue to
roll."[5]*

The reason that Dresser wants to keep its role from the public
is simple: according to Department of Defense expert Dr. William
Perry the Soviets "will be able to detect and monitor all US subs
using oil exploration equipment sold to them by the US."[6]

KISSINGER AND SOVIET MILITARY BUILD UP

Henry Kissinger has been intimately connected for two decades with the **Rockefeller** family as a family advisor before going
to Washington in 1970. In the March 1979 issue of *The Trilateral
Observer* the annual cash payments from Nelson Rockefeller to
Henry Kissinger were listed from 1958 to 1969 (**Kissinger** entered the White House as National Security Advisor to President
Nixon in 1969).[7] Each year, cash payments averaging at least $12,000
were made to **Henry Kissinger**. An official report on these transactions concluded that the payments "were for work done for the

family rather than on a consulting basis through any governmental agency."[8] **Kissinger** can be described as the intellectual hired hand of the **Rockefellers Kissinger** was responsible for brushing aside information that our exports to the Soviets had military potential and for forcing US government officials to approve export of equipment with military potential.

The co-author's (Sutton) personal knowledge of the role of **David Packard** (later Secretary of Defense, from 1969 to 1971) in suppressing information of military potential, and the intimate relations of **David Rockefeller** and **Henry Kissinger**, suggests that the Trilateral group was the origin of the 1970's phase to profit from the building of the military power of the Soviet Union.

Kissinger's personal role can be gleaned from documents leaked to columnist Jack Anderson, which read in part:

"At the time (1972) some officials, including then Secretary of Defense, Melvin Laird, voiced concern that the Russians might use the central Asian truck plant the biggest in the world - to produce military equipment."[9]

Kissinger brushed the misgivings aside. A confidential Commerce Department memorandum states that in 1971 **Kissinger** "ordered the Secretary of Commerce to grant three pending applications" for construction of the Soviet plant.[10] Another secret memo set the final value of US-licensed equipment and technology at $1.5 billion. Others notably our Western European allies - were not so sure. On March 20, 1975, **Kissinger** cabled US officials in Paris on the best way to quiet such doubts. "Kama trucks are not tactical military vehicles with cross- country capabilities," the secret cable said. "Some may ultimately be outfitted with front-wheel drive for muddy or icy environment. However, trucks will not be equipped for deep fording or have other features typical of military models." **Kissinger's** cable concluded that "we see little likelihood of diversion to military uses"[12] even though there was ample evidence on file in Washington that diversion to military uses would be made.

THE TRILATERAL VIEW OF COMMUNISM

In the light of the above material it becomes critical to know the Trilateral opinion of Communism.

In *Triangle Paper No. 13, Collaboration with Communist Countries in Managing Global Problems: an Examination of the Options,* we find the Trilateral view of cooperation with Communist countries.

The objective for making the report was prompted "by a desire to exploit any opportunities with the Communist countries for cooperative management of certain international problems".[13] The report did not have the objective of finding if such "cooperative management" would be advantageous to the United States or if it would enhance or reduce the security of the United States or whether it would lead to a more peaceful world. The objective *assumes* that "cooperative management" with Communist countries would be advantageous and beneficial to the United States.

On the questions of whether such cooperation would strengthen the Soviet Union, the report makes statements flatly inconsistent with well- documented fact. For example: "Some analysts have expressed concern about the consequences that are likely to flow from successful East- West collaboration in strengthening the economic capacity and therefore the international power of the Soviet Union."[14]

To which question the report answers, "These consequences are likely to be limited."[15]

ESTABLISHMENT COVER UP

Today the massive contribution of the Eastern Establishment to Soviet military development is widely known. It can no longer be suppressed as it was in the early 1970's.

Since previously "well-kept secrets" have leaked out, the new tactic is to mislead the American public into believing that it was an innocent mistake on the part of Washington policy makers. Specifically, when Jim Gallagher in the *Chicago Tribune* cites the Bryant Grinder case (precision ball bearing grinding machines were supplied to the Soviets and these machines assisted and enabled Soviet development of a family of MIRV nuclear missiles with multiple war heads) and cases where electronic equipment was converted for use in missile guidance systems he says, "In both of these cases the Soviets were able to overcome serious gaps in technology with the inadvertent assistance of the United States."[16]

"Inadvertent," indeed! Many credible and acknowledged experts were vocal in the early 1970's concerning these precise shipments and identified the exact military end uses. At the Republican Convention in Miami Beach (1972) the co-author (Sutton) explained at length how such shipments would be used by the Soviets. The shipments were not inadvertent: they were deliberate and made with the full forewarning of military end uses. In the past, warnings of the possible consequences of technological aid to the Soviets have fallen on "tuned-out" ears. As the criticism became more adamant, specific attempts were made to silence it.

So we can conclude:

1. The military build-up the Soviet Union by *some* "American" multinationals through technological transfers goes back 60 years, and today is centered in the Trilaterally represented companies.

2. The blame lies almost entirely with a few international banks and big business interests. Most important among them are Chase National (now Chase Manhattan) and the Rockefeller- influenced General Electric and RCA complexes.

3. Warnings of the expansion of the capabilities of the Soviet military inevitably resulting from American technological aid have either been ignored, suppressed or those daring to criticize have been vilified.

4. These elitist interests are the prime source of virtually every major crisis facing the United States today. Their greed and shortsightedness has placed the United States in the most precarious position in its entire history.

DAVID ROCKEFELLER AND SOVIET MILITARY POWER

There is no question that Trilaterals - David Rockefeller included - have been stung by repeated strong and widespread criticism of the Trilateral Commission.

At a 1980 World Affairs Council luncheon in Los Angeles, **Rockefeller** voiced concern that "Misrepresenting the motives of good and dedicated people will only narrow instead of broaden participation in the group's discussion of international affairs."[17]

Rockefeller specifically and at length denied that Trilateral multinationals deal with the Soviet Union for "the sake of financial gain." The *Wall Street Journal* excerpts from the Los Angeles speech boxed this **Rockefeller** comment to emphasize its importance:

> *"To some extremists, the Trilateral Commission is pictured as a nefarious plot by an Eastern Establishment of businessmen in the service of multinational corporations who will do almost anything including going into cahoots with the Kremlin for the sake of financial gain.* "[18]

These are strong words. The use of buzz words such as "extremists" and "nefarious" suggests an attempt is under way to cover facts with diversionary tactics.

The weak position of Trilaterals in general is reflected in their treatment of objective, factual criticism. The usual Trilateral response to *any* criticism, whether valid or not, is to label it "extremism." The critic is immediately tagged either "far right" or "far left" or, if the facts are too accurate for comfort, the critic is merely ignored.

David Rockefeller argued further:

> *"Far from being a coterie of international conspirators with designs on covertly ruling the world, the Trilateral Commission - like the Los Angeles World Affair Council - is, in reality, a group of concerned citizens interested in fostering greater understanding and cooperation among international allies.* "[19]

Examine the facts above and compare them to the **Rockefeller** rhetoric. The co-author (Sutton) has written five books since 1968 on the build-up of the Soviet Union by Western capitalists. Three of the books are academic in nature, published by the Hoover Institution at Stanford University. No one, including **David**

Rockefeller and **David Packard,** has denied the factual basis of these books. The Soviets have also remained silent. They know the facts are accurate. Moreover, Commissioner **David Packard,** a Trustee of the Hoover Institution, is well aware of the Stanford books. Hoover Institution financed part of the research and in the early 1970's **Packard** was personally involved with suppressing those parts that dealt with the build-up of Soviet military power.

ENDNOTES

1. British War Cabinet Papers, 24/49/7197 Secret, April 24, 1918.
2. Ibid.
3. Antony Sutton, *Western Technology and Soviet Economic Development 19/7 to 1930,* p. 290.
4. *Soviet Union Vital Goods Still Flow Despite Carter's Curbs,* BusinessWeek, April 28, 1980, p. 42.
5. Ibid.
6. W.A. Johnson, *Daily News Digest,* July 4,1980.
7. Antony Sutton and Patrick Wood, *Influence of the Trilateral Commission-Part I,* Trilateral Observer, Vol. 2 No.3 (March 1979), p. 20. Trilateral Observer, P.O. Box 582, Scottsdale, AZ 85252.
8. *Nomination of Nelson A. Rockefeller of New York To Be Vice President of the United States,* Hearings before the Committee on Rules and Administration of the United States Senate. 93rd Congress 2nd Session September 23, 1974), p.883.
9. Jack Anderson, U.P., February 8,1980.
10. Ibid.
11. Ibid.
12. Ibid.
13. Chihiro Hosoya et ai, *Collaboration with Communist Countries* in *Managing Global Problems,* p. I.
14. Ibid. 15.
15. Ibid.
16. 16. Jim Gallagher, *Bryant Grinder Case,* Chicago Tribune, April 6, 1980. 17. *Letters to the Editor,* Wall Street Journal (April 30, 1980).
17. Ibid.
18. Ibid.

CHAPTER FIVE

ELITIST FRIENDS OF TRILATERALISM

We have previously discussed the power and membership of the Trilateral Commission, and we now need to discuss the use of this power and the influence of the Commission in a broader framework of associated elitist institutions. The Trilateral Commission does not exist in a political vacuum; it co-exists with a group of organizations which have, since about 1920, effectively taken over political power in the United States, dominated domestic and foreign policy and presently appears to be totally unrepresentative of American society as a whole.

In addition to the influence of the Trilateral Commission we have:

- The Council on Foreign Relations
- The Foreign Policy Association
- The Atlantic Council
- The Commission on Critical Choices for Americans

Together with think tanks such as Brookings Institute and Hoover Institution, these organizations constitute the source of foreign and domestic policy making in the United States. This is where ideas are generated, policies discussed, and subsequent reports written. Ideas, policies and reports are subsequently considered and discussed by all interested members of the above organizations and sooner or later a large proportion of the proposals find their way into executive decisions and/or Congressional legislation.

The overriding characteristic of this procedure is one of intellectual closed-mindedness - intellectual incest might be the best way to describe these policy creating "backwaters."

The dismal failure to create a prosperous and peaceful world during the decades-long era of American supremacy is obvious.

THE COUNCIL ON FOREIGN RELATIONS

Founded after World War I, the Council on Foreign Relations (CFR) has been for fifty years the undisputed creator of American foreign policy.

As far back as 1959 the CFR was explicit about a need for world government:

> "The U.S. must strive to build a new international order... including states labeling themselves as 'socialist'... to maintain and gradually increase the authority of the United Nations."[1]

The site for UN headquarters in New York was donated by John D. Rockefeller, Sr., and the CFR world architects for many years tried to use the United Nations as a means to develop an image of world order. Recently the focus of world order action has shifted to the Trilateral Commission, and CFR members have complained they have lost power and prestige. *"We don't have the cutting edge we once had. We're not really in the center of things,"* stated one CFR member.[2]

The problem with the CFR is that it became too large and too diverse to act as a "cutting edge" in policy creation. With several thousand members and an internal policy of bringing in membership from a diverse geographical and racial standpoint, the CFR lost its foreign affairs expertise and prestige. Today the political action has moved from the CFR to the Trilateral Commission, as aptly described by *Newsweek:*

> "Since the end of World War II U.S. foreign policy has been dominated largely by the circle of influential men who belong to New York's Council on Foreign Relations. From Franklin

D. Roosevelt to Jimmy Carter, every President has recruited council luminaries - its membership roll is a sort of Who's Who of the Eastern Establishment elite - for high level diplomatic trouble-shooting missions or for top jobs in his Administration. But the council is not universally admired. Some outsiders view it as a kind of shadow government; others dismiss it as a private club where aging foreign-policy mandarins pontificate over tea and cookies. Both views are exaggerated, but of late even some of the council's elders have grown alarmed by a sense of their organization's waning influence. The result has been a genteel furor within the book- lined confines of the council's four-story headquarters on Park Avenue."[3]

THE FOREIGN POLICY ASSOCIATION

Founded in 1918 a little before the CFR, the Foreign Policy Association (FPA) is a tax exempt educational organization supposedly to inform citizens on "challenges and problems of the United States foreign policy."[4] The FPA is purely an elitist organization. Out of fifty-six board members no fewer than twenty-nine (fifty-two percent) are members of the Council on Foreign Relations.

However, only one FPA member, **Robert R. Bowie**, is a Trilateral Commissioner, so the interlock with Trilateralism is minor.

THE ATLANTIC COUNCIL OF THE UNITED STATES

The board of directors of the Atlantic Institute is comprised as follows:

Chairman: Kenneth Rush, former Deputy Secretary of State and Ambassador to France and Germany.

Vice Chairman: Henry H. Fowler, partner, Goldman Sachs & Co. and former Secretary of the Treasury.

W. Randolph Burgess, former Under Secretary of the Treasury and Ambassador to NATO and the OEEC.

Theodore C. Achilles, former Counselor of the State Department and Ambassador to Peru.

Harlan Cleveland, director, Aspen Program in International Affairs, and former Ambassador to NATO.

Emilio G. *Collado,* former executive vice-president, Exxon Corporation and executive director, World Bank.

Andrew J. Goodpastor, former Supreme Allied Commander Europe.

Wm. McChesney Martin, former chairman, Board of Governors, Federal Reserve System.

David Packard, chairman, Hewlett-Packard Company, and former Deputy Secretary of Defense.

Eugene V. Rostow, professor of law, Yale University, and former Under Secretary of State.

The chairman of the Atlantic Council, Kenneth Rush, was formerly of Union Carbide Corporation. He is remembered for his actively vocal role in aiding transfer of technology with military capabilities to the Soviet Union. Union Carbide is part of the "revolving door" between Washington and the New York elite.

A vice-chairman of the Atlantic Council is **David Packard**, a prominent supporter of subsidization of the Soviet Union.

A comparison of the general directors of the Atlantic Council (not on the board) compared to the Trilateral Commission is significant.

The following 11 Atlantic Council directors are also Trilateral Commissioners.

David Packard	Vice-chairman of Atlantic Council
David M. Abshire	Director, Atlantic Council
Anne Armstrong	Former US Ambassador
Sol C. Chaikin	Trade unionist
George Franklin, Jr.	Coordinator of Trilateral Commission
Thomas L. Hughes	President, Carnegie Endowment
Henry A. Kissinger	Exec. board, Trilateral Commission

Winston Lord	Chairman, Council on Foreign Relations
Charles W. Robinson	Under Secretary of State
Robert V. Roosa	Brown Brothers, Harriman
Philip H. Trezise	Former Assistant Secretary of State
Marina v.N. Whitman	Vice-president of General Motors

Also, **George Ball** is an honorary director of The Atlantic Council. What are the objectives of the Atlantic Council? In its own words:

"The Atlantic Council, established seventeen years ago, seeks to promote closer mutually advantageous ties between Western Europe, North America, Japan, Australia and New Zealand. The objective is greater security and more effective harmonization of economic, monetary, energy and resource policies for the benefit of the individual in his personal, business, financial and other relations across national boundaries."[6]

Then comes a key phrase:

"In an increasingly interdependent world where 'foreign' policy is ever more closely intertwined with 'domestic' policies there is a clear need for both official and private consideration of means of dealing with problems which transcend national frontiers."[7]

Note the assumption of an "increasingly interdependent world." By placing "foreign" and "domestic" in quotes, Atlanticists are clearing the way to destroy the distinction between foreign and domestic policies, a vital step in the road to a unified world under elitist control.[8]

THE COMMISSION ON CRITICAL CHOICES FOR AMERICANS

In its own words,

"The Commission on Critical Choices for Americans is a nationally representative, bipartisan group of 42 prominent Americans, brought together under the chairmanship of

Nelson A. Rockefeller. Their assignment: To identify the critical choices which will confront America as it embarks on its third century as a nation and to determine the realistic and desirable objectives this nation can achieve by 1985 and the year 2000.

"Because of the complexity and interdependence of issues facing the world today, the Commission organized its work into six study panels, which emphasize the interrelationships of the critical choices rather than studying each one separately.

"The six study panels are:

Panel I -- Energy and Its Relationship to Ecology: Economics and World Stability.

Panel II -- Food, Health, World Population and Quality of Life.

Panel III -- Raw Materials, Industrial Development, Capital Formation, Employment and World Trade.

Panel IV -- International Trade and Monetary Systems, Inflation and the Relationships Among Differing Economics Systems.

Panel V -- Change, National Security and Peace, and Panel VI -- Quality of Life of Individuals and Communities in the U.S.A."[9]

In brief, the Commission is a **Rockefeller** study group funded by a **Rockefeller** organization:

"The Third Century Corporation, a New York not for-profit organization, was created to finance the work of the Commission. Since the start of its activities in the fall of 1973, the Corporation has received contributions and pledges from individuals and from foundations well-known for their support of public interest activities. "[10]

The membership of the Commission reflects this **Rockefeller** influence:

MEMBERS OF THE COMMISSION ON CRITICAL
CHOICES FOR AMERICANS

Chairman - Nelson E. Rockefeller *Executive Director* -
Henry L Diamond

Members Ex-Officio
- Gerald R. Ford
- **Henry A. Kissinger**
- **George P. Shultz**
- Mike Mansfield
- Hugh Scott
- Thomas P. O'Neill, Jr.
- John J. Rhodes

Members
- Ivan Allen, Jr.
- Martin Anderson
- **Robert O. Anderson**
- William O. Baker
- Daniel J. Boorstin
- Norman E. Borlaug
- Ernest L. Boyer
- Guido Calabresi
- John S. Foster, Jr.
- Luther H. Foster
- Nancy Hanks Kissinger
- Belton Kleberg Johnson
- Clarence B. Jones
- **Joseph Lane Kirkland**
- John H. Knowles, M.D.
- David S. Landes
- Mary Wells Lawrence
- **Sol M. Linowitz**
- Edward J. Logue

- Clare Boothe Luce
- Paul W. McCracken
- Daniel Patrick Moynihan
- Bess Myerson
- William S. Paley
- Russell W. Peterson
- Wilson Riles
- Laurence S. Rockefeller
- William J. Ronan
- Oscar M. Ruebhausen
- Joseph C. Swidler
- Edward Teller
- **Marina v.N. Whitman**
- Carroll L. Wilson
- George D. Woods

Of the above members an unusual number received personal gifts from Nelson Rockefeller and were consequently under some obligation to the Rockefeller family. We know of the following cases:

- **Henry A. Kissinger**. Received a $50,000.00 gift in January 1969.
- Nancy Hanks. Later married to **Henry A. Kissinger**.
- Edwin J. Logue. In 1968 received a gift of $31,389 followed by another $145,000 of which $45,000 was repaid.
- William J. Ronan. Received a gift of $75,000 in 1958 and $550,000 in 1974.
- Henry L. Diamond. Executive Director of the Commission, received a gift of $100,000 in December 1973. [11]
-

ELITIST CONTROL OF U.S. POLICY MAKING

To identify precisely elitist control over independent policy research organizations, we compared the membership of the Atlantic Council, the Council on Foreign Relations, the Trilateral Commission and the Commission on Critical Choices for Americans to find out how many members of one organization served with other organizations. (the Foreign Policy Association appears to be a special case which we will note only briefly.)

We grouped the interlocks into three categories: *Quadruple, Triple* and *Double Hats* - depending upon his/her membership in these organizations.

QUADRUPLE HATS

The Rockefeller family is represented directly in all four organizations, and also indirectly, as will be discussed later.

David Rockefeller is chairman of both the Trilateral Commission and the Council on Foreign Relations. The late Nelson Rockefeller was an honorary director of the Atlantic Council and created the Commission on Critical Choices for Americans. In addition, Laurence Rockefeller served on the Commission on Critical Choices.

In brief, there is direct, at-the-top **Rockefeller** family participation in all four organizations. Logically, these organizations do not reflect American society as a whole, but presumably those interests represented by the **Rockefeller** family - whatever those interests might be.

This extraordinary influence cannot be denied except by some intellectually dishonest mind "blank." Those researchers and journalists who choose to ignore this unparalleled influence over domestic and foreign policy making need to reconsider their basic moral position.

Without doubt, the influence of the **Rockefeller** family on US policy making is now and has been for many decades a topic demanding urgent and thorough investigation.

Apart from the **Rockefeller** family, the most notable "quadruple hat" is that of **Henry Kissinger.** Let's briefly look at the

Kissinger- Rockefeller ties:

- In 1955, **Kissinger,** then an obscure Harvard professor, was chosen to head the Rockefeller Brothers Fund. Objective? To develop studies to formulate American foreign policy for the 1960's. An ambitious and farsighted project; however, we are unable to determine what constitutional or moral sanction gave the **Rockefeller** family the right to determine US policy.

- Nelson Rockefeller has described **Kissinger** as a "close personal friend and associate for more than eighteen years." (1974).

- In January 1969, **Kissinger** resigned as a personal foreign policy consultant to Nelson Rockefeller and became assistant to President Nixon for national security affairs. Nelson Rockefeller presented **Kissinger** with a gift of

- $50,000 at that time. The gift was made in Rockefeller's own words as a token of "my affection and appreciation."

- The amount paid by Nelson Rockefeller to **Kissinger** over the period 1958 to 1968 is a matter of public record. These amounts are not unsubstantial:

1958	$3,000	1959	$7,000
1960	12,000	1961	12,000
1962	12,000	1963	14,000
1964	18,000	1965	11,250
1966	9,000	1967	15,500
1968	28,000	1969	50,000
(The last gift was on joining President Nixon.)			

The official report notes that these payments were for work "done for the family rather than on a consulting basis through any governmental agency."[12]

In summary, quadruple hat **Kissinger** can without prejudice be described as a hired intellectual servant of the **Rockefeller** family.

TRIPLE HATS

When we come to look at triple hats, we notice at least two interesting facts: 1) There are seven triple hats, compared to only three quadruple hats and 2) with minor exceptions, these triple hats have a Rockefeller or international banking association.

The triple hats that sit on the Trilateral Commission, Council on Foreign Relations and the Atlantic Council include: **George S. Franklin, Winston Lord, Robert Roosa, George Ball, Thomas L. Hughes, Charles W. Robinson** and **Philip Trezise**.

George S. Franklin was formerly coordinator of the Atlantic Council, executive director of the Council on Foreign Relations and is presently coordinator of the Trilateral Commission. Thus, in one pair of hands, there is concentrated the executive power, wielded by the secretary of a committee of three policymaking organizations. Since the Committee on Critical Choices was a temporary organization, there was no coordinating required and presumably no requirement for **George Franklin's** talents.

Winston Lord is president of the Council on Foreign Relations (**David Rockefeller** is chairman), a director of the Atlantic Council and a Trilateral Commissioner.

Robert Roosa is a trustee of the Rockefeller Foundation and shuttles between a partnership in Brown Brothers, Harriman (Harriman is prominent in the military buildup of the Soviet Union through US technology) and sub-cabinet posts in Washington.

George Ball is a partner in another international Wall Street banking firm - Lehman Brothers - and a long time shuttler between Washington political and banking circles.

The remaining triple hat is **Marina v. Neumann Whitman**, a former professor of economics at the University of Pittsburgh and recently a vice president at General Motors.

Apart from virtually unknown **Whitman**, the Rockefeller interests are the *only* individual interests represented on all four policy-making bodies.

We might ask how the impressive investigative powers of *The Washington Post* and the *New York Times* managed to miss such an obvious conflict of interest; or, for that matter, we might ask the same question about the *Conservative Digest.*

DOUBLE HATS

When we get to double hats, the extraordinary overlap among these organizations is identified. No less than sixty-five percent of the directors of the Atlantic Council are also members of the CFR, including its chairman Kenneth Rush, a key supporter of aid to the

Soviet Union - and all seven vice-presidents except for **David Packard**, who is a double hat on the Trilateral Commission and CFR.)

Out of eighty-two directors of the Atlantic Council, no fewer than fifty-three members of the CFR and out of twenty-four honorary directors, fourteen are also members of the CFR. That gives us a total of seventy-four members out of a total of one hundred fourteen Atlantic Council directors.

Name of Member	Atlantic Council	Council on Foreign Relations	Trilateral Commission	Commission on Critical Choices
David Abshire	X		X	
Anne Armstrong	X		X	
George Ball	X	X	X	
Sol Chaikin	X		X	
George Franklin	X	X	X	
Thomas Hughes	X	X	X	
Henry Kissinger	X	X	X	X
Winston Lord	X	X	X	
David Packard	X		X	
Charles Robinson	X	X	X	
Nelson Rockefeller	X	X		X
Robert Roosa	X	X	X	

Philip Trezise	X	X	X	
Marina v.N. Whit-man	X	X	X	X

The interlock that will interest most readers is that between the traditional elitist foreign policy base (CFR) and the newer elitist vehicle, the Trilateral Commission. The authors compared the 1977-78 CRR and the 1978 Trilateral Commission membership lists.

The highlights of the interlock are as follows:

- Out of ninety-one North American Trilateral Commissioners, forty-eight (fifty-three percent) are members of the CFR. (Remember this also includes Canadian Commissioners, so the purely US figure is closer to sixty percent.)

- When we come to the category "Former Members in Public Service," the percentage is almost unbelievable. Of eighteen Commissioners who served in Washington in the Carter administration, fifteen were members of the CFR - This is eighty-three per cent!

The three Trilateral Commissioners *not* members of CFR but who were in Washington are **Jimmy Carter**, **Walter Mondale** and **Lucy Wilson Benson**, who later became US Under-Secretary of State.

In conclusion, we can readily see the tremendous overlap in membership and control of these important policy-making organizations.

ENDNOTES

1. Study No. Seven, quoted in *Organization* #11, Network *of* Patriotic Letter writers.
2. New York Times, November 21,1971, p. 2 co!. 1.
3. Angus Deming and Tony Fuller, *Foreign Policy: Mandarins in Trouble.* Newsweek, March 28, 1977.
4. Whitney H. Shepardson, *Early History of the Council on Foreign Relations.* p.8.
5. See information contained in footnote number 8.
6. Ibid.
7. Ibid.
8. For further information, contact The Atlantic Council of the United States, 1616 H Street, NW, Washington, DC *20006* and *Report on the Foreign Policy Association*
9. Helen Kitchen, *Africa: From Mystery To Maze.* Critical Choices for Americans, Volume XI, pp v-vi.
10. Ibid.
11. Ibid.

Chapter Six:

Tilateral Foreign Policy and Human Rights

Trilateral foreign policy as it was implemented in the **Carter** administration appeared to be intent on donating American assets and enterprises to the Marxist world as rapidly as public awareness will allow. This observation is not limited to this author. In fact, Vermont Royster writing in *The Wall Street Journal* made a new high for that publication, which is normally subservient to Trilateral ambitions; Royster commented on the new **Carter** agreement with Communist China:

> "The Carter administration has agreed to normalization of relations with the People's Republic - i.e., full diplomatic recognition - on terms no different from those the Chinese would have welcomed at any time since 1972.

> "Moreover, we suddenly accepted the Chinese terms, previously rejected by Presidents Nixon and Ford, not because of any new necessity for the U.S. to normalize those relations at this time. The U.S. could have continued the existing relationship, awkward though it was, almost indefinitely without any injury to our national interests.

"Instead we simply accepted every condition the People's Republic has demanded all along, including a formal acceptance by us, without any qualification, of the People's Republic claim that Taiwan is an integral part of Mainland China."[1]

In short, we have one more example of the American proclivity to think that reaching an agreement is somehow more important than what's in the agreement.

Moreover, this inclination toward giving everything away is seen by Trilaterals as an imperative. Witness **Zbigniew Brzezinski** writing at the time of the Communist China debacle:

"And, last but not least, we have to accommodate very broadly with the People's Republic of China. It represents one-fourth of humanity, and as extremely gifted and creative segment of humanity, with whom we have many common interests. These interests are long-term, not tactically anti-Soviet; they are much more connected with our fundamental view of a world of diversity and not a world dominated by this or that power.[2]

THE U.S. - COMMUNIST CHINA AGREEMENT

The Carter administration agreement with Communist China, the so-called normalization of relations, was an extraordinary treaty. All the Chinese terms, including those rejected by Presidents Nixon and Ford, were totally accepted in the Trilateral negotiations (the negotiators were all Trilaterals). On the spot in Peking was **Leonard Woodcock**. In Washington were **Cyrus Vance** and **Warren Christopher** (Under Secretary of State for East Asian and Pacific Affairs.)

There was no pressure to make an agreement at this time from the strategic or political viewpoint - so we must look to the multinationals for an answer. What do they gain? Is the China treaty a duplicate of the early 1920-30 Soviet agreement? A device to fill multinational order books and expand the loan base of international banks?

The United States was in an extremely strong bargaining position. The Chinese need US technology to survive and US credits to buy technology. They need the US as an ally against Russian intrusions over the Chinese border and recognition by the US gives the Chinese Communists a status they can achieve in no other way.

Yet the United States capitulated without a whimper, very much like the Vietnamese situation when the US got sucked into a major war without plan or purpose where some 50,000 Americans were killed. The battlefield was abandoned at a time when America still had the absolute capability to finish the military job. In other words, we apparently did not know why we were in Vietnam in the first place. When we were involved, we spent billions on war materials and even then lacked the will to use those weapons.

In this instance and others we can find a common thread, a common explanation. In science, the answer that most likely is true, is that answer which fits the largest number of cases or events. Is there profit for Wall Street in recognizing Communist China? Was there also profit in $300 billion of Vietnamese military contracts? In the same way, there was profit in saving the Soviets and building the Soviet Five-Year Plans in the 1930's?

This is the simplest, most plausible answer. It fits the greatest number of cases - and this is where Trilateralism comes in. Trilateralism is the vehicle by which *some* banking interests and multinationals carry out their policy objectives.

The Trilateral opening to Communist China also reveals a total failure to recognize the human cost of Chinese Communism: 200 million Chinese dead in the thirty years of the Revolution. During one particular campaign, *Let a Million Flowers Bloom,* Chinese Communists lifted their restrictions on freedom of speech and action. Many Chinese then took the bait to criticize the regime. After a few months of freedom of speech the Chinese government promptly arrested the dissidents and used their own words as evidence to send them to labor camps, prisons, or to their death.

Internationalist businessmen are adept at telling each other how non- political and smart they are to ignore civil and social conditions while concentrating on the business at hand. The profit statement is the guide: hard-core amorality.

The dangerous illusions Trilaterals hold about Russia and China do not therefore stem from ignorance of the facts - their actions stem from extreme shortsightedness and amorality. An upcoming contract for a multinational corporation has total precedence over any nonsense about human rights. While, for example, Trilateral **J. Paul Austin**[3] may want to sell Coca-Cola to 800 million Chinese, Austin seems to have little interest in what happened to tens of millions of the less fortunate Chinese.

The outright betrayal of Taiwan in the clear, stark words of the official agreement reads as follows:

> *"The government of the United States of America acknowledges the Chinese position that there is but one China, and Taiwan is part of China."*[4]

It is difficult to find any historical parallel where a country has acknowledged the slaughter of 200 million people by creating an alliance with that country. Possibly the closest parallel is Hitler's alliance with Stalin in 1939 after Stalin had murdered millions of peasants and Hitler had begun to move against his enemies.

For Trilaterals, human rights are subordinate to their objective of world control. Witness the following statement:

> *"...the support for human rights will have to be balanced against other important goals of world order. Some Trilateral conceptions of detente with the Soviet Union and other communist states tend to conflict with a policy promoting human rights."*[5]

The drive to open up Communist China as a captive market for globalist corporations has its parallel in the early days of the Soviet Union.

THE HISTORICAL PARALLEL

Many of the same companies now in China (some have since changed their names or merged with other companies) were equally responsible for rescuing the infant and collapsing Soviet Russia in 1922. In the early 1920's the Soviet Union was on the verge of collapse. The only industrial structure was that of the Czars. Industry was dormant, not destroyed as Soviet propagandists would have us believe. Foreign firms, mainly American and German, came in to start up the sleeping Czarist industry and remained to build the Five-Year Plans. Why? Because the Soviets had killed or dispersed the skilled engineers and managers needed to run industry. As Soviet Commissar Krassif phrased the problem:

"Anyone can help pull down a house; there are but a few who can rebuild. In Russia there happened to be far fewer than anywhere else."[6]

Communist China today is in the same situation as Soviet Russia in the 1920's. To quote a recent statement by Chaing Ching-Kuo of Taiwan:

"The Chinese Communists are on the verge of collapse at this moment. The United States' establishment of relations with the Communist is to help save a bandit regime that massacres millions and millions of compatriots. Therefore, America is the biggest sinner in history. "[7]

The same multinationals that built the Soviet Union into a vast military power are now doing the same with Communist China. China suffers from widespread electricity shortages and has had to buy Westinghouse-engineered nuclear reactors from France. The iron and steel industry is backward and inefficient. Planned increases are based on use of Western technology, as were the Soviets' in the early 1920's and 1930's. The following table illustrates how American firms involved in the USSR - even before establishment of diplomatic relations - have also been negotiating with Communist China, and in some cases, like Coca-Cola, well before the establishment of diplomatic relations.

	Soviet Russia 1920-1930	Communist China 1978
Ingersoll-Rand	Represented by Armand Hammer from about 1918 onwards	Dec. 1978 order for 2 large water well drills for $1 million
Boeing Aircraft	Technical assistance	Sales of 4 jumbo jets 747-SP
Universal Oil Products	1938 contract for hydrogenation and iso-octane plants.	Petrochemical plants

Take the example of Boeing Aircraft (**T .A. Wilson** is chairman of the board). In the 1930's Boeing supplied technical assistance to the growing Soviets. The Soviet I-16 fighter was patterned on the Boeing P-26. The Soviet TU-4 four-engine bomber was a copy of the Boeing B-29 and could only have been reproduced with US assistance. Boeing is now selling to Communist China.

Another example is UOP (Universal Oil Products), now a subsidiary of Signal Oil Company. In the 1930s UOP had contracts in the USSR for construction of hydrogenation plants, which were of vital importance for military purposes. Up to 1938 the Soviets were unable to produce 87-94 octane gasoline for aviation use. Hydrogenation plants built by UOP converted 85 octane gasoline from the Saratov and Grozny refineries into 95 octane avgas. Currently, UOP is one of the first American firms in China to develop petrochemical industry - also vital for war purposes.

Yet another example is Ingersoll-Rand which was represented in the Soviet Union by Armand Hammer (now chairman of Occidental Petroleum Corporation) as early as 1918. At that time Armand Hammer's father, Julius Hammer, was secretary of the Communist Party USA. Ingersoll-Rand became a prime seller of technology to the USSR. In 1979, Ingersoll Rand is following the same road with Communist China.

Dozens of firms can be cited with similar stories. As previously noted, US multinationals built Soviet power. This has cost the United States hundreds of thousands of lives in Korea and Vietnam. Now these same multinationals have begun to build Communist China. The following table demonstrates the widespread fundamental nature of the early Chinese contracts. Apart from Coca-Cola, they involve advanced technology with outright military application.

US Firm	Work in Communist China	Comments
Coca-Cola	Monopoly of soft drinks	Chairman J. Paul, was prime Atlanta backer of Jimmy Carter.
Control Data	12 CDC Cyber computers	$69 million
U.S. Steel	One of the world's largest ore mines	Probably over $1 billion. **Packard** and **Shepard** are directors.
Pullman,Inc Hercules, Inc UOC	Petrochemical facilities	Multimillion dollar
Mitsui Petro Chemical	Four petrochemical plants	$205 million (**Ikeda** is chairman and a Trilateral)

US Firm	Work in Communist China	Comments
Boeing Aircraft	Three 747-SP Jumbos	$156 million (**Wilson** and **Weyerhaeuser** are directors)
LTV Corp.	Oil drilling equipment	$40 million

THE CHASE MANHATTAN BANK

Chase Manhattan was the first bank into Communist China and probably has the most to profit from its build-up. Back in the 1920's the forerunner of the Chase Manhattan Bank, Chase National Bank, was deeply involved in building the Soviets - some of this activity was called illegal and was certainly against US official policy.

Both Chase National and Equitable Trust were the leaders in the Soviet credit business at a time when the State Department had specifically banned credits to Soviet Russia. Chase evaded the ban by accepting platinum from Soviet mines and advancing credit on the basis of these shipments. Again, this was strictly against US policy in the 1920's.

The president of the American-Russian Chamber of Commerce in the 1920's was Reeve Schley, also a vice-president of Chase National. The Chamber was a pressure group which sought to change US policy into recognition of the USSR and open up the Russian market for some major American firms and banks. To this end, the Chamber used known Communists as agents; for example, a Chamber delegation to Russia in 1936 was lead by Charles Haddell Smith, previously described by the State Department as "in the employ of the Soviets and a member of the Soviet Peasant International."[8] Members of the Chamber in the 1920's included many of the firms opening up the China trade today, including Deere & Co., Westinghouse and Chase National.

THE NEW CHINA POLICY IS A TRILATERAL POLICY

- Some major important China contracts link to Trilateralists and their corporate affiliates are:
- The key financial backer of **Jimmy Carter** was Coca Cola chairman and Trilateral Commissioner **J. Paul Austin**,

Coca-Cola will have a soft drink monopoly in China.

- Maybe the Chinese don't yet know what a soft drink tastes like, but 800 million Chinese are prime market for the 21st century. Coca-Cola has been negotiating for ten years with the Chinese, i.e. long before any public surfacing of a "new" China policy and presumably while the Chinese aided the killing of Americans in Vietnam.

- A consortium of US oil companies in negotiating development of Chinese petroleum resources. These include Exxon (**David Rockefeller** has dominant interests), Pennzoil, Phillips and Union Oil.

- *Time* magazine Man-of-the-Year was the Chinese Communist leader, Teng Hsiao-Ping. Trilateralist **Hedley Donovan** was editor-in-chief of *Time*.

- The first American banks into China were Chase Manhattan and the First National Bank of Chicago.

- Japanese Trilaterals are heavily involved in construction of Communist China - as described below.

Trilateral policy on Communist China has been spelled out clearly. Trilateral-Chinese cooperation has been proposed in the following areas, but not limited to them:

1. Earthquake warning

2. Energy: Above all, it is emphasized that China's oil potential can only be exploited by developing the offshore reserves on the continental shelf. "This would probably require outside technology. US oil companies have shown interest in investing in continental shelf oil exploration. "[9]

In brief, Trilateral publications outlined the **Carter** administration policies were later and still are being followed.

JAPANESE TRILATERALS AND CHINA

Japanese members of the Trilateral Commission reflect the Japanese establishment to an extraordinary degree. This is significant because Japan is now in the forefront of building Communist China.

The breakdown of Japanese Trilaterals is as follows:

	Trilateral Commissioners	Executive Committee
Business	37	1
Banks	14	3
Education	13	2
Government	5	3
Media	2	0
Unions	2	0

The previous chairman of the Japanese Trilateral Executive Committee is **Chujiro Funjino**, chairman of the Mitsubishi Corporation. Mitsubishi has contracts in China including a large contract to modernize the Shanghai shipyards, the largest in Communist China.

Three Japanese banks are represented on the Executive Committee of the Trilateral Commission: The president of the Bank of Tokyo, **Yusuka Kashiwagi** is a former special advisor to the Minister of Finance, **Saburo Okita** is president of the Overseas Economic Cooperation Fund, and **Takeshi Watanabe** is chairman of Trident International Finance, Ltd., based in Hong Kong.

Former Japanese government officials comprise more than one-third of the executive committee: **Kiichi Miyazawa** is a Minister of State and Chinese Cabinet Secretary, **Ryuji Takeuchi** is advisor to the Minister for Foreign Affairs and a former ambassador to the United States and **Nobuhiko Ushiba** is also a former ambassador to the United States. Japanese trade unions have two representatives, **Kazuo Oikawa**, who is president of the Japan Telecommunications workers union and **Ichiro Shioji**, president of the Confederation of Japan Automobile workers union.

The opening up of Communist China is a vital Trilateral policy and Japanese Trilaterals are in the forefront of the rush for contracts:

- **Yoshizo Ikeda** is president of Mitsui & Co., which has numerous Chinese contracts. Mitsui Petrochemical Industries Ltd. is involved in construction of polyethylene plants.

- **Seiki Tozaki** is president of Itoh & Co., which is involved in trading contracts with Communist China.
- **Hirokichi Yoshiyama** is president of Hitachi Ltd. His firm has a $100 million contract to supply equipment for the Paoshan steelworks and will expand the Hungchi Shipyards at Luta.
- **Yoshihiro Inayama** is chairman of Nippon Steel which is also aiding development of the Communist steel industry, including a $3 billion steel plant just outside Shanghai.

In brief:

1. The current China policy is Trilateral policy.
2. The 1978 agreement was complete capitulation to Chinese Communist terms.
3. The only rational explanation for capitulation is that the power elite is focusing more on the contracts to be won than on the long-run strategic impact on our world.

THE CASE OF THE PANAMA CANAL

The Panama Canal Treaty handed over US property, bought and full payment made, many decades ago. The zone was under US sovereignty but handed over to a Marxist (Torrijos) regime.

Some 76% of America disapproved of the Panama treaties. Those Americans who supported the Treaties are usually described as either liberals who believe Panama is a "have not" nation more deserving of the Canal Zone or those who wish to ignore the fact of legal US ownership, although this ownership has been precisely documented to Congress.

In 1977, Congressman Robert K. Dornan identified a third group of treaty supporters - what Dornan called "the fast-money type of international banker." Dornan demonstrated that the Panama overseas debt required 39% of the Panamanian gross national product. Further, the Torrijos government was far from stable and the banks participating in this debt wanted to protect their investment. Consequently, the Panama Canal treaties gave Torrijos a much needed boost to keep his Marxist regime in power and keep the bank debt from default.

Here is an excerpt from Congressman Dornan's report to Congress:

> "The most visible and known of this third type are the fast-money type of international banker. The Torrijos dictatorship is up to its ears in debt to banks. The debt of the Torrijos regime has now reached such proportions that 39 percent of the Panama GNP repeat 39 percent - goes to debt servicing alone. This might not cause the extreme consternation in the banking circles that it does if it were a debt owed by a stable government. But the Torrijos regime is far from stable.
>
> The dictator was nearly ousted a few years ago by an abortive coup and there are few wagers on his staying in power long if the treaties are rejected by the Senate. And if he is not in power, the banks do not have much chance of getting their money.
>
> "Some Members of Congress and Americans are aware of the conflict of interests involved in some of the banks' support of the Panamanian treaties. They are aware of the Marine Midland connection through negotiator Sol Linowitz. But there are many other banks whose endorsement of the giveaway of the canal may be motivated by monetary interests. Unlike Marine Midland, they have been able to keep a lower profile. They are not generally known to be part of the banking group with a lucrative stake in the ratification of the treaties. "[10]

Dornan published a list of banks participating in the Torrijos debt and also pointed out that **Sol Linowitz**, the US negotiator, was a director of Marine Midland Bank that held part of two Panamanian loans - thus establishing clear conflict of interest for **Linowitz**.

The authors examined the list of banks (thirty-one for one loan and fourteen for another loan) publicized by Congressman Dornan and traced the Trilateral links to these participating banks. The results are truly astounding. There are only three hundred Trilateral Commissioners worldwide, of which about one-third are from Japan, one-third from Europe and one third from the United States, i.e., about 90 from each region. For the two Panamanian loans cited by Congressman Dornan we found:

1. No fewer than thirty-two Trilaterals are on the boards of the thirty-one banks participating in the Republic of Panama $115 million 10-year Eurodollar loan issued in 1972.

2. Also, fifteen Trilaterals were on the boards of fourteen banks participating in the Republic of Panama $20 million floating rate promissory note issued in 1972.

3. These links suggest conflict of interest on a gigantic scale, involving not only the Carter administration but the Japanese government and less importantly some European governments.

To quote Congressman Dornan again:

"But there is a third type of pro-treaty person whose motives should be impugned. These persons are well aware of the facts of the 1903 treaty and the importance of the canal to the security of the Western World. They do not endorse the treaty out of undue love of the Panamanian people or out of confusion -- they do so out of self-interest. They have something to gain from the giveaway of the American people's canal. [d1]

TRILATERAL ASSUALT ON HUMAN RIGHTS

Trilateral writings on human rights is notable for its paucity. No Trilateral Task Force Report has been devoted to the basic question of individual freedoms and survival in an age of ever-increasing government. On the contrary, Trilateral writing has focused on the rights and powers of governmental authority rather than the rights of the governed.

In the arena of public discussion and political maneuvering, some rather transparent lip service is given to human rights. Trilateralists and the Carter administration expressed a superficial "deep concern" for human rights and they convinced many that human rights are a fundamental objective of Trilateralism. For example, as proclaimed by Trilateral **Warren Christopher**, Deputy Under Secretary of State:

"The major accomplishment of the [President's human rights] policy is that we've helped to create a concern all around the world for basic human rights."[12]

We have to presume that **Warren Christopher** and the State Department public relations officials kept straight faces when they released that statement. In fact, nothing could be further from the truth. A few examples demolish **Warren Christopher**'s expression of concern.

PROPERTY RIGHTS SUBORDINATED

In October 1977, President **Carter** signed the Soviet version of the UN Universal Declaration of Human Rights. Seven previous Presidents had refused to sign the Declaration because it excludes *the right to own property.* Traditional American philosophy is that without property rights there can be no "human rights."

RUSSIAN CHRISTIANS AND THE US EMBASSY IN MOSCOW

For two years a group of seven Russian Christians have been isolated in the US Embassy in Moscow - the same State Department that **Warren Christopher** says has a concern for human rights. According to Associated Press:

"They pray, read their Bibles, beset by fears and doubts. On one side of the room a Russian barber loudly slurs them to customers and on the other side through an iron grilled window Soviet guards occasionally shout taunts. "[13]

Why are these Russian refugees slurred and taunted on US property? Because US Embassy officials want them to return to the Soviets, even though they have already been granted political asylum. Why? Because the **Carter** administration found the presence of these Russian Christians to be embarrassing. They are kept exposed to threats and taunts to "encourage" them to return to a Soviet prison rather than refuge in the US Embassy.

Comments Rev. Blakhoslav Hruby, director of the Research Center for Religion and Human Rights in Closed Societies:

"It's a real scandal...their refuge has become a prison... although there are thousands of worse cases of human rights

*violations in the world this one is particularly shameful be-
cause these people are suffering- and for so long - in U.S.
hands.* [14]

Hruby adds:

*"The fate of these gentle, courageous, but defenseless
Christians depends in a large part on how we in the West respond to their tragic predicament. There is no place for them
to turn and nowhere for them to go. America is their last hope.*

*"But the embassy seems more embarrassed by their presence
than concerned. They're being treated as expendable in the
name of so-called 'broader' diplomacy. But these are specific
human lives and they aren't being treated like human beings.*

*"Every week, embassy officials advise them to go, and they're
becoming terribly depressed and discouraged. Yet if they finally give up and decide to go because they're being made so
miserable, they'd be sent to Siberia to die of an 'accident'.* [15]

This was the situation in the US Embassy in Moscow while
Trilateralists **Carter** and **Christopher** pontificated to the world
about human rights. And at the beginning of the Reagan administration, those Russian Christians *still* remain in captivity!

Trilateral involvement in human rights is an exercise in double
standards. Some countries are criticized, some countries are not
- depending on political objectives.

The double standard on human rights necessitated by Trilateralist objectives, was vividly demonstrated in 1978 by State
Department spokesman John Trattner. The administration decided to return the Crown of St. Stephen to Communist Hungary
after safekeeping in the US since 1951. At a press conference,
Reed Irvine of *Accuracy in Media,* Washington, D.C., pinned the
administration to the wall on the double standard with dagger-
like questions:

*Irvine: The State Department is very much concerned with
representative government these days. They are concerned
in Rhodesia and South Africa. Are you at all concerned with
whether the government of Hungary is representative of the
people?*

Trattner: Our concern about representative government around the world does not also mean that we stand up here and make judgments from this podium as to the question you are asking here.

Irvine: I see. Could you tell us when the last free election was held in Hungary?

Trattner: I would have to go back and look at the history books. I don't really know.

Irvine: Has Janos Kadar ever submitted himself to a free election?

Trattner: I think what you ought to do is ask the Hungarians.

Irvine: You know that. You know he hasn't.

Trattner: Well, then, why do you ask the question?

Irvine: I wanted to get the State Department's view of why they feel that this government ...

Trattner: My answer is that from this podium we are not in the habit of making judgments on other people's governments however much we may have opinions about them and however much to you the answer may be obvious, or it may be obvious to you that I know what the answer is. On the record, up here, up here, I am not going to give an answer.

Irvine: You don't have opinions about representative governments in Rhodesia and South Africa?

Trattner: No, I am not saying that at all.

Irvine: You say you are returning the crown to the Hungarian people. You are returning it to the government, to Janos Kadar, who obviously doesn't represent the people, because he

has never submitted himself to an election. Therefore you are saying, it seems to me incorrectly, that the government of Hungary represents the people, and by this action you are indicating to everyone in the world that this government has your approbation.

Trattner: No, I would contest that strongly. I don't think I am making that kind of statement at all.

Irvine: Are we getting any quid pro quo for this? Are the Hungarians doing anything - relaxing any restraints on human rights in return for this action?

Trattner: There are many Hungarian-Americans who have been in touch with us who have suggested that we should seek some concessions from the Hungarian government in return for the crown. Others in the Hungarian-American community have told us that because of the unique significance of the crown to all Hungarians, they feel it would be inappropriate and disrespectful to a centuries-old tradition to trade the crown for anything of that kind could possibly have an equivalent or comparable significance. We agree with the latter point of view, and recognizing that we received the crown for safekeeping without any other conditions, we stated our willingness to the Hungarian government to return it in the same manner.

Irvine: Could you tell us why we didn't return it much earlier then?

Trattner: We have always said that the return of the crown would be done in the context of an improvement in relations bilaterally, and we feel that that point has been reached.

Irvine: Has there been some remarkable change in the last year that would have altered...?

Trattner: Yes, I can cite you a few things... The overall record of Hungary in implementing the Helinsinki Final Act has been among the best in the Warsaw Pact, although its performance still falls short of Western standards.

Irvine: How does it compare with South Africa?

Trattner: I am not in the business right now, at least, of making a comparison with South Africa for you.

Irvine: Do they have as much freedom of the press as South Africa?

Trattner: I can't make a comparison for you.

Irvine: Do they have any freedom of the press? Are there any

*free newspapers in Hungary that are not run by the govern-
ment?*

Trattner: I really don't know.

Irvine: Could you find out?

Trattner: It might be possible to find out, yes [16]

For those readers who may not know the answers evaded by
the State Department, the Hungarian press is *totally* controlled
by the Hungarian government, and no opposition newspapers or
publications are allowed. South Africa, on the other hand, has one
of the most vocal and critical presses in the world: read a few
issues of the *Rand Daily Mail* or the *Cape Times* and this point is
made amply clear.

IDI AMIN AND TRILATERALISM

Remember Idi Amin, the Ugandan leader, who systematically
butchered his own population?

Far from Trilateral protests over Amin's butchery we find official US government support, as reported by Jack Anderson:

*"With great show of disapproval, the U.S. cut off Amin's
foreign aid in 1973. Yet he flies around in grand style in a
Grumman Gulfstream jet that is serviced every year at the
company plant in Savannah. Georgia Page Airways, another
American company, has provided flight crews to maintain
Amin's imperial plane.*

*We reported last fall that still another American company,
Bell Helicopter, was training 20 police pilots at Fort Worth.
They now operate at least nine Bell helicopters, which were
sent unarmed to Uganda, but could easily have been converted into para-military aircraft.*

*We have now learned that the 20 pilots, who hastily returned
to Uganda after our report was published, were admitted to
the U.S. on A-2 priority diplomatic visas. Confidential sources
say 82 Ugandans entered the country on diplomatic visas.
Several of them belong to Amin's notoriously brutal State
Research Bureau."*[17]

What is the Trilateral comment? **Warren Christopher** merely had this observation to Anderson's revelations:

> "A small number of Ugandan pilots are being trained by private U.S. firms."[18]

And Jimmy Carter then handed out a weak-handed slap officially, while unofficially allowing the training of Ugandans to continue:

> "We must strengthen our efforts to condemn the practices of that government. "[19]

RELEVANCE OF HUMAN RIGHTS

The Fall 1978 issue of *Trialogue,* official organ of the Trilateral Commission, was devoted to "The Politics of Human Rights."

A leadoff interview with Trilateral **Henry Kissinger** summarized the Trilateral use of human rights as a policy subordinate to other policies and a tool to be used to achieve overall objectives.

Kissinger expressed it this way in reply to a question:

> Q. What are the merits and chances of successes of a vocal human rights policy on the part of the U.S. Administration [sic]?
>
> A. It has some merit for the United States to stand for its principles: the United States should definitely do so and indeed, we tried to do this also in the administrations with which I was associated. However, I think that making this a vocal objective of our foreign policy involves great dangers: You run the risk of either showing your impotence or producing revolutions in friendly countries, or both... I think that fundamental goals of American policy, no matter how they are defined, should be linked to other elements of interest to the Soviets. Either a policy has relevance to other areas of national strategy, or it has no meaning whatsoever. Linkage, therefore, is synonymous with overall strategic view. It is inherent in the real world, and if we ignore it, it is only at our peril.[20]

That's it in a nutshell. "Either a policy has relevance to other areas of national strategy, or it has no meaning whatsoever." In brief, human rights have no meaning for **Kissinger** and his Trilateral friends - human rights are gambling chips to be used as, and when, the elitists see fit.

SLAVES IN COLOMBIA

Trilaterals Over Washington, Volume I, detailed the links between some US multinationals and international banks with Trilateralism and argued that Trilateral objectives are no more than self-interested objectives for some MNC's and international bankers.

Stark evidence for this argument was revealed in 1975-6 by the use of "slave-labor-at-a-profit" by Trilateral multinationals in Colombia, Latin America. While the slave labor system is not widely known even among public officials in Colombia, it apparently has widespread use.

Under the Colombian system of law an accused person can be kept in prison without bail for periods which may extend up to ten years. About 6,000 such "prisoners," actually political detainees, work on "prison labor projects" run by corporations, including prominent US multinationals. As the knowledge of this forced labor surfaced, comments by both American residents and Colombian officials support the authors' argument on Trilateral human rights policy:

"It's especially bad for multinationals to do this in an underdeveloped country," said Fernando Umana, head of Colombia's only public interest law firm.

Oscar A. Bradford, President of the Colombian/American Chamber of Commerce, hadn't heard of the practice until 1975. He commented at that time, "If I were a corporate executive, I'd be inclined to look for something a little less controversial. God knows there are enough other areas of social reform in which to apply corporate efforts and resources. "[21]

On June 20, 1975 the *Wall Street Journal* reported this detail:

"Now there are plans afoot to turn the entire prison population into 'employees' of national and multinational companies. This is a proposal of Action in Colombia, a non- profit group backed financially by 70 large Colombian and

U.S. concerns ranging from Avianca, the national airline, to local units of Bank of America, Dow Chemical Co. and International Business Machines Corp. So far, an Action of-

ficial says, Colombian and US businessmen have responded 'very favorably' to the plan, which is put forward as a program for rehabilitation and improvement of the prisoners' lot."22

The MNC's and banks who use slave labor in Colombia while trumpeting "human rights" to an unsuspecting American public, include Trilateral members:

- Bank of America (Trilateralist Clausen and Wood) which is backing Action in Colombia to turn "the entire prison population of Colombia into employees of national and multinational companies."[23]

- Container Corporation of America (100% owned by Mobil Oil) has operated a "slave labor" production line for many years. Container Corporation is also affiliated with Marcor Inc., another Mobil subsidiary. A Trilateralist in this group is Robert S. Ingersoll (First Chicago Corporation), also a trustee of the Aspen Institute for Humanistic Studies.

- Chase Manhattan owns 5.2 percent of Mobil Oil stock, and there are six Trilaterals on the Chase board. IBM is also cited as a supporter of Action in Colombia. Trilateralists on the IBM board include W.T. Coleman, Jr., William W. Scranton, Harold Brown, Carla Hills and Cyrus Vance, former Secretary of State. IBM operates in Colombia through a 90%-owned subsidiary, IBM de Columbia S.A.

And note this:

"Few of the prisoners working for private companies have been convicted. Rather, they are caught up in the Colombian system of justice, in which the accused usually stays in prison until tried or until he serves time equal to the term he would have received if tried and convicted. Since bail is practically nonexistent, about 75% of the inmates fall into this category. Some have been jailed 8 to 10 years without a trial."[24]

The slave labor program is well described by the previously cited Fernando Umana:

"This isn't a rehabilitation program at all, just window dress-

ing for what almost amounts to slave labor. "[25]

Only time and space limit expansion on this theme of Trilateral anti- human rights activities.

TRILATERALS VS. A FREE AMERICA

Trilateralism is the creation of a group of international bankers and multinational corporations. One should not hesitate to criticize these bankers and multinationals for what they are - perverters of individual freedom, and subverters of the Constitution of the United States. But one must not mistake limited criticism of *some* bankers and *some* multinationals for an attack on *all* bankers and multinationals. It is painfully clear that *most* bankers and *most* corporations are not in the slightest involved in the end-run takeover of political power in the United States. The distinction the authors have made is between *most* bankers and businessmen (who operate more or less in a free enterprise system, and respect and want this system) and a small self-perpetuating group that has perverted the system to its own narrow and feudalistic aims.

Take a well-accepted speech by Dr. J. Kirchhoff, president of Castle & Cook Inc., that was reprinted in *Barrons.* In this speech, Kirchhoff lists the "enemies" of capitalism but omits the most important of these enemies - his capitalist peers who have subsidized and nurtured the enemies of the free enterprise system. Says Kirchhoff:

"Until the mid 1950's we had a good image. Capitalism could rest on its own merits. We were effective and efficient. No one quarreled with that thesis. Visible proof of its success was witnessed in a high standard of living, political freedom and unlimited economic opportunity. We had no specific five-year plan of action. We did not program the lives of others. We were free to build and to create wherever a free market existed. We were accepted or rejected based on the quality of our performance and workmanship.

Such is not the case today: We are required to defend our very existence to a carping melodramatic 'elite minority' that produces absolutely nothing for its fellow man. Few, if any, of this elite ever developed blisters on their hands from any honest, productive labor. I personally refuse to accept the principles of this minority and I refuse to accept as part of corporate life increased government control, corporate abuse, terrorist attacks or other pressure which are being generated by this pseudo elite."

Apparently some church-related groups, which also happened to be supported by totalitarian capitalists, were attacking Castle and Cooke. Kirchhoff said,

"When a church related [sic] group contributes $85,000 to terrorist revolutionaries in Rhodesia, who oppose the concept of free elections in a multi-racial society, it forfeits any immunity from criticism. "[26]

We agree. But wait! Who are the prime supporters of these church groups who support terrorism? None other than *some* of Kirchhoffs' fellow capitalists. In fact, the speech touches on this:

"The guises frequently used are 'The New International Economic Order,' 'Alternative Economic and Social Solutions' and 'Economic Democracy.' These buzz words are palatable, at least on the surface. They are, nonetheless, the siren songs of the Marxist ideologues who have simple, uncomplicated goals: the destruction of the world's most efficient economic machine and the assumption of political power through default. "[27]

Trilateral Paper No. 14 is entitled *Towards a Renovated International System* and outlines a "global strategy" for the "New International Economic Order" castigated by Kirchhoff.

Other criticism is directed at the World Council of Churches. For example, **J. Irwin Miller** is chairman of the board of Cummins Engine (Cummins has been a prominent subsidizer of the Soviet Union) as well as a member of the central and executive committees of the World Council of Churches. The WCC regularly votes funds for Marxist terror groups around the world. In addition, the president of Cummins Engine is Trilateral **Henry Schach**t and **William Scranton** is a director.

The World Council of Churches also has a long record of financial support from the Communist world. For example, between

1970 and 1976 East Germany contributed almost $1 million to the WCC. Holland has contributed even more than this to "The fund to combat racism." In practice, of course, the fund has nothing to do with combating racism. Black Africans were threatened with death by WCC-subsidized Marxist groups such as SWAPO, ZANU and the Pan-African Congress: all nine black ministers in the former Rhodesian government received death threats from WCC-supported ZANU, a black Marxist-terrorist group.

This is well documented. Individual members of Western churches affiliated with the WCC must take personal responsibility for this financial support of murder.

Targeting the WCC Kirchhoff comments:

"We must overcome Western civilization's growing sense of guilt. There is nothing evil about profit in spite of the semantic games played by the agitators. If it were not for profit and incentive, the Western world would not be providing food, hard and soft goods, technology, services, and loans to the rest of the world...

"The survival of truth and common decency are never certain, and must be fought for constantly. We are at war, but it is a guerilla war. It is being fought in the courtroom, the board room and the media. The enemy is organized, discernible and has ample resources.

"Castle & Cooke does not intend, after 127 years, to forfeit its principles to guerrillas of any political stripe. "I am convinced that our path, rather than theirs, is the one that offers more hope for the future, but it cannot be accomplished in a vacuum or by one corporation. Let's revitalize our corporate leadership and take the offensive, in the best tradition of American capitalism.[28]

If American capitalists want *public* support they must first clean house. While Mr. Kirchhoff makes good sense, he needs to name names, point out responsibility and challenge **J. Irwin Miller** and his fellow revolutionaries before calling on aid from the American society at large.

ENDNOTES

1. Vermont Royster, Orient Express, Wall Street Journal, February 12, 1980 p. 1.
2. Zbigniew Brzezinski, Washington Star, December 31, 1978, E4.
3. J. Paul Asutin retired as president and operating officer of Coca-Cola on March I, 1981.
4. The Washington Post, December 24, 1978, p. 04.
5. Richard Cooper, et aI., Toward a Renovated International System, p. 30.
6. New York Times, June 12, 1921, p. 2 column 3.
7. Reported by AP (Taipei, Taiwan) December 24, 1980.
8. Antony C. Sutton, Western Technology and Soviet Economic Development, 1917 to 1930, p. 284.
9. Chihiro Hosoya et ai, Collaboration with Communist Countries in Managing Global Problems: and Examination of the Options.
10. Robert K. Dornan, Banking Interests in Panama, Congressional Record (September 15, 1977).
11. Ibid.
12. Uneven Justice?, Wall Street Journal, May 11, 1978, p. 1.
13. George Cornell, AP Report, Arizona Republic, March 10, 1979.
14. Ibid.
15. Reed Irvine, Behind the News. Accuracy In Media (1978).
16. Jack Anderson, EI Paso Times, April 27, 1978.
17. Ibid.
18. Ibid.
19. Francois Sauzey, Henry Kissinger. Trialogue No. 19 (Fall 1978), p. 3.
20. Wall Street Journal, June 20, 1975, p.l.
21. Ibid. p. I.
22. Ibid. p. 10.
23. Ibid. p. 10.
24. Ibid., p. 25.
25. Dr. J. Kirchhoff, Corporate Missionary: those who believe in Capitalism must fight back, Barrons (February 19, 1979), p. 3.
26. Ibid., p. 3.
27. Op. cit., p. 3.

CHAPTER SEVEN

THE PACIFIC BASIN PHENOMENON

Analysts are predicting that the 1980 Reagan presidential election will be a boon for Western states, particularly California. These claims are not unreasonable, for Reagan will naturally sympathize with Western issues much more than Carter did. Conversely, Carter clearly favored some Southern states during his administration.

But things were already shifting westward, well before Reagan and **Bush** (from the Southwest) were elected. For instance **Alden Clausen**, the chairman of San Francisco-based Bank of America, was appointed by **Carter** (with Reagan's tacit approval) to head the World Bank. Another example is Arizona Governor **Bruce Babbitt's** invitations to join the Trilateral Commission and the Council on Foreign Relations in mid 1980.

While traditionally Westerners have stayed aloof from the Eastern Establishment, it seems that the Eastern Establishment is moving in on the West. Western Trilaterals, notably **David Packard**, **George Weyerhaeuser**, **Caspar Weinberger** and others, have grown rapidly in national and international prominence and influence as a result of this transition.

There is a reason for this shift in power, and as always, it is related to economic trade and profits.

In 1979 the dollar amount of US trade with Pacific Basin countries outstripped trade done with Atlantic nations. (This refers to the countries that border the Pacific and Atlantic Oceans, respectively.) One major reason for this is the rapidly expanding Japanese economy; for instance, Japan recently surpassed the US in auto production. The boom in the electronics industry in Taiwan, Korea and other oriental countries is also expanding every month.

To multinational elitists, the hope of the future lies in Mainland (Communist) China, with its 800 million population and virtual slave labor market. There is interest in selling goods and services to the Chinese population, of course, but the potential for making goods in China for export to the rest of the world is overwhelming. Low cost department stores in the US are already carrying Chinese made textile goods that are priced thirty per cent or more *below* any other brands.

China will be a profit bonanza for the multinationals, but a depression for American labor forces who cannot possibly compete with the Chinese wage market. Indeed, China proves to become the great "equalizer" between the "haves" and "have-nots" in the world.

International interest is high also. In February 1980 *Business Week* reported:

> *"Japanese Prime Minister Masayoshi Ohira is being urged by some of his liberal, English-speaking advisors to take the initiative in setting up a Pacific Community, modeled on the European Economic Community... The Japanese, enthusiastic about the Pacific Community idea, have set up a meeting in Canberra, Australia, this fall to discuss the project."*[1]

In May 1980, one of the first steps in that direction took place with the response of the Pacific Basin Economic Council (which met in Australia) to a proposed think tank. On May 15, 1980, the *Arizona Republic* reported the following story which was not seen elsewhere. It quoted a prospectus of that planned think tank, the Pacific Basin Institute:

> *"'The Pacific Basin Institute will be a private, nonprofit research center serving as a focal point for the business communities of North America, South America and Asia, with*

*special emphasis on applied studies concerning trade, invest-
ment and economic development in the Pacific Region.*

*"'PBI is strategically located in Arizona, which borders
Mexico and is the center of the most dynamic growth area in
the United States.*

*"'The Southwestern site offers easy accessibility for Pacific
Basin leaders of business, government and education to come
together in an ideal climate with excellent resorts and meeting facilities.'*

*"The proposed research center is the brainchild of Mallery,
who refused to comment on the results of the trip to Australia.*

*"Gov. Bruce Babbitt, who said Phoenix business and govern-
ment leaders have been working intensively on the idea for
a year, said the prospects of the research center becoming a
reality look favorable.*

*"'Arizona must get into the arena of international trade on
a large scale,' he* **[Babbitt]** *said. 'It must have the academic
and research capacity to underpin that kind of effort. That's
what this is all about.*

*"'The underlying philosophy behind the concept is to look at
the Pacific Basin region for data gathering and economic de-
cision-making in partnership with business and government,'
he said.*

*"The prospectus says a site for the center 'has been donated
and sufficient financing has been committed to construct and
operate the facility.'*

*"...The prospectus says the business activity and financial af-
fairs of the institute would be directed by a board of trustees
made up of 45 persons 'who hold business, government and
academic positions is throughout the Pacific region.' "*

This sounds similar to many other elite organizations that
desire to make decisions for the rest of the world, but would be
of little consequence if the people involved were of little consequence.

The others involved with PBI were revealed in the same article:

> "The Pacific Basin Economic Council, a federation of pri-
> vate-sector businessmen representing 20 countries, includ-
> ing Canada, Japan, China and New Zealand, met in Sydney,
> Australia, last week and responded 'very positively' to the
> concept, said Larry Landry, director of the state [Arizona]
> Office of Economic Planning and Development.

> "Landry, along with Phoenix lawyer Richard Mallery and
> Roger Lyon, president of Valley National Bank, went to
> Australia last week to gain acceptance of the proposed Pacific
> Basin Institute...[2]

The four principals here are Larry Landry, Richard Mallery,
Roger Lyon and **Bruce Babbitt**.

Arizona Governor **Bruce Babbitt's** appointment to the
Trilateral Commission coincided with the announcement of
PBI. **Babbitt** is an old-line Arizona Democrat with direct ties to
Washington. He received his degree from Harvard Law School,
but only after receiving an advanced degree in geology. He was
the only public official appointed by **Carter** to the Kemeny
Commission (which investigated the Three Mile Island Incident)
and later **Carter** named him to chair the Nuclear Safety Oversight
Committee on May 7, 1979.

As head of the Arizona Office of Economic Planning and
Development Department, Larry Landry serves directly under
Babbitt.

Richard Mallery is part of **Babbitt's** tight-knit "Kitchen
Cabinet", all of whom were classmates at Harvard. Mallery is
described by the March 2, 1980 *Arizona Republic* as" A partner
in the prestigious Snell and Wilmer law firm. . . shuns active involvement in the Democratic Party. He is viewed as non-partisan,
moves well in both party circles and is more concerned about issues than party dogma."[3]

Roger A. Lyon however, reveals the most interesting back
ground. Lyon is president of Valley National Bank of Arizona,
the 28th largest bank in the country and the largest in the Rocky
Mountain Region. The largest individual shareholder in VNB is investment banker J.P. Morgan & Co. of New York, with a whopping

4.2% of VNB's outstanding shares.

In late 1980, Lyon was elected to serve as chairman of the powerful Western Regional Council, which represents "40 of the largest corporations, banks, utilities and other businesses in the Western States," according to the *Arizona Republic.* Lyon had this to say about Western regional interests:

> *"We are different from the east...in water, clean air, our vistas, national parks, wildernesses, recreation we have different values and standards. We have to convince Washington and the rest of the country of that. "[4]*

Few asked how Lyon happened to come to Arizona. From 1950 to 1976 (26 years), Lyon served at **David Rockefeller**'s Chase Manhattan Bank in New York! Lyon is the third generation of a banking family from New Jersey.

It would appear that Lyon has renounced the East for the sake of Western living, but one might remember the old proverb about a leopard changing its spots.

After analyzing the people who promoted Pacific Basin Institute through the Australian conference, we can see a heavy-weight connection to the Trilateral elite and a typical modus operandi. PBI will have a membership similar to the Trilateral Commission: academics, politicians and multinational corporation "heads of state." Its goal appears similar as well: to foster economic cooperation and trade.

Certainly Pacific Basin Institute is neither a copy nor replacement of the Trilateral Commission. Far from it. More likely it is the result of the same Trilateral policy that opened China up in the first place. Remember, *all* five of the original China negotiators (who worked in secret and included Carter), were current or former members of the Trilateral Commission. China is exclusively a Trilateral phenomenon.

Pacific Basin Institute is seen to be the natural extension of that phenomenon. It is certainly something to watch in the future.

It should also be noted at this point that it was very difficult in obtaining information regarding PBI. Governor **Babbitt's** office was totally uncooperative and gave us no information. In fact, after his T.C. appointment was made public in 1980 by the

Commission itself, **Babbitt** received so much harsh criticism from Arizonans that his staff responded to callers with "I have no personal knowledge of that." This is a standard dodge when a politician doesn't want to answer the question; they now acknowledge his membership.

Valley National Bank and Roger Lyon's office have also been wholly uncooperative in releasing information on PBI. When asked for a "history sheet" on Lyon (a customary handout for top corporate executives, his aide became defensive and refused to release *any* information.

A contact was made with the Japanese embassy in Washington, D.C., who acknowledged that they had information on PBI. While they had originally agreed to send us information, after two months and two more phone calls, nothing was received.

Finally, after contact with Richard Mallery's office, the prospectus for PBI was obtained. According to that report, Mallery is president of PBI and Lyon is chairman of the board.

There is a substantial link to Stanford University: Weldon B. Gibson is vice-chairman of the board and is executive vice president of SRI International (Stanford Research Institute). Trilateral **Arjay Miller** is a director of SRI International. **Philip Habib**, a senior fellow at Hoover Institution at Stanford is vice president of PBI.

Acknowledgements and thanks were given to heavyweights like **Winston Lord,** president of the Council on Foreign Relations, and Robert Macy, Jr., managing director of Lehman Brothers, Kuhn Loeb.

CONCLUSIONS:

- The West is rapidly growing in Trilateral influence. The election of Reagan and **Bush** will accelerate this trend.
- As China's manufacturing capacity is brought on line by Trilateral multinational corporations, America (and the rest of the world) will be flooded with noncompetitively priced goods.
- American labor will feel the biggest brunt of this and will lose countless jobs at the expense of Chinese slave

labor.

- The Pacific Basin Institute is the main instrument that will be used by the Trilateral elite to coordinate the Pacific Basin and to devise and recommend "policies" for participating countries in the Basin.

ENDNOTES

1. Maryanne McNellis, *Japan's Push for a Pacific Community,* Business Week (February 25, 1980), p. 72.
2. Joel Nilsson, *Pacific Region Businessmen Back Idea of State-Based Trade Institute,*
3. Arizona Republic (May 15, 1980), p. A-I.
4. *Richard Mallery: Bridge to the business community,* Arizona Republic (March 2, 1980), P. A-I.
5. J.J. Casserly, *Bank Chief to Lead Regional Council,* Arizona Republic (December 6 , 1980).

CHAPTER EIGHT

BACKWARD AND FORWARD

At this point we should step back and look at the Trilateral Commission in the light of history. The Commission represents the third attempt by the New York international banking fraternity to create a New Economic World Order under their control. When we look at this third attempt within the context of history, it is clear why the Commission (or its equivalent) will continue.

THE ORIGINS OF GLOBALISM

It was Thomas Jefferson, writer and signer of the Declaration of Independence who first warned a newly independent America about the powers behind the scenes of government:

"If the American people ever allowed the banks to control the issuance of their currency, first by inflation and then by deflation, the banks and corporations that will grow up around them will deprive the people of all property until their children will wake up homeless on the continent their fathers occupied. The issuing power of money should be taken from the banks and restored to Congress and the people to whom it belongs.

"I sincerely believe the banking institutions are more dangerous to liberty than standing armies."[1]

The "banking institutions" are represented today by Trilateralism. What was true in 1790 is true in 1980.

Out of seventy-seven Trilateral Commissioners from the U.S., well over one-half are either directors of banks, or have been directors of the Federal Reserve System (which is owned and controlled by private banks). We also must recall that **David Rockefeller**, chairman of Chase Manhattan Bank, founded the Trilateral Commission.

To follow through on Thomas Jefferson's prophetic warning, "the American people" have not merely allowed "banks to control the issuance of their currency," but almost unbelievably they have allowed banking interests to control the domestic and foreign policies of the United States.

ATTEMPT #1: THE LEAGUE OF NATIONS

The formal attempt to extend control of the United States to the world was the League of Nations. The idea for the League of Nations came from Cecil Rhodes' Round Table groups and was proposed to Woodrow Wilson at least as early as September 1915 by Sir Edward Grey, a member of the Round Table, in a letter to Colonel M. House:

"Would the President propose that there should be a League of Nations binding themselves to side against any power which broke a treaty."[2]

What went wrong with the League of Nations? Elitists blame the failure on Woodrow Wilson. For example, elitist academic Harlan Cleveland wrote:

"The first try, the League of Nations, was the product of Woodrow Wilson's strong initiative and the victim of his weak follow through: the United States wrote most of the club rules, then decided not to join the club. In its weakened condition, it could not survive the rise of fascism, Nazism and militarism."[3]

This statement is typical of elitist evasion and distortion of truth. Cleveland makes at least the following errors:

- The League did not survive Hitler to be sure, but who financed and nurtured Hitler? None other than key members of the Council on Foreign Relations, the successor to the Inquiry which promoted the League. (See Antony Sutton, *Wall Street and The Rise of Hitler.*)

- Cleveland does not mention that the rise of Communism was also financed and nurtured by the same key members of the Council on Foreign Relations. (See Antony Sutton, *Wall Street and the Bolshevik Revolution.*)

- It is more valid to argue that the first try at New Economic World Order failed because the "club" saw more profit (both financially and for the goal of New Economic World Order) in the Second World War. This aspect of world history has to be buried because it would highlight the amoral character of elitists.

ATTEMPT #2: THE COUNCIL ON FOREIGN RELATIONS

In New York, July 29, 1921, the elite founded a semi-secret organization called The Council on Foreign Relations. The CFR evolved out of the American Delegation to the Paris Peace Conference in 1919, which later merged with the American Branch of the British Institute of International Affairs. This culminated with the formation of the United Nations. The report of the founding committee for the CFR contained the following statement of purpose:

"Until recent years it was usual to assume that in foreign affairs each government must think mainly, if not entirely, of the interests of its own people. In founding the League of Nations the allied powers have now recognized that national policies ought to be framed with an eye to the welfare of society at large."[4]

Here we have precisely the same globalist objective to be found in the Trilateral Commission today.

What is important is the makeup of the board of directors of the Council on Foreign Relations during the 1920's and 1930's. It was dominated, as is the Trilateral Commission, by Wall Street banking interests.

Prominent among the early directors was Paul M. Warburg, partner in the firm of Kuhn-Loeb and the first member appointed by Woodrow Wilson to the Federal Reserve Board. In fact,

Warburg was the brains behind the Federal Reserve System. Warburg was also chairman of the International Acceptance Bank, Inc. and (much less known) a director of American I.G. Chemical Corporation which was the American branch of I.G. Farben that had so much to do with the rise of Hitler.

In the Trilateral Commission today we find Kuhn-Loeb and the Federal Reserve System well represented. **Charles W. Robinson**, former managing director of Kuhn-Loeb, was in the **Carter** administration. Links between Trilateralism and Federal Reserve System include **Arthur F. Burns, Andrew Brimmer, David Rockefeller, Paul Volcker, Bruce K. MacLaury, Alden Clausen** and **Robert V. Roosa**.

Another Wall Street financier on the board of the CFR was Otto H. Kahn. Like Paul Warburg, Kahn was a former partner in the private banking company of Kuhn-Loeb. Russell C. Leffingwell was a director of the Council on Foreign Relations during the inter-war years. In 1919 he held the office of Secretary of the Treasury and had been in partnership with J.P. Morgan and Company.

Another director of the CFR was **Owen D. Young**, chairman of General Electric Company (which was dominated by the J.P. Morgan interests) and the German Reparations Committee (which drew up the so-called Young Plan). CFR director Allan W. Dulles served during the inter-war period. During the same time, Dulles was also a director of J. Henry Schroeder Banking Corporation and a partner in the establishment law firm of Solomon and Cromwell. It is recorded that the J. Henry Schroeder Banking firm was one of the key elements behind the rise of Hitler in Germany.

Another inter-war director of the CFR was Norman H. Davis. According to Quigley, Davis was a "non-legal agent of the Morgans."[5] He had represented the US Treasury on the Paris Peace Delegation. Woodrow Wilson himself owed his 1913 financial backing for the Presidency to his "classmate and life long friend." Cleveland Hoadley Dodge was a director of National City Bank and the Russell Sage Foundation.

The CFR exerted its major influence during the period from 1940 through the mid 1960's, and its members reflected almost all of the establishment leaders particularly people like Wall

Street banker John J. McCloy, John Foster Dulles, Allen Dulles and so on. The high point of the CFR undoubtedly was the creation of the United Nations. John Rockefeller, Sr. donated the New York site and was instrumental in getting the United Nations off the ground in San Francisco in 1945.

At the height of CFR powers in 1971, a dispute over the editor of the Council's quarterly *Foreign Affairs* magazine marked the end of the second attempt for new world order. Under President Bayless Manning, a former dean of the Stanford Law School, the CFR tried to broaden its membership from a geographical, age, racial and sexual standpoint. By the 1970's the CFR had sixty women and twenty-two blacks on its rolls; but these new members were not selected as carefully as in the past and the expertise and prestige traditionally associated with the CFR was diluted. When Manning attempted to appoint William P. Bundy to the editorship of *Foreign Affairs,* he (Manning) was eased out of the CFR presidency by **David Rockefeller**.

ATTEMPT #3: TRILATERALISM

In 1973 the third attempt at new world order came under the guise of the Trilateral Commission. It had different short- and medium-term objectives than both the League of Nations and United Nations.

Trilateralism abandons the concept of bringing together nations into a *political* world society in one giant step. Instead, it proposes to first create regional economic groupings and then link the three most important of these regional groupings (North America, Europe and Japan) into a *new economic world order.* The discussion and policy- making steps necessary for this objective are known as the "Trilateral process." Incorporation of Communist societies and the Third World is desired but is left for a more distant date.

In brief, Trilaterals are more pragmatic than their CFR allies in the United Nations and the League of Nations.

Even this limited Trilateral objective has major problems, not least of which is that it requires abandonment of American independence and national sovereignty.

It is no surprise to find Trilaterals eager to change the Constitution into a document more malleable to their ends. *Volume I* quoted **Brzezinski's** statement *(Between Two Ages,* p. 258):

> *"Either 1976 or 1989 - the two-hundredth anniversary of the Constitution - could serve as a suitable target date for culminating a national dialogue on the relevance of existing arrangements..."[6]*

The Trilateral Commission's New Economic World Order is impossible as long as the Constitution exists in its present form. More dictatorial powers are needed to function as revealed in an official Commission report:

> *"If a more effective and equitable economic order is to emerge, national policies and programs must be subject to moderation and adjustment to take into account probable adverse international ramifications. This can be accomplished only if powerful domestic agencies are brought under control and sensitized to the international consequences of their policies."[7]*

The Trilateral Commission here proposes that our domestic policies be subordinated to international policies.

In *The Crisis of Democracy* (funded and written by the Trilateral Commission) evidence is found that Trilaterals need to restrict Constitutional freedoms. For example, the right to free speech is protected under the First Amendment to the Constitution. Yet the following concerning freedom of the press is found:

> *"... it is a freedom which can be abused... the responsibility of the press should now be increased to be commensurate with its power, significant measures are required to restore an appropriate balance between the press, the governments and other institutions in society.[8]*

How does the Commission propose to do this?

> *"...beginning with the Interstate Commerce Commission and the Sherman Anti-Trust Act measures had to be taken to regulate the new industrial centers of power and define their relations to the rest of society. Something comparable appears*

to be now needed with respect to the media."[9]

Of course, monopoly of industry and commerce is not the same as freedom of speech. The break-up of monopoly cannot in any way be compared to restrictions on expressions of ideas. It is a logical absurdity, yet an excellent example of Trilateral use of non sequiturs.

THE 1980's PROJECT

Continuation of the Trilateral Commission is almost a foregone conclusion. The Trilateral process is simply another attempt in almost 100 years of new world order plans.

There are subtle but important changes in Trilateralism to be noted. Not only is the immediate objective limited to regional groupings but the Trilateral program is carefully balanced on two key hinges:

a. That a New Economic World Order is inevitable. For example, "The management of interdependence has become indispensable for world order in the coming years. Its origins lie in the extraordinary expansion of interaction between modern states and societies."[10]

b. That the objective can be attained through propaganda techniques. To this end, almost endless studies and reports are published assuming that the New Economic World order is inevitable for the survival of mankind. This assumption is critical because it has no basis in fact.

It is notable that the major propaganda effort is still centered within the Council on Foreign Relations i.e., the 1980's Project. But the clue to Trilateral involvement is their dominance of the CFR Committee on Studies responsible for the 1980's Project.

So far, the project consists of twenty-five volumes released by McGraw-Hill. They lay down the "steering trends" to new world order in the 1980's. Of the ten members of the CFR Committee on Studies, four were Trilaterals (**Kissinger, Volcker, Whitman, Perkins**). The chairman was **Perkins**. **Kissinger** and **Volcker** dominated the other members (pedestrian academics without fame or notoriety).

TRILATERAL MONEY MANAGEMENT

No doubt by this time readers will have grasped the fundamental observation that the Trilateral New Economic World Order is intended for the private benefit of Trilateral Commissioners at the expense of everyone else. This is the secret of monopoly, possibly age old, but certainly rediscovered by the Rockefeller-Morgan financial elite at the end of the 19th century.

Trilaterals are just following the golden rule of John D. Rockefeller, Sr. and John Pierpoint Morgan: *gain political power and use it for financial objectives.*

If this is the fundamental Trilateral rule, what can be said about the future of our society? Specifically on monetary affairs, the following can be projected:

- A fiat currency. This is absolutely essential for the New Economic World Order, and must be coupled with international fiat "reserve" assets.

- Gold will continue to be centralized into a few hands. Gold in the hands of the many is out of the question if Trilateralism is to succeed. As gold provides for personal economic sovereignty, it must be retained in the hands of the elitist few and directly or indirectly be controlled.

The Treasury campaign to demonetize gold, formerly led by Trilateral **W. Michael Blumentha**l, is an admission that Trilaterals are having problems in this segment of their program.

Gold has been removed from our monetary system in order to remove the shackles from "management" (manipulation) of the monetary system for elitist objectives. This policy was begun by Franklin D. Roosevelt in 1933 and it must not be forgotten that Roosevelt himself, far from being a man of the people, came from the old established banking family that created the Bank of New York in 1784.

The Repeal of the 1933 *Joint Resolution* by Congress in 1974 has allowed American citizens to privately own gold, but was coupled with a Treasury program to sell gold and depress its price.

Under US dominance, the International Monetary Fund joined in the gold-selling campaign. These selling pressures temporarily held down the price of gold.

Crisis management (or problem management) is an essential Trilateral tool to build a New Economic World Order. Problems do not exist to be solved or ameliorated. Problems exist to exasperate, knowingly or unknowingly, in order to advance basic world order objectives.

Monetary management is no exception. Trilateralist proposals for monetary management will not solve the questions of inflation, federal intervention, burdensome taxation, interest rates or any other matter.

One may be justified in thinking that academic experts in the Trilateral Commission are chosen because their "solutions" coincide with the objectives of the power elite. An excellent example is found in the views of **Gardner Ackley** who is a member of the Commission as well as having held the position of professor of political economy at Henry Carter University and the University of Michigan. An interview with **Ackley** presents **Ackley** as a valuable asset for Trilateralism. His proposals advance New Economic World Order objectives:

> *"There are many occasions in which deficits are appropriate and necessary. . . There are many occasions in which deficits are unavoidable.* "[11]

THE 1980 PRESIDENTIAL ELECTIONS

Trilateralism was heavily represented in every major political campaign in 1980. **John Anderson** - running on an independent ticket - was a member of the Commission and was duly financed by many individual fellow members. **Jimmy Carter** and **Walter Mondale** both had definite connections with the Commission.

While Ronald Reagan was not a member of the Trilateral Commission, many of his top campaign advisors were. We want to demonstrate how Trilateralism "covered all the bets" in the political arena, and how its resulting influence on Ronald Reagan - the victor - will all but guarantee the success of their New Economic World Order plans.

By the time the Republican National Convention met to nomi-
nate a candidate, Ronald Reagan had no serious rival. Excitement
was high because for the first time in a long time there was a
unified party. Senator Barry Goldwater delivered a well-cheered
speech stating the dangers of elitist influence in government - he
also said that this might be the last election America faces.

Goldwater's recent book, *With No Apologies,* devotes an entire
chapter to the Trilateral Commission. Without judging his intent,
we can safely say that Goldwater well understands the Trilateral
Commission and its goals.

Goldwater's speech was cheered but his warnings were ignored. After the convention forcefully rejected **Kissinger**'s proposal for a "split Presidency" (with **Kissinger** being the "other"
president), it turned right around and nominated Trilateral
George Bush for Reagan's vice-presidential running mate.

After this, many prominent and hopeful conservatives
"counseled" the authors that Reagan was not connected to the
Trilaterals and would "use" anything or anybody he could to get
elected. In the Trilaterals' case, it was OK because Reagan would
quickly dispense with them once he was elected.

One of the largest pro-Reagan forces in the country was Moral
Majority, a quasi-Christian political action group originally brain-
stormed by Paul Weyrich in Washington. Other groups like Moral
Majority (Round Table and Christian Voice, for example) were
wooed by Reagan in typical political fashion.

After the election, millions of Americans (many of whom *are*
fundamental Christians) were looking to Reagan to support their
positions. But the November 24 issue of *U.S. News & World Report*
revealed the hard reality:

> *"Top officials of the Reagan team have sent a message to the
> Moral Majority: 'It isn't your administration.' These advis-
> ers to the President-elect are urging him to ignore political
> threats of punishment by the religious right if he does not
> support their policies.* "[12]

The article went on to say:

> *"Reagan's first moves after the November 4 election gener-
> ally pleased moderate Republicans and Democrats, some of*

*whom feared he would follow the dictates of his most con-
servative supporters. 'Hell with them,' Vice President-elect
George Bush declared on November 10 in Houston, referring
to right-wing groups that supported the President-elect."*[13]

In perspective then one must ask, "Who is going to throw
whom out of where?"

America had bought the "anti-elitist" story once more, like
they did with CFR member Franklin Delano Roosevelt in 1934
and Trilateral **Jimmy Carter** in 1976. The facts cannot be ignored: Reagan's campaign was engineered and operated by
Trilaterals **David Packard, George Weyerhaeuser, Bill Brock,
Anne Armstrong** and **Caspar Weinberger**, and a large assort-
ment of CFR members, Reagan was personally supported by
David Rockefeller.

WILL THE REAL REAGAN PLEASE STAND UP?

On November 6, 1980, the following Reagan quote was widely
reported in the nation's press:

*"I think there is an elite in this country and they are the very
ones who run an elitist government. They want a government
by a handful of people because they don't believe the people
themselves can run their lives...Are we going to have an elitist government that makes decisions for peoples' lives, or are
we going to believe as we have for so many decades, that the
people can make these decisions for themselves?"*[14]

Reagan certainly cannot claim ignorance of the scope and influence of the Trilateral Commission. Indeed, he has been rubbing
elbows with the Eastern elite for many years as a member of the
exclusive male- only Bohemian Grove Club in Northern California.

The San Mateo Times quoted Irving Stone, the author of *The
Origin,* a biographical novel of evolutionist Charles Darwin - and an
ardent evolutionist. In light of Reagan's wooing non-evolutionists
(i.e., the before-mentioned 'fundamental groups) during the campaign, Stone's comments serves as another warning that things might
not be as they appear.

*"I've known Ronald Reagan for 35 years. He's a very' warm,
personable man. But Ronnie doesn't have the mind to make*

independent judgments... he has to have a script which he will memorize perfectly.

"I'm a little frightened to have a man in the Oval Office who can't make independent judgments...

When he made that statement about evolution in Houston, he was talking to a large crowd of Fundamentalists. Apparently, he wants their votes very badly. ["15]

After the election, Reagan assembled a "transition team" which would later select, screen and recommend appointees for major administration posts. According to a compilation by *Research Publications* of Phoenix, of the fifty-nine people Reagan named to that team, twenty-eight were members of the CFR, ten belonged to the secret and elite Bilderberger group, and no less than ten were Trilaterals.

There are two particular "brain trusts" that will fuel Reagan's foreign policy. The first is Stanford University's Hoover Institution on War, Revolution and Peace in Palo Alto, California. The other is Georgetown University's Center for Strategic and International Studies (CSIS) in Washington, D.C. Almost forty of the total transition team had been associated with one or the other of these "think tanks." Reportedly, fifteen of Reagan's advisors came from CSIS. (**Henry Kissinger** is a professor at CSIS, for instance.)

The chairman of CSIS is Trilateral **David M. Abshire**, who also headed Reagan's foreign policy and defense transition staff.

David Packard is the most influential overseer at the Hoover Institution at Stanford.

In short, the reader can see that regardless of good intentions or wishful thinking, Reagan appears to be totally consumed by Trilaterals. This is the Trilateral way of political "protection." A Reagan-**Bush** administration will result in further progress for Trilaterals toward their New Economic World Order:

- Reagan will stress business and economics, and "business" is the Trilaterals' expertise.
- The new Republican majority Senate will be very cooperative with the administration as far as an economic policy is concerned.

- Under Democratic control, Trilateral headway was stagnating; it has a "fresh start" with Republican control. Here we apply the principle that a ship will not respond to rudder control unless substantial movement is present.

Looking to the next ten years in light of the last sixty years does not promise anything but "business as usual." The same type of elite groups that dominated in the 1920's *are* dominating today. They are moving forward today with no less resolve than they were then. And prospects for their success never looked brighter.

ENDNOTES

1. Thomas Jefferson, *The Writings of Thomas Jefferson,* (Autobiography, correspon- dence, reports messages addresses and other writings.) vol. 7, p.685.
2. Jennings C. Wise, *Woodrow Wilson: Disciple of Revolution,* p.382.
3. Harlan Cleveland, *The Third Try at World Order,* p.2.
4. Whitney H. Shepardson, *Early History of the Council on Foreign Relations,* p.3.
5. Carroll Quigley, *Tragedy and Hope,* p.50.
6. Zbigniew Brzezinski, *Between Two Ages: America's Role in the Technetronic Era,* p.258.
7. Egidio Ortona and et.al., *The Problem of International Consulations,* p.17.
8. Michael Crozier and et.al., *The Crisis of Democracy,* p.18!. 9. Ibid., p. 182.
9. Richard Cooper and et.al., *Toward a Renovated International System,* p.4.
10. *A Constitutional Ban On Red Ink?,* U.S. News & World Report, January 29, 1979, p.27.
11. *Washington Whispers,* U.S. News & World Report vol. LXXXIX, No.21 (November 24, (980), p. 20.
12. 13. Ibid., p. 22.
13. San Jose Mercury, November 6, 1980.
14. San Mateo Times, October 16, 1980.

CHAPTER NINE

TRILATERALISM IN EUROPE

Trilateralism, as its name suggests, is a three-sided affair:

a. The United States

b. Japan

c. Western Europe (excluding Austria, Greece, and Sweden)

This area includes eighty percent of the economic power in the non-Communist world and is the source of virtually all of the world's new technology.

The basic Trilateral concept is to link the three economic power areas in the world into a united international force. US dominance would mean Rockefeller-Chase Manhattan dominance because Trilateralism was created by **David Rockefeller** and continues to be dominated by him.

The European segment of the Commission shares the same goals for a New Economic World Order, but they would envision themselves as the ultimate dominating factor (likewise for the Japanese Trilaterals).

The political gaps in Trilateral distribution are more than noticeable. Africa is not included. Neither is the Far East, Latin America or Australasia.

Trilaterals want to build a unified Trilateral force, then draw in the last named areas on a piecemeal basis. Africa (apart from South Africa) is undeveloped and contributes talk rather than power. The Far East is a complex emerging economic force. Australasia is not powerful in global terms.

Latin America includes some powerful countries (Brazil; Argentina and Mexico) - yet is ignored because the Latin cultural tradition has kept Latin leaders aware of Chase Manhattan-**Rockefeller** activities. In general, Europe has a residue of gratitude for World War II, while Latin America has a long standing cultural antipathy towards anything smacking of international banking operators: Catholic bankers, for instance, are bound by religious precepts to lend money for productive purpose only. New York bankers use money and debt for political control.

Each Trilateral area has a chairman and a deputy chairman. **David Rockefeller** is North American chairman and **Mitchell Sharp** of Canada is North American deputy chairman.

Europeans hold these positions for their Trilateral side:

Georges Berthoin is European chairman

Egidio Ortona is European deputy chairman

Berthoin is president of the European Movement and one time aide to Jean Monnet, father of "One Europe." **Egidio Ortona** is president of Honeywell Information Systems, Italia, which is closely linked to Trilateral **Edson W. Spencer**, president of Honeywell in the US.

The geographical distribution of Trilateralists in Europe is shown in Table 1.

TABLE 1

Country	Trilateral Commissioners	Executive Committee Members	Number in Public Service
United Kingdom	26	2	2
W. Germany	21	3	2
France	18	3	4
Italy	14	3	2

Eire (Ireland)	7	1	2
Norway	3	1	1
Netherlands	6	1	0
Denmark	3	1	2
Spain	12	2	0
Portugal	3	0	0
Total	**114**	**17**	**15**

TRILATERALISM AND "ONE EUROPE"

The link between "One Europe," or a United States of Europe and Trilateralism is important. To move from three regional groupings to "One World" requires that each region be cohesive and unified. (Authors' note: "One Europe" is an established term created by the people associated with it. "One World" is the authors' coinage to compare and describe the larger concept.) This is impossible with the current state of the United Nations. It is much more plausible in the Trilateral process.

US-Trilateral intent is to build "One Europe" to be merged into a global society. Oddly, this is not the view from Europe, which sees "One Europe" as a final goal. Wall Street sees "One Europe" as a stepping stone to One World.

When links between the European Economic Community (EEC) and Trilaterals are described, the step by step movement towards One World becomes apparent.

There may well be economic arguments for reducing European customs barriers to encourage free trade. But European political disadvantages have been obscured by more superficial economic benefits. To avoid sinking into the Trilateral morass, Europe will have to restrict cooperation to economic and military activities. To extend the cooperative process into the political arena invites loss of European sovereignty to a Trilateral global society. Traditional French hostility towards American political moves is not altogether without foundation.

So with this in mind, the coauthors feel it is important to take a look at European Trilaterals and their links to EEC and "One Europe."

THE EUROPEAN ECONOMIC COMMUNITY

The European Economic Community currently consists of ten countries: Belgium, Denmark, Ireland, France, Germany, Italy, Luxembourg, Netherlands, United Kingdom and Greece. (Greece became an official member as of January I, 1981.) Spain and Portugal are tentatively slated to join the EEC in 1983.

BELGIUM

Out of ten Belgian Trilaterals, two are prominently connected with Europeanization and two more are connected with international banking.

Henri Simonet is foreign minister of Belgium and immediately before that (1973-1977) was vice president of the European Economic Community (EEC).

Jean Rey was Belgian minister for economic affairs from 1954-1958 followed by a long career at various European Community posts:

- 1958-1967, president of external relations of EEC
- 1967-1970, president of the executive committee of EEC

Two prominent Belgian Trilateral bankers include **Baron Leon Lambert**, president of Groupe Bruxelles Lambert, SA, which is affiliated with the Rothschilds, and **Luc Wauters**, chairman of Groupe Almanij-Kredietbank of Brussels.

DENMARK

There are three Danish Trilaterals. **Svend Auken** is Minister. of Labor and was a member of the Committee of Social Democrats *against* EEC to 1971-72. On the other hand, Trilateral **Ivar Norgaard** is Minister of Environment and was vice president of the European Parliament in 1974. **Norgaard** was a member of the Danish National Bank in 1968 but otherwise Danish Trilaterals are politicians rather than bankers.

EIRE (IRELAND)

There are seven Irish Trilaterals including prominent members of European organizations.

Michael O'Kennedy is the Irish Minister for Foreign Affairs and a former vice president of the Irish Council of the European Party in the senate. Another politician, **M.T.W. Robinson,** is a member of the executive committee of the European Movement. **F. Boland,** chairman of IBM-Ireland and a director of the Investment Bank of Ireland, is a former representative to the United Nations (1956-1964).

The key statement on "Political Cooperation" in the European Community was published by an Irish Trilateral **Garret FitzGerald,** former foreign minister of Ireland and current leader of the Fine Gael opposition party. He asserts that most European political activity is not part of the formal structure of EEC!

Political cooperation is centered in the office of the revolving post of president of the EEC Council of Ministers. A permanent secretariat of some 200 committees is constantly at work and meets on a continuing basis. **FitzGerald** is one-time president of the EEC Council of Ministers and claims that considerable political activity is taking place towards "One Europe." It is notable that according to **FitzGerald, Henry Kissinger** found Europeanization too complex to grasp: *it is a groping, slow movement toward a declaration of European identity.*

FitzGerald concluded:

> *"...the work of political cooperation is important because it is only through this pragmatic process of seeking on a piecemeal basis to harmonize foreign policy that that foundation can be laid for a European Community that can eventually develop into a genuine federation or confederation."[2]*

FRANCE

The French Trilateral component is not truly French but represents mainly the French connection to international and European organizations plus French banking interests.

Trilateralism is totally inconsistent with a deeply held sense of French nationalism. French Trilaterals are much further from the cultural soul of their country than perhaps any other Trilaterals.

The three French Trilateral-European Community links are of

major significance. **Raymond Barre**, prime minister and Minister of France, was formerly vice president for Economic and Social Affairs at EEC.

Georges Berthoin, Trilateral European chairman, was the chief EEC representative to the United Kingdom, and was private secretary to the father of the One Europe concept - Jean Monnet. **Robert Marjolin** was formerly vice-president of the Commission of the European Communities and was a member of the International Advisory Committee of the Chase Manhattan Bank. **Marjolin** was for many years connected with the EEC and the organization of the OEEC, and with **Berthoin**, he forms the core link between French Trilateralism, the European Economic Community and **David Rockefeller**.

Why does France, the most independent nationalistic nation in Europe - almost the world - produce the strongest single Trilateral link to **David Rockefeller**? The answer might be that the Trilateral Executive Committee recognized the problem of French nationalism as standing in the way of One Europe and One World; perhaps special efforts were made to ensure a powerful French connection.

This French Trilateral triad is backed up by numerous lesser French Trilaterals with One Europe connections. They include **R. Bonety**, formerly with the EEC, **Paul Delouvrier**, formerly with the European Iron and Steel Commission, a part of EEC, and **Francois Duchene**, a French Trilateral residing in England as director of the Center for Contemporary European Studies at the University of Sussex. (This might be termed a European Trilateral think tank on a minor scale.)

Michel Gaudet was formerly director general of the EEC legal service. **Thierry De Montbrial** is director of the Institut Francais des Relations Internationales in Paris. This is the French affiliate to the Royal Institute of International Affairs with Trilateral connections through **Sir Andrew Shonfield**. Lastly, there is **Roger Seydoux**, formerly with UNESCO and UN.

Out of twenty-seven French Trilaterals we find that nine have strong One Europe connections.

WEST GERMANY

The West German team of twenty-one Trilaterals includes **Count Otto Lambsdorff**, the German Minister of Economics. In general, West German Trilaterals stress industrial and trade union connections rather than One Europe connections.

Trade unionists include **K. Hauenschild** (Chemical, Paper and Pottery Workers), **E. Loderer** (Metal Workers Union) and **H.O. Vetter** (Federation of Trade Unions).

Industrialists with U.S. connections include **Otto Wolff**, a director of EXXON and a member of the secret Bilderberger group.

Bank directors include **H.K. Jannott**, **A. Munchmeyer** and **N. Kloten**.

No German Trilaterals have more than incidental connections with One Europe. Even politician Trilaterals in Germany are domestically oriented, for example, **K.H. Narjes**, **H.J. Junghans** and **O. Sund**. The only major exception to this observation is **Karl Kaiser**, director of the Research Institute of the German Society for Foreign Policy and who is widely reported abroad and in West Germany.

ITALY

By contrast to West Germany, Italy has a major EEC and One Europe representation.

These Italian Trilaterals include:

- **F. Bobba**, in 1950, was with the Italian Ministry of Foreign Affairs with responsibility for European integration. Later, **Bobba** became director general of Economic and Financial Affairs at EEC.
- **Guido Carli** is a longtime member of the EEC Monetary Committee.
- **Umberto Colombo** is a director of the Committee for Scientific Policy at OECD.
- **G. Colonna Di Paliano** has been with a variety of European organizations since 1964, including EEC, ECSC and Euratom. He is also a director of EXXON.
- **E. Ortona** is a former president of the UN Security

Council and a president of Honeywell Information Systems (Italia).

- **Giovanni Agnelli** is a key Trilateral, president of Fiat and on the International Advisory committee of Chase Manhattan (**Henry Kissinger** is chairman of the IAC).

LUXEMBOURG

Although an important member of the European Community, Luxembourg has no Trilateral members.

NETHERLANDS

With six Trilaterals, Netherlands has several connected with One Europe including:

- **M. Kohnstamm**, a civil servant with the ECSC in the 1950's and a vice-president of the Action Committee of the United States of Europe since 1956.
- **J. Loudon** is a member of the Atlantic Institute and Ford Foundation, a member of the Chase Manhattan International Advisory committee and chairman of Royal Dutch Shell.
- **E. Wellenstein** was with ECSC from 1953-1967 and director General of External Relations at EEC from 1973-1976.

UNITED KINGDOM

With twenty-six Trilateralists, Great Britain has several with a close connection to EEC Affairs. These include:

- **R.H. Grierson**, director general of Industrial and Technical Affairs at EEC in 1973-74.
- **R. Maudling**, with EEC in 1958-59.
- **C. O'Neill**, ambassador to EEC in 1963-66 and a director of the "Britain in Europe Campaign" 1974-75.
- **Lord Harlech**, chairman of the European Movement.
- **A.L. Williams**, deputy director of European Movement 1970- 71.

In brief then, there is (a) except in the case of West Germany, a major connection between One Europe and Trilateralism, and (b) a rather deep connection between Chase Manhattan and the European side of Trilateralism.

HOW EUROPE SEES THE POLITICAL PROCESS

In some ways Europeans have a more sophisticated understanding of the realities of the world political process than many Americans. Yet in other ways Europeans are quite deficient in their understanding of the political workings of both the United States and the Soviet Union.

Historically, Europe has usually been run by elites. Populism in the American tradition does not exist in Europe - it is more of a frontier phenomenon, in the Jefferson-Jackson tradition. Elites are known and hardly mysterious for Europeans. In Britain, for example, the word "establishment" is generally accepted, if not approved, and no one uses the label "paranoid" or "conspiratorialist" to an argument based on acceptance of an Establishment.

For many years in the United States any talk of "elites" or "establishment" put the speaker into the "kook" category. Europe doesn't have to be convinced of the existence of an elite; it is accepted.

From a European perspective, the distinction between Republican and Democrat has always been elusive. The major American parties are seen as merely different sides of the same coin, and the existence of a supra-party elite is quite acceptable.

So it is easier for Europeans to accept the concept of Trilateralism as a verifiable fact. Trilateral human rights policies are seen more clearly in Europe as a pragmatic diplomatic tool. Consequently Germany and France have been major supporters of South Africa, knowing full well that the US elitist attack on South Africa has been motivated by self- interest, not human rights.

Where Europe is weak is in its knowledge of the *details* of American elitism. While the concept is acceptable, knowledge of the details is vague, hazy and perhaps largely unknown.

EUROPEAN BLOCKAGES TO INFORMATION

Rather ironically though, Europe has greater blocks to details of US elitist operations than the United States. Governments own most of the radio and television industry this means censorship. A program on French radio or television exposing Trilateralism and its meaning for Europe is unthinkable; after all, an important part of the European elite is also Trilateral. French critics such as Pierre de Villamarest have a harder time disseminating information than critics in the United States.

Elitism in Europe is more securely entrenched than in the US. Both the US Constitution and American traditions frown on aristocracies and the flowering American aristocracy that stems from Alexander Hamilton.

ASPEN INSTITUTE BERLIN

The implementation of the concepts of secular humanism in Europe is being achieved through a branch of the Aspen Institute for Humanistic Studies, Trilateralists and other elitists. (See Chapters Two and Three.) This is a major connection between European Trilateralism and American Trilateralism. In 1974, the Aspen Institute Berlin was founded as "an integral part of the Aspen Institute for Humanistic Studies" and serves as the European and non-US funnel through which Trilateral ideas flow. In particular, the Aspen Institute Berlin states its purpose "as a flexible and experimental effort to articulate and to strengthen individual and social *adherence* to humanistic values."[3] (Emphasis added.) In other words, they are trying to force their values on Europe as well.

Members of the board of Aspen Institute Berlin include a host of Trilateralists, humanists, elitists and "One Europe" advocates: **Georges Berthoin** fits all those labels. Another board member is Marion Countess Donhoff, the publisher of *Die Zeit,* whose editor-in-chief is Trilateralist **Theo Sommer**, a participant in **Henry Kissinger**'s International Seminar in 1960. **Thierry De Montbrial** was at one time affiliated with the University of California at Berkeley and is the author of books on world economy and energy policy. **Richard Lowenthal**, a professor emeritus at the Free University of Berlin, has taught at elitist schools like

University of California at Berkeley, Columbia (where **Brzezinski** had planned to return in January, 1981), Harvard and Stanford, and is an expert on foreign policy, especially in regard to the Communist bloc.

Other Trilateral elitists on the board of Aspen-Berlin whom we wish to mention are: **Robert McNamara**, president, World Bank; **Robert O. Anderson**, chairman, Aspen Institute and Atlantic Richfield; **Pehr Gyllenhammaer**, president, Volvo; **Conor Cruise O'Brien**, editor-in-chief, *The Observer*, London; **Jean-Francois Revel**, editor, *L'Express*, Paris.

Additionally, we find the two most prominent German politicians of our time on the honorary board. First, there is **Willy Brandt**, former Federal Chancellor, chairman of the ruling Social Democratic Party and chairman of the United Nations' Independent Commission on International Development Issues (which included **Peter G. Peterson**, **Henry Kissinger** and *Washington Post* publisher **Katherine Graham**).

Secondly, there is **Helmut Schmidt**, Chancellor of the Federal Republic of Germany, a close friend of **Valery Giscard d'Estaing**.

Willy Brandt, in describing the reasoning for the Aspen Institute Berlin's location, gave away his own lack of understanding of the threat of the Communist bloc when he stated, "The choice of Berlin is not accidental - we regard it as a crossroads and touchstone of the new relationship between East and West." More recently, a publication of the Aspen Institute Berlin reported, "Scholars and public figures from the Soviet Union and other countries of Eastern Europe actively participate in the work of the Aspen Institute Berlin."[5] Once again, we view the Trilateralist's naiveté and self-serving attitude.

In sum, The Aspen Institute Berlin is a European mirror image of Trilateralist thought and practice.

ENDNOTES

1. Garret FitzGerald, *"Political- Cooperation: Towards a Common Policy",*
2. Commission of the European Communities, European September-October 1978, p. 18. 2. Ibid., p. 20.
3. *Aspen Institute of Berlin Catalogue.* p. 2.
4. Ibid., p. 2.
5. Ibid., p. 3.

CHAPTER TEN

CONCLUDING THOUGHTS

There is no doubt that the Trilateral Commission exists: it is not a figment of a wild imagination as some of its supporters claim. Further, this Commission has written policies and set objectives. During the Carter administration, members of the Commission had the majority of executive branch power under their control, and it doesn't look like much is changing under the new Reagan administration.

At this point, it is useful to address the criticism of the Trilateral Commission, and the counter-criticism from the Commission itself.

David Rockefeller's feelings about Trilateral critics have been amply demonstrated: he views himself as the "moderate middle," and puts his critics on the "far right." This same theme was used in the November 24, 1980 issue of *Forbes Magazine:* Washington Bureau Chief Jerry Flint titled his article *What's a Trilateral Commission?* and captioned it "Why Marxists and Birchers love to hate the Trilateral Commission."[1]

Flint stated,

"On the Right radical end of the political fringe, for example, is Patrick Wood, co-author of the book Trilaterals Over Washington - 53,000 sold, he says, who has a new expose coming and who publishes a monthly newsletter, The Trilateral

Observer, from Scottsdale, Ariz. He warns that the Trilaterals want to trade America's economic independence for some kind of new, world economic order, a playground for the multinationals, manipulating governments for their profits. "[2]

The article then talked about the John Birch Society (rightwing), Laurence Shoup (a Marxist writer) and *Penthouse* magazine. Flint interviewed Commission coordinator and member **George Franklin** who claimed "We haven't a single advocate of world government..."[3]

One of Flint's concluding thoughts was "Alas, people and their conspiracy theories are not easily parted. It is much easier to imagine a villain than to think things through."[4]

When this coauthor (Wood) was interviewed, Flint was pointedly told that neither Sutton nor Wood advocate, teach or believe in a "conspiracy" theory as such. This position has been expounded on dozens of radio and TV shows all over America, and on numerous of prestigious speaking platforms.

A conspiracy is defined by Webster's as "a secret agreement to do something legal or illegal." Since the coauthors have had little trouble in acquiring information on Trilateral activities and positions, it can hardly be called a secret organization. Further, who has a right to act as judge and jury to determine legality or illegality of specific acts by members of the Trilateral Commission? (This requires a Congressional investigation into the facts presented in *Trilaterals Over Washington.*)

The Forbes article is significant for the following reasons:

- Flint ignored the reasons given for the coauthors' refusal to be involved with "conspiracy" tactics.
- He arbitrarily placed the authors in the "Right radical end of the political fringe," implied to be even to the right of the John Birch Society.
- He *did not mention* Professor Antony Sutton's name anywhere in the article, nor the fact that he was formerly a research fellow with Hoover Institution for War, Peace and Revolution at Stanford University - hardly the "Right radical end" of anything!
- Ignored was *The Nation's* recent article attacking the

Trilateral Commission. *The Nation* is one of the most prestigious *liberal* publications in the country.[5]

- Also ignored was the suppressed criticism of the Commission by Nobel Laureate Professor George Wald in August 1980[6] - the reader may not agree with the criticism, but certainly cannot discount the source and the platform.[7]

The *Forbes* article typifies "establishment" handling of critics of the Commission. Responsible and researched criticism is "associated" with various minority radical elements in the country.

Since the truth of the matter (the facts) cannot be discredited, they attempt to discredit the critic. This is a shallow and weak ploy, not too difficult to see through.

To be fair though, some credit can be given the Commission in sending representatives to participate in public debates around the US with the coauthors. North American Secretary **Charles Heck** appeared with Patrick Wood on the nationally broadcasted *Larry King Show* on the Mutual Broadcasting System, among others. Commissioners **George Franklin** and **Phillip Trezise** debated with Antony Sutton at different times. **George Franklin** has debated with left-wing Trilateral critic Howard Katz on an influential T.V. program in Florida.

It is the personal experience of the authors that when public response was measured (i.e., on "call-in" radio, T.V. shows or public speaking events), sentiment was at least 95% hostile to the position of the Trilateral Commission and only 5% against the position taken by the coauthors. While Commission members have no reason to admit it, overwhelming public antipathy against the Commission has stung deeply.

It has never been the coauthors' intent to unfairly discredit a person in contrast to the philosophy that person holds. People are people but ideas differ. When facts don't line up with a person's philosophy, and this discrepancy is pointed out, it is difficult for the person to resolve the discrepancy. The reaction will most likely be negative, ranging from ignoring the facts to lashing out at the person(s) delivering the facts.

The coauthors readily admit that a certain amount of their

own bias shows in their writings, but this is only natural. Despite this, these works have been used by both conservative and liberal writers around the world. The reason is the coauthors' integrity for reporting facts is unquestioned, even if the reader disagrees with the conclusions offered.

As you have read this book, you may have arrived at different conclusions than the coauthors; in any case, you are probably antithetic to the Trilateral Commission and to the proposed *New International Economic World Order*. You are urged to further your information gathering in your own community or sphere of influence. Share what you find with others, including the coauthors.

Freedom of the press is predicated on a free interchange of ideas and information. Any attempts to suppress either must be protested to the limit of moral restraint.

All in all, the information in this book (and in Volume I, as well) shows a very bleak picture of politics and the economics in the United States. Even so, it is a mistake to just abandon the field to the elite. God gave you a thinker (your brain) that is able to discern reality from fiction and fantasy; don't be swayed by psychological pressure designed to discredit what you think. Even if your thinking is *wrong,* if you let someone browbeat you out of your position, you will still be wrong. Test every thing weigh, digest, chew, mull over, check, re- search, etc.

Then stand on *your* findings and decisions.

Finally, the coauthors believe that once the American in the street realizes the full implications of the Trilateral process, then Trilateralism will receive outright rejection. The reason is simple: Trilateralism is diametrically opposed to the US Constitution and will ultimately require removal of the Constitution if the New Intrnational Economic World Order is to succeed.

ENDNOTES

1. 1. Jerry Flint, *What's a Trilateral Commission?,* Forbes (November 24, 1980), p. 45. 2. Ibid., p. 45.
2. 3. Ibid., p. 46.
3. 4. Ibid., p. 49.

APPENDIX I

1979 INTERVIEW WITH GEORGE S. FRANKLIN, JR.

COORDINATOR OF
THE TRILATERAL COMMISSION

Introduction

In the original analysis of the Trilateral Commission in the 1970s, the only persons to actually interview and debate members of that elite group were Antony C. Sutton and me, Patrick Wood. From 1978 through 1981, we together or individually engaged at least seven different Commission members in public debate.

On July 27, 1979, Radio Station KLMG, Council Bluffs, Iowa aired a highly informative interview with George S. Franklin, Jr., Coordinator of the Trilateral Commission and long-time associate of David Rockefeller.

Joe Martin, the commentator on the program, invited authors Antony Sutton and Patrick Wood to participate in the questioning. The program was probably the most penetrating view of Trilateralism yet uncovered.

Only one complete transcript remains intact from those interviews, and it is reproduced below. Hopefully, this will give you some insight into the inner workings, attitude and mindset of Commission members.

Lest anyone make accusation that this transcript was selectively edited to show a "bad light" on the Commission, it is reprinted in full, without edit. Editor's comments are added in certain places to clarify the facts, when appropriate, and are clearly identified to the reader as such. Members of the Trilateral Commission are noted in bold type. The entire interview was first and only published in the *Trilateral Observer* in 1979, which was published by Patrick Wood and The August Corporation.

The Interview

Commentator: Hello.

Wood: Hello.

Commentator: Is this Mr. Wood?

Wood: Yes, it is.

Commentator: Patrick Wood, we have Antony Sutton on the other line. You two are there now, right?

Wood: Yes.

Commentator: Are you there too, Mr. Sutton?

Sutton: Yes.

Commentator: All right. Before we get Mr. Franklin on the phone, tell us, what is your concise opinion of the Trilateral Commission?

Sutton: It would seem that this is **David Rockefeller**'s concept, his creation; he financed it. The Trilateral Commission has only 77 or so American members. It's a closed elitist group. I do not believe that they in any way represent general thinking in the United States. For example, they want to restrict the rights of the media in violation of the Constitution.

> *[Ed: Compare this initial statement to Franklin's admissions during the interview.]*

Commentator: They want to restrict the rights of the media?

Sutton: Yes.

Commentator: All right, we have Mr. **George Franklin** on the phone right now, okay? Hang on, gentlemen. Hello, am I talking to Mr. **George S. Franklin**?

Franklin: That is right.

Commentator: You are coordinator of the Trilateral Commission?

Franklin: That is right.

Commentator: Mr. Franklin, my name is Joe Martin. I have two other gentlemen on the line and I have listeners on the line too, who would like to ask a few questions regarding the Trilateral Commission. Are you prepared to answer some questions, sir?

Franklin: I hope so.

Commentator: Is the Trilateral commission presently involved in any effort to make a one-world?

Franklin: Definitely not. We have not. We have no one-world doctrine.

Our only belief that is shared by most of the members of the Commission itself is that this world will somehow do better if the advanced industrial democracy that serves Japan and the United States can cooperate and talk things out together and try to work on programs rather than at cross purposes, but definitely not any idea of a world government or a government of these areas.

> *[Ed: "Definitely not," says Franklin. Numerous statements in Trilateral writings show Franklin is in error. For example: "The economic officials of at least the largest countries must begin to think in terms of managing a single world economy in addition to managing international economic relations among countries," Trilateral Commission Task Force Reports: 9-14, page 268.]*

Commentator: Why is it, in the Trilateral Commission that the name **David Rockefeller** shows up so persistently or [the name of] one of his organizations?

Franklin: Well, this is very reasonable. **David Rockefeller** is the Chairman of the North American group. There are three chairmen: one is [with] the North American group, one is [with] the Japanese group, and one is [with] the European group. Also, the Commission was really **David Rockefelle**r's original idea.

> *[Ed:Note that Franklin does not say (at this point) that the Trilateral Commission was financed and established by David Rockefeller.]*

Commentator: On President **Carter**'s staff, how many Trilateral Commission members do you have?

Franklin: Eighteen.

Commentator: Don't you think that is rather heavy?

Franklin: It is quite a lot, yes.

Commentator: Don't you think it is rather unusual? How many members are there actually in the Trilateral Commission?

Franklin: We have 77 in the United States.

Commentator: Don't you think it is rather unusual to have 18 members on the Carter staff?

Franklin: Yes, I think we chose some very able people when we started the Commission. The President happens to think well of quite a number of them.

Commentator: All right, we would like to bring in our two other guests -

men who have written a book on the Trilateral Commission. You may be familiar with Mr. Antony Sutton and Mr. Patrick Wood?

Franklin: I have not met them, but I do know their names, yes.

Commentator: Mr. Sutton and Mr. Wood, would you care to ask Mr. Franklin a question?

Sutton: Well, I certainly would. This is Tony Sutton. You have 77 members of which 18 are in the Carter Administration. Do you believe that the only able people in the United States are Trilateralists?

Franklin: Of course not, and incidentally, the 18 are no longer members of the Commission because this is supposed to be a private organization and as soon as anybody joins the government they no longer are members of the Commission.

Sutton: Yes, but they are members of the Commission when they join.

Franklin: That is correct.

Sutton: Do you believe that the only able people in the United States are Trilateralists?

Franklin: Of course not.

Sutton: Well, how come the heavy percentage?

Franklin: Well, when we started to choose members, we did try to pick out the ablest people we could and I think many of those that are in the Carter Administration would have been chosen by any group that was interested in the foreign policy question.

Sutton: Would you say that you have an undue influence on policy in the United States?

Franklin: I would not, no.

Sutton: I think any reasonable man would say that if you have 18 Trilateralists out of 77 in the Carter Administration you have a preponderant influence.

Franklin: These men are not responsive to anything that the Trilateral Commission might advocate. We do have about two reports we put out each year, and we do hope they have some influence or we would not put them out.

> [Ed: The Trilateral Commission puts out considerably more than two reports each year. In 1974 and 1976, it was four in each year plus four issues of "Trialogue"]

Sutton: May I ask another question?

Franklin: Yes.

Sutton: Who financed the Trilateral Commission originally?

Franklin: Uhh. . .The first supporter of all was a foundation called the Kettering Foundation. I can tell you who is financing it at the present time, which might be of more interest to you.

> [Ed: This is what Franklin said in another interview: *"In the mean-time, David Rockefeller and the Kettering Foundation had provided transitional funding."*]

Sutton: Is it not the Rockefeller Brothers' Fund?

Franklin: The Rockefeller Brothers' Fund? The North American end of the Commission needs $1.5 million over the next 3 years. Of this amount, $180,000 will be contributed by the Rockefeller Brother's fund and $150,000 by David Rockefeller.

Commentator: Does that mean that most of it is being financed by the Rockefellers?

Franklin: No, it means that about one fifth of the North American end is being financed by the Rockefellers and none of the European and Japanese end.

Commentator: Do you have any further questions, Mr. Sutton?

Sutton: No, I do not.

Commentator: Do you have a question, Mr. Wood?

Wood: Yes, I have one question. In reading your literature and reports, there is a great deal of mention of the term "Interdependence".

Franklin: Right.

Wood: While we can see that there is some need for the world to cooper-ate in many areas, this system of interdependence seems to have some very profound effect on the United States structure as it is today. For instance, our national structure versus the interdependent structure in the world. Now, do you feel that this interdependent structure has been properly presented to the American public for approval or disapproval?

Franklin: Well, I don't think that it is a question of approval or disap-proval altogether. For example, we get a great deal of our natural re-sources from abroad. Everybody knows that we get a great deal of oil from abroad. So, whether we like it or not, we are much more dependent on other nations that we used to be. Now, this does not mean that they make our decisions for us on what our policies are going to be, and our energy policies are made here by the President and Congress. Now, they do consult others about them because they have to, because unfortunately we are forced to become interdependent.

> *[Ed: The term "interdependent" is a key word in Trilateralism. Think for a moment: The known world has always been more or less interdependent. Trilateralists use "interdependence" in a manner analogous to the propaganda methods of Goebbels: if you repeat a phrase often enough people will begin to accept it automatically in the required context. The required context for Trilaterals is to get across the idea that "one-world" is inevitable."]*

Commentator: Does that answer your question, Mr. Wood?

Wood: Well, perhaps not completely, let me phrase that another way. Do you feel that your policy - that is, those who represent the Trilateral policy as well as interdependence - do you feel that that philosophy is in accord with the typical American philosophy of nationalism and democracy and so on?

Franklin: Well, I think I would answer that this way. First, we are in fact interdependent. I say, unfortunately, we depend on much more that we used to. Therefore, we have to cooperate far more than we used to. But, that does not mean that we are giving other people the right to determine our policy and we do not advocate that. You will not find that in any of our reports.

> *[Ed: Notice how Franklin ducks around the key issue presented by Wood, i.e., whether the concept as used by Trilaterals is inconsistent with generally accepted American ideals. Wood said nothing about "... giving other people the right to determine our policy." This is a straw man erected by Franklin to duck the issue.]*

Wood: Do you feel that the Trilateral Commission position has been publicized really at all around the country?

Franklin: We try to publicize it, we do not altogether succeed because there are so many other people who also want publicity, but we do try. Anything we do is open to public scrutiny.

> *[Ed: The August Corporation had recently commissioned a thorough search of the massive New York Times computerized data base. We came up with a very meager list of references to Trilateralism. Only 71 references in the past six years in all major U.S. and foreign pub-*

lications. Many of these were no more than short paragraphs. We know that the Trilateral Commission mailing list has only 4,000 names including all its 250 members and 600 or so Congressmen and elitists. In brief, media coverage has been - and is - extremely small. The 71 citations by the way include mostly critical articles from independent authors. It also includes such efforts as the Time front-page promotion of Jimmy Carter for President - probably the key effort on Carter's behalf. **Hedley Donovan** *was then Editor-in-Chief of Time.]*

Commentator: Mr. Sutton?

Sutton: **Paul Volcker** was a member of the Trilateral Commission and has just been appointed Chairman of the Federal Reserve Board. Does **Paul Volcker** have any connection with Chase Manhattan which is dominated by Rockefellers?

Franklin: He was, quite a long time ago, on the staff of [Chase] Manhattan.

[Ed: **Paul Volcke**r has twice worked for Chase Manhattan Bank. In the 1950s as an economist and again in the 1960s as Vice President for Planning. We cannot deny that Volcker "knows about (Trilateral) financial policies" as stated by Franklin.]

Sutton: Don't you think that this is quite an unhealthy situation, where you have a man connected with Chase who is now Chairman of the Federal Reserve Board? Doesn't this give some credence to the criticism of elitism?

Franklin: Conflict of interest?

Sutton: Yes.

Franklin: It does give some credence to it. On the other hand, it is very important that the Chairman of the Federal Reserve Bank know about our financial policies and, therefore, will certainly have been connected to some financial institution. This has not always been the case. I think that anyone who knows **Paul Volcker**, knows that he is an extraordinarily objective person. I think if you would notice, that the editorial comments on his appointments were almost uniformly favorable, there must have been some that were unfavorable, but I have not seen them.

Sutton: May I ask another question?

Commentator: Go Ahead.

Sutton: Mr. **Donovan**, of Time-Life, has just been appointed Special Assistant to President Carter. Mr. Donovan is a member of your Commission.

Franklin: That is correct.

Sutton: Does this not emphasize the fact that the Carter Administration is choosing its administration from an extremely a narrow range. In other words, the Trilateral Commission?

Franklin: I do not think that that needs any confirmation. That is a matter of fact that he has chosen most of his main foreign policy people, I would have to say, from the people he got to know while he was on the Trilateral Commission.

> [Ed: Franklin admits that the "Carter Administration is choosing its administration from an extremely narrow range."]

Sutton: Well, I can only make the statement that this leaves any reasonable man with the impression that the Carter Administration is dominated by the Trilateral Commission with your specific ideas which many people do not agree with.

Franklin: Well, I would certainly agree that people who were members of the Commission have predominant places in the foreign policy aspects of the Carter Administration. They are not, because they are members of the Commission, controlled in any sense by us. I do think that they do share a common belief that is very important that we work particularly with Europe and Japan or we are all going to be in trouble.

Sutton: But this common belief may not reflect the beliefs of the American people. How do you know that it does?

Franklin: I do not know that it does. I am no man to interpret what the people think about.

Sutton: In other words, you are quite willing to go ahead [and] establish a Commission which you say does not necessarily reflect the views of the people in the United States? It appears to me that you have taken over political power.

Franklin: I do not think this is true at all. Anybody who forms a group for certain purposes obviously tries to achieve these purposes. We do believe that it is important that Europe, Japan, and the United States get along together. That much we do believe. We also chose the best people we could get as members of the Commission. Fortunately, nearly all accepted. The President was one of them and he happened to have thought that these were very able people indeed, and he asked them to be in his government, it is as simple as that. If you are going to ask me if I am very unhappy about that, the answer is no. I think that these are good people.

Wood: May I ask a little bit more pointedly, if Carter got his education from the Trilateral Commission, was not his dean of students, so to speak, Mr. **Brzezinski**?

Franklin: I cannot tell you exactly what role Brzezinski had, but certainly he did have considerable effect on the education Carter received on foreign policy.

Wood: Mr. Brzezinski is on record in more than one of his books as being a proponent of rejuvenating or redesigning the U.S. Constitution, is this correct?

Franklin: I have not read all his books, I have not seen that statement, and I have worked with him very closely for three years and he has not said anything of that sort to me.

Wood: As a matter of fact, he is on record and in one of his books as indicating that the U.S. Constitution as it is today is not able to lead us into an interdependent world and that it should be redesigned to reflect the interdependence that we must move ahead towards.

Franklin: As I say, if you tell me that, I must believe it, and I have not read that book and I have never got any inkling of that between 1973 and 1976.

[*Ed: Here is what Brzezinski writes in one of his books Between Two Ages: America's Role in the Technetronic Era:*

Tension is unavoidable as man strives to assimilate the new into the framework of the old. For a time the established framework resiliently integrates the new by adapting it in a more familiar shape. But at some point the old framework becomes overloaded. The new input can no longer be redefined into traditional forms, and eventually it asserts itself with compelling force. Today, though, the old framework of international politics - with their spheres of influence, military alliances between nation-states, the fiction of sovereignty, doctrinal conflicts arising from nineteenth century crises - is clearly no longer compatible with reality."

and specifically on changing the U.S. Constitution:

The approaching two-hundredth anniversary of the Declaration of Independence could justify the call for a national constitutional convention to re-examine the nation's formal institutional framework. Either 1976 or 1989 - the two-hundredth anniversary of the Constitution could serve as a suitable target date culminating a national dialogue on the relevance of existing arrangements... Realism,

however, forces us to recognize that the necessary political innova-
tion will not come from direct constitutional reform, desirable as that
would be. The needed change is more likely to develop incrementally
and less overtly ... in keeping with the American tradition of blurring
distinctions between public and private institution.

Obviously Franklin is either unaware of the writing of his "close" as-
sociate Brzezinski or is evading the question.]

Commentator: I would like to interject a question if I could. Mr. Franklin, within the Trilateral Commission, are there any Trilateralists who have control of the energy resources in this world?

Franklin: No. We have no major oil companies represented on the Commission.

Commentator: I mean stockholders in oil companies.

Franklin: I am sure that **David Rockefeller** must have some stock in an oil company. I do not know.

Commentator: Doesn't **David Rockefeller** have stock in Chase National Bank?

Franklin: Definitely

Commentator: Doesn't Chase National Bank have stock in Exxon?

Franklin: Honestly, I do not know.

Commentator: Standard Oil? Mobil?

Sutton: Well, I do.

Franklin: I would be certain that some of their pension trusts and some of the trusts that they hold for individuals, undoubtedly do.

Commentator: So, the Trilateral Commission has no effect at all in the energy field at all?

Franklin: Yes, the Trilateral Commission has written a report on energy. There were three authors, there were always three authors. The American author was **John Sawhill**, who was formerly head of the Energy Administration and is now presently of New York University.

Commentator: I have read where the oil and gas world is dominated by seven major firms, do you agree with that?

Franklin: I do not have expertise in this field, but I think it sounds reasonable.

Commentator: Well, a listing of controlling ownership in these major oil and gas companies by banks - by Trilateral Commissioners - is listed as Manufacturer's Hanover, Chase Bank, Wells Fargo Bank, First National Bank of Chicago, and First Continental of Illinois. And these all supposedly are of Trilateral representation. Is that true, sir?

Franklin: No, sir, it is not true. Give me the list again. I think I can tell you which are and which are not.

Commentator: Manufacturer's Hanover.

Franklin: No, sir, it is not.

Commentator: There are no stockholders in that, who are members of the Trilateral Commission?

Franklin: Wait a minute. I cannot tell you whether there are no stockholders in Manufacturer's Hanover. I might even be a stockholder in Manufacturer's Hanover. I am not.

Commentator: Chase Manhattan figures prominently.

Franklin: Chase Manhattan certainly.

Commentator: ...which is David Rockefeller's Bank!

Franklin: There is no question about that.

Commentator: So there is some connection with the energy field.

Franklin: Well, yes.

Commentator: So, if Chase Manhattan has stock in Exxon, Mobil, and Standard Oil, then there is a direct connection there?

Franklin: I am sure that is true. Every bank runs pension trusts, so it must have some of its trust money in some of those companies.

Commentator: I have read, and I do not know if it is true, you may answer this, that Chase Manhattan is a number one stockholder in Exxon, number three in Mobil, and number two in Standard Oil.

Franklin: I just would not know.

Commentator: Do you have any questions, Mr. Sutton?

Sutton: Yes, the figures you have just quoted about Chase Manhattan stock ownership in the oil companies: these were published by the U.S. Senate some years ago. There is a series of these volumes. One, for example, is entitled *Disclosure of Corporate Ownership*.

[Ed: Any reader investigating further should note that the ownership is heavily disguised by use of nominee companies. For example "Cudd & Co." is a fictitious nominee name for Chase Manhattan Bank.]

A partial list of nominees which have been used by Chase Manhattan Bank includes the following:

Andrews & Co.	Elzay & Co.	Reeves & Co.
Bedle & Co	Gansel & Co.	Ring & Co.
Bender & Co.	Gooss & Co.	Ryan & Co.
Chase Nominees Ltd.	Gunn & Co.	Settle & Co
Clint & Co.	Kane & Co.	Taylor & Witt
Cudd & Co.	McKenna & Co.	Timm & Co.
Dell & Co.	Padom & Co.	Titus & Co.
Egger & Co.	Pickering Ltd.	White & Co.
Ehren & Co.		

Franklin: I am sure that these banks could run billions of dollars through trusts and some of the trusts must be invested in some of these major oil companies.

Commentator: Then the Trilateral Commission member who has stock in the bank and who is also a high-ranking Trilateral Commission member, would have some jurisdiction over energy?

Franklin: No, not really. I know some of the management of these companies. They are not controlled by the stockholders the way they used to be.

Wood: Let's put that question another way if we might. It perhaps would be erroneous to say Chase Manhattan Bank controlled Exxon, because in fact, they do not. However, Chase Manhattan Bank is the largest single shareholder that Exxon has. Considering the discussion going on about the major oil companies, and their part in this energy crisis, don't you think that it would be possible to exercise control from Chase Manhattan Bank to put pressure on Exxon to help alleviate the energy crisis?

Franklin: Well, I think you could answer that kind of question just as well, as I can. Everybody has their own views on these things.

Commentator: You must be familiar with the members of your

Commission, especially with Mr. Rockefeller and his various holdings?

Franklin: I am extremely familiar with Mr. Rockefeller. I have known him for nearly 50 years.

Commentator: ... and his holdings?

Franklin: I am not at all familiar with his holdings.

Commentator: I think everybody is familiar with his holdings. I thought everybody was familiar with his holdings, I know he owns Chase Manhattan Bank.

Franklin: No, that is not true.

Commentator: I mean, he is the largest stockholder.

Franklin: That, I would agree to. I would say that he has about five percent, I am not sure.

Commentator: Five percent? Would you agree with that, Mr. Sutton?

Sutton: Yes, plus he is chairman of the board.

Franklin: Yes, that is correct. I have no doubt that he does control Chase Manhattan Bank.

Commentator: You have no doubt about that?

Franklin: No, basically, no. Directors are important.

Commentator: Do you have any doubt that as chairman, he controls the bank and Chase Manhattan also controls or at least partly controls the American Electric Power [the utility company]?

Franklin: I do not know anything about it.

Commentator: You are not sure about that?

Franklin: I just don't know. These things do not ever really enter into consideration. If you look at our energy report that will tell you whether you think this is an objective or effective document or not.

[Ed: Chase Manhattan Bank owns 1,646,706 shares of American Electric Power Company through two nominees, <Kane & Co. (1,059,967 shares) and Cudd & Co. (586,739 shares)>. This gives it a direct 2.8 percent of the total. However, numerous other holding in American Electric Power are maintained by banks and firms where Chase has some degree of control. For example, Morgan Guaranty has almost 500,000 shares and is dominated by J.P. Morgan; the second largest stockholder in J.P. Morgan is Chase Manhattan Bank.]

Commentator: Mr. Sutton?

Sutton: Can we go off energy for a while?

Commentator: Yes.

Sutton: I have a question for Mr. Franklin. Who chooses the members of the Trilateral commission?

Franklin: The Trilateral Commission's Executive Committee.

Sutton: Who comprises the committee?

Franklin: Who is on that committee?

Sutton: Yes.

Franklin: Okay. **William Coleman**, former Secretary of Transportation, who is a lawyer; **Lane Kirkland**, who is Secretary-General of the American Federation of Labor; **Henry Kissinger**, who does not need too much identification; **Bruce McLaury,** who is president of the Brookings Institution; **David Rockefeller**; **Robert Ingersoll**, who was formerly Deputy Secretary of State and Ambassador to Japan; **I. W. Able**, who was formerly head of United Steelworkers; and **William Roth**, who is a San Francisco businessman and was chief trade negotiator in the previous Kennedy trade round.

Sutton: May I ask a question? How many of these have a rather intimate business relationship with Mr. Rockefeller?

Franklin: **Henry Kissinger** is chairman of Mr. Rockefeller's Chase Advisory Committee.

Sutton: **Coleman**?

Franklin: Coleman, I don't think has any business relationship with him, he is a lawyer.

> *[Ed: In fact William Coleman is a Director of Chase Manhattan Bank which Franklin has already admitted to be controlled by **David Rockefeller**.]*

Sutton: Mr. **Ingersoll**?

Franklin: Mr. Ingersoll, I don't think has any business relationship.

Sutton: Isn't he connected with First Chicago?

Franklin: He is vice chairman of the University of Chicago.

Sutton: No, what about the First Bank of Chicago? [First Chicago Corp.]

Franklin: I don't believe that Ingersoll has any relationship with banks in Chicago, but I don't know for certain on that.

[Ed: Robert Stephen Ingersoll before joining the Washington "revolving door" was a director of the First National Bank of Chicago, a subsidiary of First Chicago Corp. The largest single shareholder in First Chicago is David Rockefeller's Chase Manhattan Bank. Ingersoll has also been a director of Atlantic Richfield and Burlington Northern. Chase Manhattan is also the largest single stockholder in these two companies. Thus, Ingersoll has a long standing relationship with Rockefeller interests.]

Commentator: We are adding another man to the interview, his name is Mr. John Rees, a very fine writer from the *Review of the News*, Washington, D.C., who is in the area right at this time to make some speeches.

Sutton: Mr. Franklin, do you believe in freedom of the press in the United States?

Franklin: Definitely, of course.

Sutton: Let me quote you from a book *Crisis In Democracy*, written by **Michel Crozier**, who is a Trilateral member.

Franklin: Correct.

Sutton: I am quoting from page 35 of his book: *"The media has thus become an autonomous power. We are now witnessing a crucial change with the profession. That is, media tends to regulate itself in such a way as to resist the pressure from financial or government interests."* Does that not mean that you want to restrict the press in some way?

Franklin: I can't quite hear you.

Sutton: Let me paraphrase this for you. I think I will be clear in my paraphrasing. The Trilateral Commission is unhappy with the press because it resists the pressure from financial or government interests. That is one of your statements.

Franklin: Now, let me say something about our book. The book that we put out, the report, is the responsibility of the authors and not of the Commission itself. You will find that in the back of a number of them, and that book is one of them, that other members of the Commission will hear dissenting views, and you will find dissenting views in the back of that book on the press question.

Sutton: I would like to quote a further statement from the same book and leave the questions at that point: "The media deprives government and to some extent other responsible authorities of the time lag and tolerance that make it possible to innovate and to experiment responsibly." What the book recommends is something like the Interstate Commerce Commission to control the press. This seems to me to be a violation of the Constitution.

Franklin: I would agree with you that we do not want something like the Interstate Commerce Commission to control the press.

> [Ed: **Michel Crozier**, et al, in Crisis In Democracy make the following statements with reference to the "Interstate Commerce Act and the Sherman Anti-trust Act":
>
> "Something comparable appears to be now needed with respect to the media.... there is also the need to assure to the government the right and the ability to withhold information at the source" (page 182).
>
> The authors go on to argue that if journalists do not conform to these new restrictive standards then "The alternative could well be regulation by the government."]

Sutton: I fail to understand why the Trilateral Commission would associate itself with such a viewpoint.

Franklin: As I just mentioned to you. We hired three authors for each report. The authors are allowed to say what they think is correct. What the Trilateral Commission does is this: It says we think this report is worthwhile for the public to see. This does not mean that all the members of the Commission agree with all the statements in the report and, in fact, a majority of them might disagree with certain things. Now, where a statement is one that many Commissioners seem to disagree with we then do put in the back a summary of the discussion. That book does have a summary of the discussion of our meeting which questions various things in the book, in the back of it.

Sutton: Would you say Mr. Franklin that the members of the Commission do have a common philosophy?

Franklin: Yes. I think a common philosophy. I think that all of them believe that this world will work better if the principal industrial powers consult each other on their policies and try to work them out together. This does not mean that they will agree on everything. Of course, they won't. But, at least they will know what the other countries feel, and why they feel it.

Sutton: *The Financial Times* in London -- the editor is **Ferdy Fisher**, a

Trilateralist. He fired a long time editorial writer, Gordon Tether, because Tether wanted to write articles criticizing the Trilateral Commission. Do you have any comments?

Franklin: I didn't know that at all. It sounds terribly unlikely, but if you say that it is so, probably it is.

[Ed: See Chapter Seven "Trilateral Censorship: the case of C. Gordon Tether" in Trilaterals Over Washington. Trilaterals see the media as the "gatekeeper" and comment as follows:

"Their main impact is visibility. The only real event is the event that is reported and seen. Thus, journalists possess a crucial role as gate-keepers of one of the central dimensions of public life."]

Rees: Frankly, Mr. Martin, with Antony Sutton on the line, I feel absolutely a novice, because Antony is a real expert on the Trilateral.

Sutton: Well, I am looking for information.

Commentator: Are you getting information?

Sutton: Yes, I am very definitely getting information.

Commentator: Do you have any other questions?

Sutton: Not at the moment. I'd rather hear someone else.

Commentator: All right.

Wood: I do have one question, if I might. You mentioned earlier that as you decided to issue a report, whether it reflected Trilateral policy or not, you felt that it was worthy to be shared with the public. Is that correct?

Franklin: We do not have a Trilateral policy, except for the very broad policy [which] is that each of these major areas ought to know what the other countries are doing and why and try to work things out as much as possible. That is our only Trilateral policy, I would say. We don't have a policy on energy and a policy on monetary reform and a policy on, etc.

[Ed: The latest issue of Trialogue (Summer 1979) has an opening paragraph as follows:

"The draft report presented in Tokyo by the Trilateral Task Force on Payments Imbalances analyzes the extreme payments imbalances which have marked the world economy throughout the 1970's and offers a series of broad policy recommendations..."

Part II of the same issue has the following opening paragraph:

"The draft report presented in Tokyo by the Trilateral Task Force on Industrial Policy... reviews the desirable aims and criteria of trilateral industrial policies and their international implications."

Yet Franklin asserts "We don't have a policy on energy and a policy on monetary reform, etc."]

Wood: Okay, let me ask a question. Based on that then, what efforts have you made, if any, to publish these articles or these studies so they might be reviewed by the general American public? For instance, I have never seen one study published in any major popular magazine, whether it be *Time Magazine*, a newspaper -- in fact, there have been very few references. Over a period of six years now, there have been few mentions of the name "Trilateral Commission" in the nation's press. This is backed up by the *New York Times* data base, which is one of the most extensive in the world. Now if these are made public, can you tell me how these are made public?

Franklin: Yes. What we do is, that we have a list of about 4,000 people, some of whom request them and some of whom we thought would be interested if we sent them -- and we send them free -- and we would be glad to send them to you, for example, if you would like to have them. Now we also, when we publish, when we send them out to a considerable list of press correspondents. We also have press lunches and things. Because of the nature of this thing, it can't be printed in full, because they are just too long. No newspaper wants to print a 40- or 50-page study. But, there have been mentions of one or two of the studies in *Newsweek*. We would like to get more published, frankly, very much more than we have been getting. Now in Japan, for example, we have done much better. At our last plenary session in Tokyo, members of the Commission who were there, gave over 90 separate interviews to members of the Japanese press who were present. In fact, there were many more requests than that which we could not honor because there was not time. We have not done anything like as well in this country.

Wood: Allow me to ask you this. This takes specifically one case, the case of *Time Magazine*. **Hedley Donovan** is the former editor-in-chief of that magazine. I understand he is recently retired, and also you have as a member of your Commission, **Sol Linowitz**, also a director of *Time*. Now, Time-Life books, of course, you have *Time Magazine, Fortune, Money and People*. Now I would ask you -- considering the special advantage you have by having such a giant as **Hedley Donovan** and **Sol Linowitz** as well, both connected to *Time* -- don't you feel that if you really wanted to publicize these "position papers" that it would only take a scratch of the pen by Mr. Donovan?

Franklin: No, I don't, and I will tell you why. **Hedley Donovan** is not only a member of the Commission, but he is one of my close personal friends. **Hedley Donovan** is also a person of great integrity. He will not publish anything we do because he is connected with it. He looks out for the interest of *Time,* and he does not feel we were worth *Time* publicity, and I am sure he will be exactly the same way in the White House. He is going to be loyal to his President and to his job.

Wood: But *Time Magazine* is the largest news magazine in the country?

Franklin: Right. We only had a little publicity, but we had only what Hedley would have given, whether or not he was a member of the Commission.

Wood: So, he basically thinks that the Commission really does not matter.

Franklin: No. He does not, or he would not be a member of the Commission at all. *Time Magazine* does give us some money, not very much, but $2,500 a year to be exact. But, his editorial judgment is not biased by the fact that he is a member of the Commission.

Commentator: Mr. Rees, would you like to ask a question?

Rees: Yes, Mr. Franklin, I noticed that you were saying that the Trilateral Commission takes no responsibility for the use of the publisher's imprimatur, but I would be interested to know about how you go about selecting your writers to put out the various positions.

Franklin: Well that is a very interesting question. We have a meeting with the chairmen. The way the situation is organized is this. There are three chairmen, one from each of the three areas. Three secretaries, one from each of the three areas, and I have got an intermediate staff job called "coordinator." Now, the chairmen and secretaries meet with what they have jointly, will discuss not only topics they think will be useful to have, but also authors for these topics. The topics are then discussed by the whole Commission and approved or changed slightly. The authors are chosen by members of the staff and consultation with the chairmen.

Rees: So, although you do not take responsibility for the finished product you are responsible for the selection of the writers.

Franklin: Very much. No question about that.

Rees: So it does have your imprimatur stamp of approval each time?

Franklin: In that sense. We certainly choose the writers, and we choose them because we think they are very good, obviously. So far, every single report that has been written by the authors has, in fact, been accepted for publication by the Commission.

Rees: Then the report on the news media was accepted?

Franklin: It was accepted, but there was a lot of disagreement with that. It was felt that it was an important statement, with quite a lot of interesting new ideas in it. It was also a very strong opposition which was reflected in the back of the report in a section, I think it is entitled, "Summary of Discussion."

Commentator: Mr. Sutton, do you have any other questions?

Sutton: I have one more question, that goes to a new field entirely: taxation. We have established that **David Rockefeller** is chairman and the single most powerful influence in Chase Manhattan Bank. Now, do you happen to know the tax rate that Chase Manhattan pays in the United States?

Franklin: I don't know . . . happen to know -- it is about 50% [fifty percent].

Sutton: I will give you some figures. In 1976, Chase Manhattan Bank's tax rate was precisely zero. I am wondering why, if you are so influential politically, why at least you cannot pay a tax rate more equivalent to that of the average American Taxpayer, which is 15% or 20% or 30%?

Franklin: I have nothing to do with Chase Manhattan Bank. But if the tax rate was zero, it must have been because it had very large real estate losses in that year, I think.

Sutton: In 1975, it was 3.4%. It is always way under 10%.

Franklin: Well, that is extremely interesting. It is a new fact for me.

Sutton: Well, my point is this, that you are willing to guide the United States into the future, but apparently you are not willing to pay your fair share of the costs.

Commentator: You are talking about the Commission members as a whole?

Sutton: Yes.

Franklin: I think you will find that the Commission members pay whatever the laws says they are supposed to pay under the circumstances. I do not know what the particular reason was on Chase. They did have heavy losses. I am not familiar enough with their situation to be able to tell it to you.

Wood: May I ask another question along that same line, please?

Commentator: Go ahead.

Wood: In that same year, 1976, it is recorded that some 78% of Chase Manhattan's earnings came from International operations. That leaves 22% from the U.S... Don't you think perhaps this might be a conflict of interest, between choosing their international policy versus their domestic policy in the United States?

Franklin: Well, I think that is true of most of the major banks. Now, that does not answer your question, I recognize.

Wood: Where would their loyalty lie? If on one hand they are trying to look out for America, yet on the other hand they are trying to look out for their bread and butter, which is not America.

Franklin: First, in the long run, I think any of our major corporations must recognize, that unless the United States does well, they are going to be in the soup. Secondly, some of these people, you may or may not believe it, have enough integrity, they can divorce their interest, like Hedley Donovan could, on the question of publicity on the Trilateral Commission.

Commentator: Gentlemen, I think we are running out of time here. I think we have reached the end of the interview. We would like to thank you, Mr. Franklin, Mr. Wood, and Mr. Sutton. Thank you for being guests on our show.

INDEX

Printed in the USA
CPSIA information can be obtained
at www.ICGtesting.com
LVHW020423190724
785880LV00001BA/28